NORTHERN TALES

The Pantheon Fairy Tale and Folklore Library

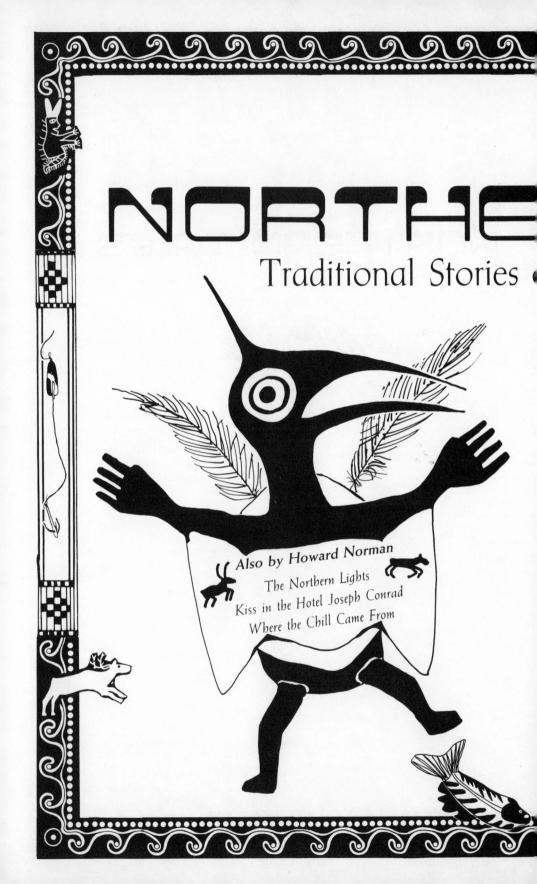

NORTHE

Traditional Stories

N TALES

skimo and Indian Peoples

Selected and edited by Howard Norman

🏛 Pantheon Books New York

All rights reserved under International and Pan-American Copyright Conventions. Published in the United States by Pantheon Books, a division of Random House, Inc., New York, and simultaneously in Canada by Random House of Canada Limited, Toronto.

Permissions acknowledgments may be found on page 345.

Library of Congress Cataloging-in-Publication Data
Northern tales : traditional stories of Eskimo and Indian peoples /
    selected and edited by Howard Norman.   p.   cm.—(The Pantheon
fairy tale and folklore library)
    ISBN 0-394-54060-3
    1. Eskimos—Legends.   2. Indians of North America—Legends.
I. Norman, Howard A.   II. Series: Pantheon fairy tale & folklore library
E99.E7N67   1990
398.2'089971—dc20   90-52531

Book Design by Fearn Cutler
Decorative art & maps by Jenny Vandeventer
Manufactured in the United States of America
First Edition

for Peter Matthiessen

Contents

PART THREE
Endless Trouble, Endless Wandering:
Tricksters and Culture Heroes   99

PART FOUR
The Stubbornness of Bluejays: Stories About Animals   141

Introduction

The native peoples of the arctic and subarctic have always had folktales at the heart of their myriad cultures. This collection gathers together only 116 tales, yet they range in geographical origin from the Japanese island of Hokkaido up through Siberia, over to Greenland, all across Canada, and on out to the Aleutian Islands in the Bering Sea. Drawing on "deep time," or "Way-Back Time," when the earth and its earliest inhabitants were ever-changing, and on events of a more recent past, northern tales are tuned to the ancient rhythms of human and animal speech and to landscape—taiga, tundra, mountains, plains, boreal forest, jigsaw coastlines, sea.

While the northern world is represented here, the astonishing richness and diversity of tale-telling, village to village, lies far beyond the pages of any book. Certainly the overarching language families are present, and there is at least one tale from 35 different tribes. Yet some Eskimo and Indian peoples are not represented. The maps of tribal territories on pages xii and xiv will at least locate them.

Although the subtitle of this collection is "Traditional Stories of Eskimo and Indian Peoples," it is meant to include indigenous peoples, worldwide, who lived or still live a hunting and fishing life through long winters, and who have always predicated much of their cultural self-definition on ancestral, sacred, "tribal" beliefs. Therefore, the native peoples of Siberia—the Yukaghir, the Chukchee, and others—are represented in these pages, as are the Ainu, a hunting-gathering people of Hokkaido and Sakhalin, who have a highly ritualized system of relationships between man and nature, including an oral literature that often features interspecies communication.

The introductions to each part are meant to generally illuminate cultural particulars—village life, origins, tricksters, animals, shamans, strange and menacing creatures, hunting, marriages—and to forecast some of the delights of the stories themselves. In addition, the parts serve as overlapping panels of mythic reality. A reader will easily dis-

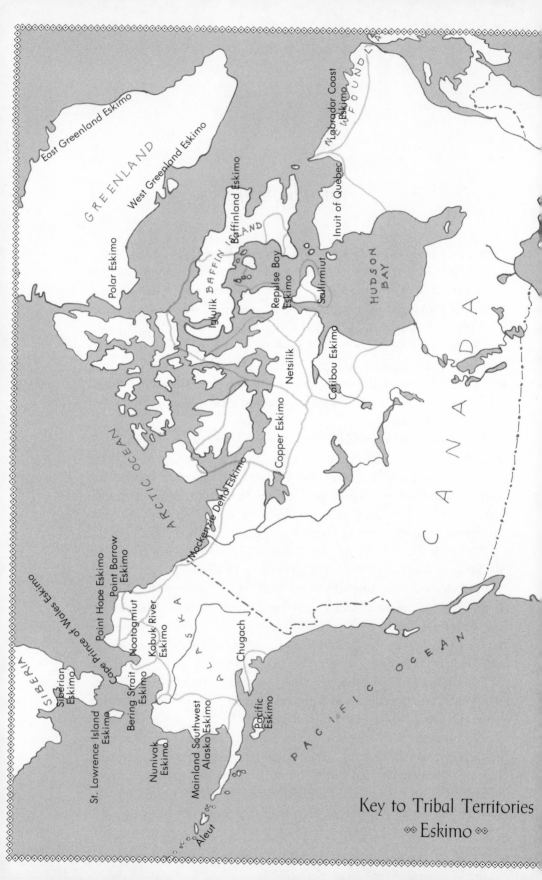

Key to Tribal Territories
⊗⊗ Eskimo ⊗⊗

cover that animals, for example, are central to tales in all the parts; a marriage takes place in the section featuring menacing neighbors; a cannibal-windigo, with its heart made of ice, makes a cameo appearance in the section focusing on shamans; and so forth. Certain fundamental perceptions provide continuity between all the tales: that the visible world can be deceptive and that certain entities are able to change form at whim; that life is often harsh and unforgiving; that with its gifts of sustenance (birds, mammals, fish) the environment may be lethally frugal one year and extraordinarily generous the next; that true power resides with the spirits of earth, sea, and air.

Be they scatological, ribald, celebratory, mournful, violent, or beau-tiful—or all these at once—northern tales enlighten an audience about the sacredness of life. In the naturalness of their form, they turn away from forced conclusions; they animate and enact, they shape and re-shape the world. They are, as Helen Tanizaki said, "an education in paradox"—the joys and terrors, triumphs and defeats, feasts and fa-mines, which throughout time have informed northern experience from the most remote hunting camps to the bustling centers of village life.

"Stories are not just about living things," said Mark Albert Blackfish, "they *are* living things." No matter how tangential in narrative pro-gression or illogical in plot they may seem to the western mind, the genius of northern tales is to be discovered in their vast emotional dimensions, in how they chronicle profound moments in tribal life, and again and again, in how they are able to orchestrate the phantas-magoric with the commonplace, offering an often strange, always com-pelling reality. "Our tales are narratives of human experience," said Osarqaq, a Polar Eskimo, "and therefore they do not always tell of beautiful things. But one cannot embellish a tale to please the hearer and at the same time keep to the truth. The tongue should be the echo of that which must be told, and it cannot be adapted according to the moods and tastes of man."

◇◇◇

Northern tales are told in tents, at kitchen tables, on hunting trips, at festivals and pow-wows, while driving along in pickup trucks. I recorded a number of Eskimo stories in the train station in Churchill, Manitoba. While in some Eskimo and Indian communities tale-telling is exclusive to or at least more frequent during winter, in others tales

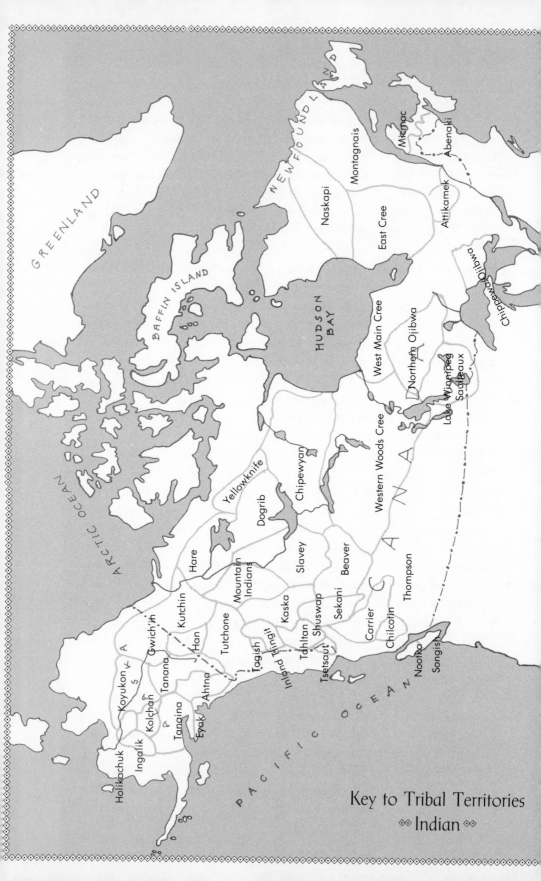

Key to Tribal Territories
◇◇ Indian ◇◇

are a year-round entertainment. Hiroko Sue Hara reported that among the Hare Indians, "storytelling is a common pastime throughout the year in the tent or cabin. Especially during long nights in winter camps Indians tell stories to each other. These stories may be accounts of the speaker's own hunting experiences, old timers' anecdotes and folktales. Stories are often told with gestures and imitative sounds. The audience utters 'e'eⁿ, e' eⁿ,' when the speaker pauses awhile after a sentence. Such interjection is considered to heighten the mood of the storyteller. Old men who can tell stories are welcome in the tents at night and are often asked to recite stories by the hosts and children."

In *The Last Kings of Thule*, his remarkable account of life among the Eskimos of Greenland from 1950 to 1951, Jean Malaurie wrote:

> Oqaluttuarpoq! Someone is telling a story. In this instance, the story is being told on Kutsikitsoq's sledge. Usually stories are told in the family igloo; people lie on the illeq, heads toward the center of the igloo, feet toward the wall; their breathing becomes peaceful and takes on the rhythm of nighttime; two people, their heads close together, tell each other their secret thoughts in low voices. Their soft murmuring does not disturb the solitary man who is slowly sinking into a half dream. The soothing flame of the oil-lamp is lowered. It is then that the mother begins to tell the story, slowly, in a low voice. Everyone listens in silence. The next morning, when the children wake up, they will ask questions about some detail, and difficult sentences they will repeat several times. Someone will correct them. And that is all. They will remember it forever.

In the early 1980s, the writer and folklorist Lawrence Millman described an enlightening happenstance.

> I was sitting in a tent in Auyittiq National Park on Baffin Island. My companion was an Eskimo storyteller from Pangnirtung named Ken Annanack. For several days, heavy rains and a howling autumn gale had been lashing our tent. At first the talk had been somewhat desultory. . . . But when Ken started to tell stories, his voice took on a new intensity. He told me about a man who tried to eat the weather. I heard about a man who was transformed into a salmon and an entire group of men transformed into bears. The wind howled and into the teeth of this wind more stories were hurled; long untold stories; half forgotten stories; mere local anecdotes (oqalualat); and even a few larger myths (oqalugtuat).

These more recent testimonies are part of a historical continuum. The past work of missionaries, ethnographers, travel writers, linguists, and native people themselves in recording folktales naturally crosses paths in the present. "In 1823," Victor Barnouw relates, "Lewis Cass, governor of Michigan Territory, sent a questionnaire about Indian customs to traders, military men and Indian agents under his jurisdiction. One of the questions was: Do they relate stories, or indulge in any work of the imagination?" For nearly two centuries there has been a vast education to be had from native tale-tellers. Many hundreds of tales were recorded one-on-one, so to speak, between teller and listener, often outside traditional settings. Pencil in hand, tape recorder on the table, the listener—who sometimes speaks the native tongue in only a limited way—is in a decidedly privileged circumstance. Such collaborations are built upon the generosity of the teller and his or her community. Malaurie says:

> As for myself, I achieved most of my progress in learning Polar Eskimo during the long winter nights in Siorapaluk by making rough translations into French of the work written in Eskimo by Knud Rasmussen about his first stay in Thule: *Auanqarnisalerssarutit Okalualut* ("Legends of the Men in the North"). I was aided immeasurably in this endeavor by my Greenlander friend John Petrussen, the catechist, and by the Polar Eskimos. The Eskimos were particularly helpful in explaining—often in long paraphrases or in pantomimes—a number of words and expressions totally unknown to me.

Malaurie acknowledges Knud Rasmussen, the Danish explorer and ethnographer, who in 1910 established an arctic trading post at Thule, from which he set out on a number of expeditions. These resulted in "descriptions of the Polar Eskimo [that] display a depth of understanding, sensitivity and insight that are unequaled in arctic literature." All recent work is in part an homage to the predecessors in the field. A concise history of northern ethnographic research can be found in *The Handbook of North American Indians*, volumes 5 and 6. Naturally, today another northern folklorist well might mention luminaries I do not include here. There is Father Jules Jette, who for thirty years around the turn of the century lived in the Koyukon village of Nulato. He left an astonishing archive of invaluable research into Koyukon linguistics and ethnography. (his "On Ten'a Folk-lore" is especially illuminating).

The Siberian folktales collected in the early part of the twentieth century by Waldemar Bogoras, on the Jesup North Pacific Expeditions, are a veritable treasure from that region. Earlier yet, Hinrich Rink's *Tales and Traditions of the Eskimo* provided the first considerable resource of Greenlandic tales. Edward Sapir, who worked with the Gwich'in dialect in the early 1920s—especially with a remarkable tale-teller named John Fredson—also worked with the Sarcee and other Athapaskan dialects. In the early 1930s, Cornelius Osgood worked among the Tanaina and Ingalik Indians, notably with an Ingalik man, Billy Williams. Lucien M. Turner, a gifted naturalist, collected tales from the Indians and Eskimos in the Quebec-Labrador peninsula, and his *Ethnology of the Ungava District* is one of the last works to depict the spiritual life of the native peoples there. Diamond Jenness, certainly one of Canada's most distinguished anthropologists, collected tales from the Copper Eskimo, the Mackenzie Delta Eskimo, the Cape Prince of Wales Eskimo, the Carrier, the Sekani, and others. Frederica de Laguna graciously turned all her materials on the Eyak Indians over to Michael Strauss, and served as an inspiration to him in his own work with the Eyak language and folklore, which in part resulted in his *In Honor of Eyak: The Art of Anna Nelson Harry*. Anna Nelson Harry, a superb Eyak tale-teller, worked with De Laguna in the 1930s and some forty years later with Krauss. Krauss poignantly recalls: "Anna Nelson Harry was one of the last of a whole nation, the Eyaks. Her death is full of meaning for all mankind. Her long, hard life spanned the unutterably tragic final chapter of the living history of her people. Anna had the gift of the Eyak language, to tell the stories of her people. The spirit of her language and people live in her art."

The abovementioned were my earliest primary sources for *Northern Tales*. All of my selections for this anthology were culled from libraries, personal archives, and correspondence. I made extensive use of the scrupulous work published under the auspices of the Alaska Native Language Center and the Ethnology Division (Mercury Series) of the National Museum of Man, Ottawa, Canada. As the editors working with these and other institutions do so expansively, so do I, first and foremost, thank the native tale-tellers across the North. Superlatives can only understate when one is trying to express an anthologist's gratitude to tale-tellers past, present, and future.

When in this book I have inadvertently trespassed on rather than illuminated what is most vital in oral traditions, I offer my apologies. I wish for this volume to exist as a spirited, if necessarily fragmented, homage to northern tales. Allow me special notes of thanks to Mary Akiose and Helen Tanizaki, both of whom have traveled extensively in Siberia and the North American North and flooded my mailbox with local anecdotes, tales, and songs. In addition, Mark Albert Black-fish, William Threepersons, and Mary Blackfish opened their homes to me on a number of occasions. Jack Trueblood and Paul Thorbjourn took me along on zoological surveys and photographic excursions, and introduced me to winter life in Churchill. Thomas Scarborough, a thoroughly obsessed bibliophile, tracked down obscure and out-of-print texts. I turned again and again to librarians in Harvard University's Tozzer Library, the Boreal Institute in Edmonton, and the Center for Northern Studies in Wolcott, Vermont. My wife, Jane Shore, listened to translations of tales sent to me with a loving and critical ear. David Wyatt and Ann Parotti let me work in their apartment in Washington, D.C., and Scott and Charlotte Bassage allowed me use of their cabin in East Calais, Vermont. There were ongoing conversations with Barbara Einzig, whose Siberian translations were inspiring. In uncanny ways, the "spirits" drawn by Edward Koren slowly evolved a kind of arctic presence. Many thanks late in this project go to Ginny Read for her keen eye and counsel. And all along, my editor, Wendy Wolf, demonstrated patience and insight; there's not a hint of gratuitousness when I say that *Northern Tales* would not exist without her.

Howard Norman
East Calais, Vermont

◇ A NOTE TO THE READER ◇

The word "Eskimo" is decidedly in great and permanent disfavor among
native peoples, and is recognized as not paying respect to their historically based, vital sense of self-definition. Today, the word "Inuit"
designates indigenous peoples of the eastern Canadian arctic. Those
of the Bering Strait region prefer to be called "Yup'ik," and those of
the north slope of Alaska are the "Inupiat." Despite my obviously
generic use of "Eskimo," which is perhaps far too deeply rooted in the
public domain of western readers, it is my true hope that the range of
tales in this collection contributes to underscoring the remarkably idiosyncratic nature of northern cultures.

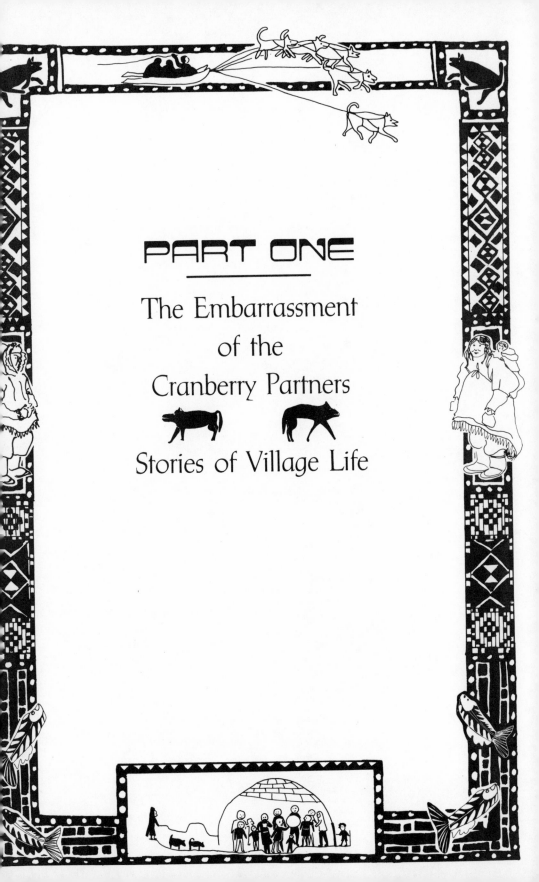

PART ONE

The Embarrassment
of the
Cranberry Partners

Stories of Village Life

THE MONTAGNAIS TALE "The Embarrassment of the Cranberry Partners" indeed takes place in a village of cranberries, though they are curiously personified as moose hunters. In this group of stories, at any rate, theirs is the only plant village. The rest are either animal or human, or villages with mixed populations, harking back to a time when people and animals had all sorts of social interaction. In the North, village-to-village visiting is almost a constant activity, so it comes as little surprise in these tales when almost anyone shows up, relative or stranger, or even supernatural being.

A village is the place where everything goes on. Here, then, we have all the buzz of human activity: cooking, gossip, births, deaths, adultery, children's mischief. Sleds get built, sled dogs are groomed, hunters come and go, and always there is the gathering of food, whether by fishing, shooting, or berry picking. We see all the various cultural particulars, interwoven with the more dramatic, even cataclysmic, events that give such vitality to tales of village life.

At their outset, many of these tales fix us in a particular topography. "Eviksheen the Grass-User," a Kobuk River story, begins: "Eviksheen and his wife are living on the Kobuk River, down there where a little creek comes out from the lakes. They live at the mouth of that creek, where fish are running back and forth every year." At the conjunction of waters, with the fishes' ancient life-cycle flowing past, Eviksheen and his family seem anchored to time itself and in that sense secure. But life, as such tales prove, is not always what at first it seems. Soon we discover that Eviksheen is hopelessly lazy and his wife does all the providing. She finds and raises an abandoned baby, who grows to be a great caribou hunter. They are a family now. Still, in the end, "nobody ever comes around to them. They still don't know anybody else. But they know they are rich people right there. No more grass bed and grass clothing—lots of caribou skins." They stay put, a village of three, yet much has happened. In their story we find interlocking motifs of

adoption, marital strife, maternal and paternal instincts drawn forth—
the world of difference a child makes.

In these tales, we see a vigilant protection of the social order, of
normal life. "A village," Charlotte Blackfish, an Ojibwa woman, said,
"is where all sorts of evil can find you at home. You have to be careful
even in your house." Human frailty and strengths are side by side in
any village. Outside forces and those born within a community can be
equally threatening. The Siberian Eskimo tale "The Girl Who Watched
in the Nighttime" depicts this movingly. Two odious crimes, kidnap-
ping and murder, are plaguing a particular family; a man has lost all
but his youngest son. That boy comes to represent the debilitating
grief and depression of the community; he seems to have lost the will
to live. His cousin tries to console him, and while there this alert girl—
in essence the hope of the people—captures a marauding fox who ad-
mits to being the murderer. The fox also reveals a bit of shocking news:
the "true enemy" is a man living *in* the village—a neighbor! This villain,
who had hired the fox, is confronted with his crime and dies of shame.
Immediately the spirit of the village is buoyed up. We're given a litany of
traditional milestones, which tell us that the social order has been restored, which equals happiness and prosperity: "They lived on. The girl
lived with the boy, and when they grew up, they married. They had
many children. All the people loved her. She was rich."

Many tales here indeed contain details of monotonous, everyday
life. But on closer look, the tales—"The Little Old Lady Who Lived
Alone," for instance—transcend a mere portrayal of domestic particulars. Yes, the old woman hermit is a village unto herself. She is self-
sufficient. We know she catches, dries, and cooks fish. She makes
"Indian ice cream." Her routines are well established for us. But in a
larger sense her life is a template for the universal themes of loneliness,
isolation, longing, and the deceptive workings of memory. While she
is said to be happy, the tale is fairly bursting with a yearning for lost
youth. A singing fish, who momentarily woos the old woman into
thinking a male suitor has called, finally is simply a singing fish. Or is
it? Could it be a mirage of hope and possibility, now lost? The flip-
side of her momentary jubilation is a heartbreaking return to the habits
of life. But a deeper chord has been struck; she tries to do the usual,
to eat Indian ice cream. But she is overwhelmed by emotion: "She got
lonely, and began to cry. Then she went off crying into the woods."

Lessons in morality and etiquette may enter some of these tales obliquely, but they are nonetheless important. Living in a village is a constant learning process; the homogeneity and cohesiveness are observed and practiced from a young age. People look to elders for all kinds of instruction and counsel. Tales can directly serve a pedagogical purpose as well. Teit wrote of this among the Thompson Indians of British Columbia:

> Some elderly man of a household, or some chief, would often speak to the people until late at night, admonishing and advising them, especially the young of both sexes, how to act and live with one another; telling them the benefits of being good and the results of being evil; also giving his ideas of the future life, etc., thus teaching them and guiding them by his knowledge and experience. In winter many nights were spent in speech-making of this kind, in relating stories of war, hunting and other experience, and telling mythological stories. The old people often took turns at telling myths and legends after all went to bed, and stayed up until all fell asleep.

"The most important reason to tell stories about life in villages," said Fanny Gulin, a part-Shasta Indian, "is to educate our children in the old ways." In this realm of tales and tale-telling the education is sometimes strict. Ceryl Guy, an Alaskan Tlingit, said that she "had to remember" what she had been told the night before. This repetitive behavior was traditional among the Shasta:

> The children repeated the story, sentence by sentence, after the storyteller, each word being repeated until they got it right. Little girls, the older ones, frequently practised telling the stories to a group of their little friends, who watched for their mistakes. This was done in daytime, but only in winter.

In tales of village life, the importance of the themes of togetherness, the centrality of family life, the sustaining of traditional beliefs, can hardly be overestimated. Even intimidation—often spiced with humor—was used as a precautionary measure. Stories about Bigfoot were sometimes told so that children would obey their parents. Bigfoot, in this case a menacing creature, gives shape to the darkness. His presence often had a shivering effect on arctic and subarctic children, much as warnings about the "bogeyman" had for European children: "Don't wander off at night, or Bigfoot will get you!"

The Embarrassment of the Cranberry Partners

◇ M O N T A G N A I S   I N D I A N ◇

The high-bush and low-bush cranberries were hunting companions, and they were also neighbors, since they lived in adjoining villages on the shore of a lake. The entrances to their houses faced the water. The cranberries could look out and see moose swimming across the lake.

The high-bush and low-bush cranberries were the best of friends, they protected each other, they were known far and wide as the cranberry partners.

They often visited each other's houses.

All through winter, spring, and summer it was impossible to embarrass the cranberry partners.

But now it was the fall of the year, and both the high-bush and low-bush cranberries were ripe. They were fat and full of juice.

One day, lying around lazily inside their houses, they suddenly heard the sound of a moose passing by.

Both the high-bush and low-bush cranberries jumped up at once and seized their bows and arrows.

They ran toward their front doors, but being so fat they all got jammed in the doorways so that none of them could get out. They couldn't get to the moose in time, and so the moose passed right on by and was soon out of sight.

Because of this, the cranberries were embarrassed. There were other ways to embarrass the cranberry partners in the autumn, but this is how the moose embarrassed them.

Eviksheen the Grass-User

◇ KOBUK RIVER ESKIMO ◇

Eviksheen and his wife are living on the Kobuk River, down there where a little creek comes out from the lakes. They live at the mouth of that creek, where fish are running back and forth every year. They use grass for bed and clothing—nothing else. This couple never take long trips to other places. They just spend their lives right there. Eviksheen is so lazy that he never does anything. He does nothing but stay home in a little house all his life. He never uses his feet on the ground—so lazy! So his wife, when the fish are running, does all the work. She cuts the fish up and puts them away. She loves her husband very much, even if he is lazy. This couple have lived there a good many years, and nobody has ever visited them, so that they don't know there are other people—they think they are the only people. Nobody visits. They never visit anybody.

So, this woman goes fishing. Once in a while she goes back up yonder to pick some berries. Up yonder she sees a lot of caribou— lots of them. When she comes home she never tells her husband about the caribou, it would be no use. He wouldn't hunt them—too lazy. When autumn comes, and snow, she begins to snare ptarmigan. She does all the work. Mrs. Eviksheen does all the work. Mr. Eviksheen never uses his feet to stand up, he lies in bed all along.

One day it is cold and she has on her grass parka with the hood up. She has snared a few birds already. She has a few ptarmigan cut up and ready to take home, when she hears some kind of noise up at the other end of the snare line. She pulls back her hood, listening. Then she hears somebody crying. Now she leaves all the birds behind, and she goes to where that crying is. Not very far off she finds a crack on the riverbank, a big crack. She looks in, and there is a baby crying right there, nobody else, just a baby. So she grabs that baby and puts it inside her grass parka, and starts to take it home.

Mrs. Eviksheen is very glad to have found that young boy about a year old. She thinks Mr. Eviksheen will be glad to have that little boy, but when she comes in with that baby crying, Mr. Eviksheen never turns his head to look at them—so lazy.

Mrs. Eviksheen still snares ptarmigan. She takes the little boy with her every time. But the boy is getting pretty good-sized now, getting too heavy to pack around, so one day Mrs. Eviksheen goes out alone to get a little wood. And while she is out she hears the boy crying inside the house. She turns and quickly goes in the house, and she sees her husband playing with the boy with one hand, like this—but he never looks around. He just keeps the boy from crying with his hand. Mrs. Eviksheen is very glad then, because her husband is at least playing with the boy.

So they lived there quite a few years until the little boy is big enough to be playing around the house. Mrs. Eviksheen starts making a bow and arrow for the little boy, little things at first, then arrowheads out of ptarmigan bone. The little boy is growing up, and big enough now to go out a little, not much, just outdoors a bit. And one day he kills a ptarmigan and brings it in. His mother is very happy then, she has got a boy she's proud of. Mr. Eviksheen is still lying in the house, never doing anything!

The little boy is growing up to be pretty good-sized now. One day he brings home a rabbit. He killed it with his bow and arrow to help his mother and father. Mrs. Eviksheen loves her husband very much, all the while.

She knows a lot about caribou, those she saw back yonder many years before. She never told her husband about them. The old man is too lazy to hunt anyhow. This time when the boy brings home the rabbit, the old man is proud too, and he sits right up and makes a good bow and arrow for him.

The boy goes back yonder and sees some caribou, and goes after them for the first time. He goes out on the tundra a ways, sees the caribou, and sneaks up to them. He gets near them, and sends an arrow flying. He wounds a caribou, who wobbles about. The boy watches, but he is afraid, and doesn't go near the caribou. The caribou dies, but the boy is still too afraid to go near it, and he goes home and tells his mother and father. He says that he killed a big thing, a great big thing, he never saw anything like it before, he doesn't know what it is! His mother gets ready and takes the stone knife and jade axe and goes out to see what it is. She takes quite a few days to get that caribou home. Every day she takes home a little, and she takes a few days at this.

The boy has no trouble hunting now. He is taking caribou right along. He is getting to be a man growing up. They do not use grass for clothing now. They are getting lots of caribou skins, getting to be rich with them. They are building up a cache on posts alongside the house. He fills up quite a few caches with meat and skin and one thing and another. No more grass for clothing! And next, he gets some fur— fox, mink, otter, and more; the country was full of fur in those days.

Nobody ever comes around to them. They still don't know anybody else. But they know they are rich people right there. No more grass bed and grass clothing—lots of caribou skins.

The Girl Who Watched in the Nighttime

◇ S I B E R I A N E S K I M O ◇

Two cousins lived in the village of Uni'sak. One had five sons, the other had a single daughter. The sons of the former began to die, and only the youngest one remained alive; and even he began to suffer. Then his mother sent for her sister-in-law, and said, "My last son is suffering. Please send your daughter to cheer him up. He feels quite ill." The other woman said to her daughter, "They have sent for you. You may go after the meal."

"No," said the girl. "Let me go at once."

The mother said, "Then at least put on your clothes."

"Why should I? It's not a long way."

She put on only her boots, and, being quite naked, went out of the sleeping-room and crossed over to the other cousin's house. She entered the sleeping-room. The suffering boy was stretched out upon the skins, moaning. He could neither drink nor eat. Night came, and they lay down to sleep. A new line, made of seal-hide thong, was lying near the entrance. The girl picked it up, made a noose in the shape of a lasso, and crouched near the entrance, watching. She was naked and had on only her boots as before.

The sun had set and it was dark. Then she heard a rustling sound from the direction of sunset. She listened attentively, and heard some wary steps. She peered into the darkness, and at last noticed a form. It was a raven. He approached noiselessly. Behind the house were some scraps of food. He picked at them, and crept slowly to the entrance. The girl threw the lasso over him and caught him.

"Ah, ah, ah! Let me alone! I have done nothing."

"And why do you steal in here in the nighttime, without giving notice to the master of the house?"

"I am looking for food, gathering meat-scraps and even excrement. Let me go."

"All right."

She let him go, and he flew away. She watched on, lasso in hand, quite naked. Then from the direction of midnight she heard a rustling noise guardedly approaching. It was a fox creeping toward the house. As soon as she approached, the suffering boy moaned louder. The fox stopped and put her nose to the ground. She listened and then said, "This time I shall probably carry him away."

The fox drew nearer, and the girl threw the lasso and caught her.

"Qa! Qa! Qa!"

"And why are you stealing in here in the nighttime? The master of the house knows nothing about you. It is you, probably, who have taken away those boys."

"Why, yes, I did it."

"Then I shall kill you."

"Why will you kill me?"

"Why, you scoundrel, you make all the people mourn. You source of trouble!"

"Oh, it is not my fault. This neighbor of yours induces me to do it, and pays me for it!"

"Is that so? Nevertheless, I shall kill you."

"Oh, I will leave here and go away!"

"No, I shall kill you!"

"I will pay you a large ransom. You shall be happy along with your husband. And I will kill your enemy."

"Ah, then, you may go."

The fox ran away. The girl entered the sleeping-room, and her body, which was quite naked in the cold, felt warmer. She woke up her cousin. "Get up! You have slept enough!" she said. The boy did not moan any more, and he asked for food. She gave him some. She cut meat into small pieces. He swallowed a morsel, then another one, and still another. He ate five pieces of meat. She gave him some water to drink. Only then did she herself eat and drink. They went to sleep. The boy slept. In the morning they awoke, and the boy was quite well.

But their neighbor came, the secret enemy. "Ah, ah! Who is this girl? I saw her going around naked, carrying a lasso. She must be my secret enemy."

The girl went out.

"You are my enemy," she said.

From mere shame, the neighbor fell down and died. The others lived on. The girl lived with the boy, and when they grew up, they married. She had many children. All the people loved her. She was rich.

Uteritsoq, the Obstinate One

◇ EAST GREENLAND ESKIMO ◇

There was once an obstinate man—no one in the world could be as obstinate as he. No one dared come near him, so obstinate was he, and he would always have his own way.

Once it came about that his wife was in mourning. Her little child had died, and therefore she was obliged to remain idle at home: this is the custom of the ignorant, and this we also had to do when we were ignorant as they.

And while she thus sat idle in mourning, her husband, the obstinate one, came in one day and said, "You must sew the skin of my kayak."

"You know that I am not permitted to touch any kind of work," said the wife.

"You must sew the skin of my kayak," he said again. "Bring it down to the shore and sew it there."

And so the woman, for all her mourning, was forced to go down to the shore and sew the skin of her husband's kayak. But when she had sewn a little, suddenly her thread began to make a sound, and the sound grew to a muttering, louder and louder. And at last a monster came up out of the sea, a monster in the shape of a dog, and said, "Why do you sew, you who are in mourning?"

"My husband will not listen to me, for he is so obstinate," she said.

And then the mighty dog sprang ashore and fell upon her husband.

But the obstinate one was not abashed; as usual he thought he would get his own way, and his way now was to kill that dog. They fought together, and the dog was killed.

But now the owner of the dog appeared, and he turned out to be the Moon Man.

He fell upon the obstinate one, and the obstinate one would as usual not give way, but fell upon him in turn. He caught the Moon Man by the throat and nearly throttled him. He clenched and clenched, and the Moon Man was nearly choked to death.

"There will be no more ebb-tide or flood if you throttle me," said the Moon Man.

But the obstinate one cared little for that; he clutched all the tighter.

"The seal will never breed again if you throttle me," screamed the Moon Man.

But the obstinate one cared for none of these things, even though the Moon Man threatened more and more.

"The day will never dawn again if you work my death," said the Moon Man at last.

And at this the obstinate one began to hesitate: he did not like the thought of living in the ceaseless dark. And he let the Moon Man go.

Then the Moon Man called his slain dog to life again and made ready to leave that place. And he took his team and cast the dogs up in the air one by one, and they did not come down again; at last there was the whole team hovering in the air.

"May I come and visit you on the moon?" asked the obstinate one. For he suddenly felt a desire to do so.

"Yes, come if you please," said the Moon Man, "but when you see a high rock in your way, take great care to drive around behind it. Do not pass it on the sunny side, for if you do you will lose your guts."

And then the Moon Man cracked his whip and drove off through the naked air.

Now the obstinate one began making ready for his journey to the moon. It had been his custom to keep his dogs inside the house, and therefore they had a thick layer of ingrown filth in their coats. Now he took them and cast them out into the sea that they might get clean again. The dogs, little used to going out at all, nearly froze to death after their cold bath. They ran about, shivering with cold.

Then the obstinate one took a dog and cast it up in the air, but it fell down heavily to earth again. He took another, and a third, but they all fell down again. They were still too dirty.

But the obstinate one would not give in, and now he cast them into the sea once more.

And when he then a second time tried casting them up in the air, they stayed there. And now he made himself a sledge, threw his team up into the air, and drove off.

When he came to the rock which he was to drive around, this obstinate one thought to himself, "Why should I drive around a rock at all? I will go by the sunny side!"

When he came up alongside, he heard a woman singing drum-songs and whetting her knife. She kept on singing, and he could hear how the steel hummed as she worked.

Now he tried to overpower that old woman, but lost his senses. And when he came to himself, his guts were gone.

"I had better go around after all," he thought to himself, and around he went by the shady side.

Thus he came up to the moon, and told how he had lost his guts merely for trying to drive around by the sunny side.

Then the Moon Man bade him lie down at full length on his back, with a black sealskin under him, which he spread on the floor. This the obstinate one did, and then the Moon Man fetched his guts from the woman and stuffed them in again.

While he was there, the Moon Man took up one of the stones from the floor and let him look down onto the earth. And there he saw his wife sitting on her bench, plaiting sinews for thread, and this although she was in mourning. A thick smoke rose from her body, the smoke of her evil thoughts, and her thoughts were evil because she was working before her mourning time was past.

And her husband grew angry at this, forgetting that he had himself newly bidden her work despite her mourning.

And after he had been there some time, the Moon Man opened a stone in the entrance of the passageway and let him look down. The place was full of walrus; there were so many that they had to lie one on top of another.

"It is a joy to catch such beasts," said the Moon Man, and the obstinate one felt a great desire to harpoon one of them.

"But you must not, you cannot," said the Moon Man, and promised him a share of a catch he had just made. But the obstinate one would not be content with this; he took harpoons from the Moon Man and harpooned a walrus. Then he held it on the line—he was a man of very great strength, that obstinate one—and managed to kill it. And in the same way he dealt with another.

After his return from the Moon Man's place, he left off being obstinate, and never afterwards forced his wife to work while she was in mourning.

The Chuginadak Woman

◇ A L E U T ◇

Mount Cleveland breathed through a woman. That woman looked at Umnak from the top of Mount Cleveland and saw Samalga Island appearing like floating kelp.

In the evening she began to descend. She came to a married man who lived in a settlement on Chuginadak Island. That man took her as a daughter.

Her foster father, who clubbed seals, once came back with a broken club, and the foster daughter stored away the half of that club. Her foster parents told her to marry, but she did not want to.

Her foster father, having been out a whole day, also brought back some sea-lion guts. She hid the one she thought was the longest. After it had dried, she put it away. When asked to marry, she said that she would only marry a man in the East who used to shoot rosy finches.

Half of her foster father's thongs, which she had put away, and all her belongings she packed into her bag and went to bed.

At night, when her foster father and foster mother had fallen asleep, she left the house and walked off. Walking a night and a day, she came to Imgaxsxix Point and went to sleep.

The next day, seeing that the weather was fine, she took from among her things the sea-lion gut and talked to it: "Gut! let me pass on you to the other side," she said and cast it out.

When she threw it, the gut became a path with horsetail grass, and walking over it she came up on Samalga. Then she looked back in the direction she had come from, but did not see land, and she wound up the gut and put it away.

Next she walked toward Idan village. When darkness came she reached Idan village, where she came upon two women. Having fed her, they went to bed with her, but she did not want to sleep. When she heard that the two women had fallen asleep, she walked off with her pack on her back. Walking the whole night, she reached Nikolski Lake at daybreak. Without stopping she walked toward the northeast, passed Uyux and Itagusix village, and reached Mid-Umnak village, where she slept.

After sleeping, just at daybreak she walked off again, heading northeast along the seashore. Having reached Atxudigan, she took out the gut from among her things and said to it again, "Gut, let me pass on you to the other side." Then it became a path with horsetail grass, and she walked over it.

Having reached land at Land's End, she gathered in the gut, put it back among her things, took her pack on her back, and proceeded along the south coast of Unalaska Island. Walking eastward, she reached Kitxalux Point. Having slept there, at daybreak she took out the gut from among her things and without talking to it threw it toward Unalga Island. It became a path, and she passed over it to the island.

After that she gathered in the gut. She tried to put it in order but saw that it was not right. Having reached Akutan Strait, she took the gut and, talking to it, threw it again. She saw that it did not reach across the strait, but when it became as it had been before, she started to walk along it. When she was not far from reaching over to Ikaaginax, she saw two murres come flying.

When they reached her, the murres picked her up in their beaks and flew with her into a sea cave. In the evening they put her to bed between them, each with one wing as a mattress and the other as a blanket for her. All night she suffered from the smell of bird.

At daybreak, she looked out from the cave, and seeing that the weather was fine she asked the murres to take her to the top of the cliff and let her see the whales breathing in Akutan Bay.

The murres flew with her in their beaks and let her down at the top of the cliff. Then she sat there watching how the whales of Akutan enjoyed breathing.

She sat there the whole day, and when in the evening the murres came to her, she did not go with them but continued to sit. When darkness came and the houses of the village began to have fires, she descended toward the village. Then she saw through the door-hole that the chief of Akutan was having a celebration.

Seeing among the dancers the man she had come for, she thought that he might come out. When somebody came out, she hid herself until he went back in, and then she returned to the door-hole.

When that man, the son of the chief of Akutan, began to go out, she stepped aside. When he came out and walked off, she seized him and they fell down. Telling him why she had come, she rolled down with him until she noticed with horror that she had killed him.

When he died, she went back to the murres and sat down on the cliff she had descended from. At daybreak the murres took her in their beaks and flew back with her into their cave.

Missing his son, the chief of Akutan had him searched for. When he was found dead outside, the chief sent for the people of his village to find out how his son had been killed. In spite of the inquiry, he did not find out who had killed his son, and sent for the old women in his land. Having fed them, in the evening he told two of them to go to bed in a small hut and find out in a dream who had killed his son. Two other ones he had enter the hut to keep awake and listen to what the sleeping ones were saying. The two who kept awake heard one of the two sleeping ones saying in a dream that a woman from the Islands of the Four Mountains had come to marry him and then had killed him.

So the chief of Akutan found out who had killed his son, and the next day began to prepare his army. The woman in the cave, learning that an army was ready to come against her, took out from among her things the half-thongs she had put away and stretched them across the entrance of the cave.

The chief of Akutan sent his men out to the cave with his magic spirits: killer whales, sea lions, and fire. Reaching the cave, every killer whale that leapt into the cave at once fell dead into the sea. When there were no more killer whales, the woman took the half-club from among her things and put it inside the entrance to the cave.

Whenever a sea lion leapt inside the cave, the woman saw that the half-club struck it and cut it in the middle.

When there were no more sea lions, the fire was let into the cave. When it began to whirl around inside the cave, the two murres let water drip from their mouths on the woman.

Having annihilated the magic spirits of the chief of Akutan, the woman said to the men from inside the cave, "You will never kill me, in vain you are trying to kill me."

The bidarka men returned to their village, and the chief of Akutan asked them, "Did you kill that woman?"

"She is not killed," they said to him. "She said that even though a woman she would never be killed, and all your magic spirits were annihilated there!"

Then the chief of Akutan sent away a bear he had as a magic spirit to bring her to him: "Tell her that I shall do nothing to her, but that I want to learn from her why she killed my son."

Reaching the cliff, the bear descended toward the cave until his claws gave out and he fell into the sea and died.

Waiting in vain for his bear, the chief of Akutan sent away a wolf he had as a magic spirit. The wolf descended toward the cave, but his claws gave out and he fell down and died.

Waiting in vain for the wolf, the chief of Akutan sent away a fox he had as a magic spirit to fetch her.

The fox went to the cave, entered, and seeing the woman, said that the chief of Akutan invited her. The woman gathered up her things and went out with the fox. When she got outside, the fox took her on his back, climbed with her to the top, and then walked with her to the village.

She arrived in the evening. Learning of her arrival, the chief of Akutan sent for her. Being invited, the woman went there and saw that the man she had killed was sitting as if alive in the back of the house, and she went over there. Then the chief ordered a meal for her. When she had eaten, he began to question her: "Why did you kill my son, tell me why?"

"From far away I came to marry him and was telling him why I came, when I noticed with horror that I had killed him," she said.

She was ready to say more, but the chief of Akutan killed her. Then he laid her on the side together with his son, covered them with their parkas, and sent out all the people of his house. Then he blew out the lamps and put his house in darkness and began to have a celebration all by himself. Singing and beating his drum, he began to palpate his son's leg. Feeling that the leg was becoming warm, he beat his drum and sang until his son and the woman came alive.

In the morning he had his son marry her, and made him chief in his stead from then on.

The Boy Who Became an Arctic Tern

◇NAUPAKTOMIUT ESKIMO◇

A grandmother and a grandson lived in a village with other people. One evening they stayed home. The boy went out to the toilet. It was moonlight. A woman came from nowhere and stood by him. She said, "I have come to get you for my husband." The boy said, "My grandmother always told me not to get married while I was young." Then the woman said, "Try to look down." The grandson looked down, and he had left his grandmother way below already. That woman had taken him up in the air.

Since he couldn't go back, he followed the woman. They came to a house and went in. The woman's parents and her three brothers were there. The woman married the boy and they lived there. But soon he started getting cranky because he didn't hunt and wanted to. When he got real cranky, he told his wife he was going out hunting. His father-in-law told him, "Don't go to those hills up there. If you do, I don't think you'll come back."

When the boy went outside he could see the hills far up there. He went hunting and got caribou from the flat. One time when he went hunting he couldn't find caribou close by, so he went up into the hills. He got one caribou and started back, but he couldn't find his way home and it got foggy. He kept walking all day, and towards evening the fog started to lift. When it lifted he saw his house close by. He went into the house and his father-in-law said, "So our son came home."

After a few days he went out hunting again. He couldn't find caribou close by, so he returned to the hills. He got caribou there and he started home again. While he was walking he got lost and couldn't find his way. He looked back and saw something just like a big black rock wall coming towards him, so he started running. After a while he looked back again and saw that it was getting closer and was beginning to close around him, so he really ran. The black rock wall started closing up until there was just enough room to run out. It looked like he might not make it out, so he put his mouth inside the shoulder of his parka and called, "Grandma, could I go home?" And she answered, "Maybe you'll come home, grandson." He ran with all his strength and he made it through the opening. When he got out he looked back and saw nothing, no rock, just the flat. He saw his house a little ways away and went over. His wife was waiting for him outside. When they went in, his father-in-law said, "Our son came home again." They didn't expect him to come home after he went to the hills.

He went out hunting again and the youngest brother came along. When he heard that they were going to the ocean his father-in-law told them, "Don't get a spotted seal. If you get one, you won't come home." They both had sleds and put kayaks on the sleds. They got to open water and started using their kayaks. They found a large round ice floe and the grandson said to his brother-in-law, "You go this way and I'll go that way." They parted and went around the ice floe. The grandson met a spotted seal. It started bothering him, so finally he killed it with his spear.

Suddenly he blacked out. When he recovered from being blacked out, he heard a noise like somebody in pain. He was in a house and a voice said, "If you take that spear out from the wounded one, maybe you'll go home." He looked around and saw a man. Then he went over to that noise like somebody in pain and found a young boy lying with a spear stuck in his back, with the harpoon line still attached. He took the spear out, and the young boy stopped suffering. The man said, "All your things are outside. Your kayak and your sled are ready to go.

Go the way that your sled points and it will take you. You will travel through the ice. If you can't use your sled and your kayak any more,

leave them and walk through the ice. If you get to open water, you'll cross it some way. There will be fishes there. Don't eat from them no matter how hungry you are. After you pass you'll find some more fishes in the water. Don't eat from them either. If you pass by those you'll get to a third bunch of fishes. You can eat from those."

After the man told him all this, the boy went out and saw his kayak and sled all ready. He put his sled towline over his shoulders and went. He kept going and when the ice got broken up he used his kayak, sometimes dragging it through the ice. When the ice got too big to drag the kayak, he left it and started walking. He walked until he came to the open water. He didn't know how to cross it. It was so far he couldn't see the other side. He didn't know what to do, and he walked around for a while. Then he thought of his *an-yuk*, his magic charm, and he took it off and then pretended to put it back on again. He became a *mitkutaylyuk*, an arctic tern, and flew around for a while.

He learned to fly, and then went into the air and started flying over the open water. Close by he saw a lot of fishes, but he thought of what the man had said, so he passed them by. He came to some more and passed them too. He was hungry, but he didn't eat. When he got to the third group, he ate from them and then flew across the water. He kept flying until he saw ice, where he landed and became a man. He walked until the going got slow, then he changed into a bird again. He flew until he saw a house close by. He landed and became a man.

When he got close, he saw that it was his house. His wife was outside waiting and they went in. His father-in-law said, "Our son came back again." He stayed there, and in a few days his brothers-in-law said, "Of all these times you have been away maybe you have a story for us, how you've hunted or where you've been, or what you did while you were away." They kept bothering him, and finally he got tired of them. He told them, "Make an *aaluyuk*. When you finish it, fill it with water, and I will tell you the story of when I was gone."

The brothers made an *aaluyuk*, finished it, and filled it with water. The boy said, "If I become some kind of animal in that water and you boys don't want me to stay here any more, don't turn the plate upside down. If you still want me, turn it upside down." Then he began telling them the story about the time he shot the spotted seal. He became a *mitkutaylyuk* in the house and started showing how he crossed the open water. He flew around the house and the brothers watched him. He said, "That's how I flew over that open water." When he was flying he got close to the water-filled plate and suddenly flew into it. The brothers turned it over right away, but it was too late. When he went through the water, he started home to his grandmother. When he got there, his grandmother was dead. The house had fallen into the ground. That boy is still a *mitkutaylyuk* now. The end.

Wanda Stalker told me this story.

The Little Old Lady Who Lived Alone

◇ A T H A P A S K A N ◇

There was a little old lady who lived alone. She always worked by herself. In summer she set a net and caught a lot of fish. She cut them and hung them up and dried them, and then she put them in her grass cache. She was happy, since she had plenty of food. When winter came, she cooked, but she cooked only bones, even though she had plenty of food. "Late winter I will run short," she thought. Sometimes she just made Indian ice cream—snow and oil mixed up—and ate that.

Every evening at dusk she opened the curtain. She made a fire and put on a pot and cooked, and dished up her food. "That's enough," she thought. "I'll close the curtain and go to bed." So then she put dirt over her fire, went out, climbed up on the roof, and closed the curtain. She went back in the doorway. She stood there, as if listening. She listened really hard. She stuck her fingers in her ears and twirled them around. Then she heard something—someone singing. She ran inside. She grabbed the washbasin out from under the shelf and poured water in it and washed her face. She combed her hair. When she was done, she reached down and got out her workbag and took out clothing, and put on her fishskin parka.

Then she went out again. In a little while, someone began to sing. Then she went back in. She got up on the shelf. She stayed there, spinning sinew. After a short time, she went out again and listened. There was someone singing. The old lady thought, "I wonder if it's a man." She went down below the house and looked around the shore. And there she saw a little fish, singing as it swam. She picked up a stick and struck the water with it. Then she went back home. She went inside. After she had sat a little while, she went back out. It was quiet. "It must have been a man," she thought. She got lonely, and began to cry. Then she went off crying into the woods.

That is the end of the story.

Qasiagssaq, the Great Liar
◇EAST GREENLAND ESKIMO◇

Qasiagssaq, men say, was a great liar. His wife was called Qigdlugssuk. He could never sleep well at night, and already being awake, he always woke his fellow villagers when they were supposed to go out hunting in the morning. But he never brought any game home himself.

One day when he had been out as usual in his kayak, without even seeing a seal, he said, "It is no use my trying to be a hunter, for I never catch anything. I may as well make up some lie or other."

And at the same moment he noticed that one of his fellow villagers was towing a big saddleback over to an island to land it there before going out after more. When he had got the seal to land, Qasiagssaq rowed around behind him and over to the seal, which he stole and towed back home. His wife was looking out for him, going outside every now and then to see if he might be near. And so finally she caught sight of a kayak coming in with a catch in tow. She shaded her eyes with both hands, one above the other, and looked through them, gazing eagerly to try and see if she could make out who it was. The kayak with its seal in tow came rowing in, and she kept on going out to look, and at last when she came out as usual she could see that it was really and truly Qasiagssaq, come home towing his catch.

"Here comes Qasiagssaq towing his catch!" cried the villagers, and when he came in, they saw that he had a great saddleback with deep black markings all over the body, and the towline was rich with trappings of the finest narwhal tusk.

"Where did you get that towline?" they asked.

"I have had it a long while," he answered, "but have never used it before today."

After they hauled the seal ashore, his wife cut out the belly-part, and when that was done, she shared out so much blubber and meat to her fellow villagers that there was hardly anything left for themselves. And then she set about cooking a meal, with a shoulder-blade for a lamp and another for a pot. And every time a kayak came in, they told the newcomer that Qasiagssaq had caught a big saddleback.

At last there was only one kayak still out, and when that one came in, they told him the same thing: "Qasiagssaq actually got a big seal!"

But the last man to arrive said this: "I got a big saddleback today and hauled it up on an island, but when I came back to fetch it, it was gone."

But the others said, "The towline that Qasiagssaq used today was furnished with toggles of pure narwhal tusk."

Later in the evening, Qasiagssaq heard a voice calling in at the window, "You, Qasiagssaq, I have come to ask if you will give me back that towline."

Qasiagssaq sprang up and said, "Here it is, you may take it back now."

But his wife, who was beside him, said, "When Qasiagssaq does such things, one feels shame for him."

"Prrr!" Qasiagssaq said to his wife, as if to frighten her, then he went about his business as if nothing had happened.

On another day, when he was out in his kayak, he said, "What's the use of my being out here? I never catch anything."

And he rowed in towards land. When he reached shore, he took his breeches down and sat on the ground, with his testicles resting on a stone. Then he took another stone to use as a hammer, and hammered until his testicles were flattened. He lay there for a long time, but finally got up and went down to his kayak, and now he could only walk with his legs wide apart. And when he came down to his kayak, he began trampling it, until all its woodwork was smashed to pieces. And then, getting into it, he heaped up a lot of ice shards upon it and even placed some inside his clothes, which were made of ravens' skins. He rowed home.

All the while, two women had been watching him.

His wife was looking out for him as usual, shading her eyes with her hands, and when at last she caught sight of his kayak, and it came nearer, she could see that it was Qasiagssaq, rowing very slowly. And when he reached land she said, "What has happened to you?"

"An iceberg calved on top of me."

Seeing her husband come home in such a condition, his wife said to the villagers, "An iceberg calved right on top of Qasiagssaq, and he just got out alive!"

But then the women who had watched Qasiagssaq came home. They said, "We saw him today. He rowed to land, took off his breeches, and hammered his testicles with a stone. Then he went down to his kayak and trampled it to bits, and when that was done he filled the kayak with ice and even put ice inside his clothes."

When his wife heard this, she said, "When Qasiagssaq does such things, we should feel shame for him."

"Prrr!" said Qasiagssaq, as if to frighten her.

After that, he lay still for a long while, waiting for his wounds to heal, and when at last his testicles healed, he went out again in his kayak. As usual, he caught nothing. He said to himself, "What's the use of my staying out here?"

And he rowed in to land. There he found an oblong stone, laid it out on his kayak, and rowed out again. When he came in sight of the other kayaks that lay waiting for seal, he stopped still, took out his two small bladder-floats made of the belly of a seal, tied his harpoon line to the stone on his kayak, and when that was done, he rowed away as fast as he could, while the kayaks that were waiting for seal looked on. Then he disappeared from sight behind an iceberg, and when he came around on the other side, his bladder-floats were gone and he was rowing as fast as he could towards land. His wife was looking out for him, shading her eyes. "What has happened now?" she said.

Qasiagssaq called out, "You don't have to be afraid of breaking the handles of your knives. I have struck a great walrus; it's gone down underwater with my two bladder-floats. Some man out after seal will be sure to find it."

Qasiagssaq didn't go out again. He remained idle. And the kayaks began to come in, and villagers went down to the shore and told them the news: "Qasiagssaq has struck a walrus!" And they said this to all the kayaks as they came home. But as usual there was one who stayed out longer than the others, and when at last he came back, late in the evening, he was told about Qasiagssaq's walrus.

"I don't believe that," the man said, "because here are his bladder-floats. They were tied to a stone, and the knot worked loose."

Everyone brought the bladders to Qasiagssaq and said, "Here's your bladder-floats. They were fastened to a stone, but the knot worked loose."

As usual, his wife said, "When Qasiagssaq does such things, you can only feel shame for him."

"Prrr!" said Qasiagssaq, to frighten her. And after that, he went around as if nothing had happened.

One day he was out as usual in his kayak, at a place of much ice. He caught sight of a spotted seal, which had crawled up on the ice. He rowed up to it, lifted his harpoon, but just as he was about to throw, he said, "Wouldn't it be a great pity if that skin, which is to be made into breeches for my wife, was pierced with holes by the point of a harpoon?" So he lay down and began to whistle to the seal. Spotted seals can sometimes be caught by whistling. And just as he was about to grab hold of the seal, it went under the ice. He watched it carefully. When it came up again, he rowed to it, lifted his harpoon. But he said, "It would be a pity to put a hole in the skin." The seal went down and didn't come up in sight.

Well, one day Qasiagssaq heard of an old couple in another village who had lost their child. So he went to visit. He arrived and went into their house, and there the couple sat, mourning. He said, "What's the trouble here?"

"They're mourning."

"Why?"

"They've lost a child. Their daughter died the other day."

"What was her name?"

"Nipisartangiaq."

Qasiagssaq cleared his throat and said in a loud voice, "Today my little daughter Nipisartangiaq is doubtless crying at her mother's side."

The mourning couple looked up excitedly and said, "Ah, we're so grateful that you gave your daughter that name. Your little girl can have all the clothes we have here. The soul of our dead girl will return into the body of your daughter, because she is named Nipisartangiaq!"

They gave him pearls and clothes.

"Here's my cooking pot, too," the mother said.

When Qasiagssaq was about to set out for home, they gave him lots of food to take to his little girl.

When he got home, his fellow villagers asked, "Where did you get all that?"

"Some people in another village set out on a journey, but they were hurried and forgetful and left all of this behind."

Towards evening, a number of kayaks arrived; they were people coming to visit and had brought meat with them. They said, "Tell Qasiagssaq and his wife to come down and fetch this meat for their little daughter."

"Qasiagssaq and his wife have no children," the villagers said. "We know them well, and they have no children."

When the visitors heard this, they said, "Then tell Qasiagssaq to return the beads and clothes and the cooking pot."

The villagers got those things and returned them.

Qasiagssaq's wife said, "Now you have lied again. I feel shame for you."

"Prrr!" said Qasiagssaq to frighten her, and went on as if nothing had happened.

It is said that Qasiagssaq's wife Qigdlugssuk had a mother who lived in another village, and she had a son whose name was Eernilik. One day Qasiagssaq set out to visit them. He arrived at their place, and when he walked into their house it was quite dark, because they had no blubber for lamp-oil, and their little child was crying because it was starving. Qasiagssaq cleared his throat and loudly asked, "What's the matter with him?"

"He's hungry as usual," the mother said.

Then Qasiagssaq said, "I should've brought some blubber with me. In our village, seals are thrown out every day. You must come home with me."

The next morning, they all set out together. When they got to Qasiagssaq's village, but before they landed with their kayak, Qasiagssaq's wife's mother saw a lot of raven bones on a refuse heap. "Agh! one has got away," Qasiagssaq cried out.

Quickly he snared the raven. His wife cooked it, and their lamp glowed dimly, and his mother-in-law was given raven meat to eat. Later, she was well fed by the other villagers, who gave her meat to take on her return journey. Qasiagssaq gave her nothing.

On another day he was out in his kayak, and when he came home in the evening he said, "I found a dead whale. Tomorrow we should all go out in the big boat and cut it up."

The next day, the big boat and the kayaks all set out to the eastward, and after a while the villagers said, "Where's the whale?"

"Over there," said Qasiagssaq, "beyond that little ness."

They rowed up, but when they reached the place there was no whale to be seen. "Where is it? Where is it?"

"Up there, beyond the ness," Qasiagssaq said.

Again, they reached the place, and no whale.

"Qasiagssaq is lying as usual," a villager said. "I say we kill him."

But Qasiagssaq said, "Wait a little, maybe a whale will wash up."

"He's only trouble to us. He's always been trouble to us. This is serious."

And at last they killed Qasiagssaq.

Witiko Father and Son Bested by a Conjuror
◇ J A M E S   B A Y   C R E E ◇

Once there were two men, a father and a son, who always went off together to do murder. They always looked for a place where people could be taken unawares.

It was nearly spring and the son walked about until he found no less than ten canoes all together at a lake. He said to his father, "I found ten canoes along the lake." The father replied, "I guess all those canoes will be in use this spring." The father and son continued on and stopped around the point to sleep.

Later, they were trying to fish and covering their lines so as not to be seen. All of a sudden they saw ten families coming across the ice to meet the summer. The ten families put up two large tents. The father said to his son, "We will not touch them until toward morning when they are sound asleep." The father had another son who was not a murderer, but the man did not know where he was.

In the morning the father and son went to look at the ten families while they were sleeping. The father said, "We will each go into a tent, you in one and I in another." And this they did until they had killed all ten families. The old man met a strong man and was nearly mastered by him, but the old man finally managed to get clear of him at last and killed him. When he was finished killing his lot he went to his son and asked, "Are you finished killing your lot?" The son answered, "Yes." The father said, "Bring a light over to this tent. I want to see who is this who is so strong." The son brought a light, and the old man came to find it was his other son. He started to cry, "You know this is your older brother?" when he saw he had killed his own son. The younger brother began to cry for his brother. Then the father said, "What good is it for us to cry like this? He is the first one we will eat. We have lots of meat now, enough to last us the whole summer."

In the summer they gave up their murdering ways and lived like other Indians and ate what other Indians ate. At last a man started to wonder how he could make away with the two murderers. This man had a daughter and two sons. The two sons tried to give the sister to the young murderer. So he married the girl. The father and the son and his new wife still traveled together. So when winter came along they started their same game of murdering and eating people, but the girl never helped them do anything like that.

The girl continued to live just as she had before. She also told her mother's people everything her husband and father-in-law were doing. When summer came again the three of them lived with the rest of the people and there was no murdering. Winter came again and they started looking around for people to kill. The son often went off and left his wife with his father. The girl and the father would camp together. Once when the son was off he found some people who were starving. When he came home he told his father, "I have found some starving people. I found some people not worth killing because they are so poor." The father said, "Do not worry about it. Hunt and give some game to these people to fatten them."

The three of them went off to see these poor Indians, and all lived together. The young man started to hunt and killed a moose. He gave this to the starving people to eat, and they started to fatten up a little. The man who was starving had a large family, including a small child still in arms. The father told a woman who was starving, "Bring the baby. I will hold it while you are eating." The woman passed the child to the old man to hold. While he was holding it the baby started to cry. The old man was feeling the child below the ribs to see if it was fat enough, and he squeezed the baby.

The starving people did not know who the murderers were. They didn't know that those who were feeding them intended to kill them. The wife of the young man told them on the sly, "You know, these people are going to kill you." The people started to think how they could save themselves from being murdered. The man thought of a plan to save his own life. He knew well enough he could save his own life by running away, but also knew he could not take his wife and children.

One morning when it was very wild, snowing, drifting, and blowing hard, the man said, "This will be a fine day for me to run off." He had a lot of moose bones still from the moose that had been killed. He told the murderers, "The tent is getting very dirty from cooking inside. I think it is time we shifted camp." The old man said, "Fine. It is time to shift the tent. The wood is getting scarce around here, too." The murderers got ready to shift the tent. The man said to them, "I will not come now to where you are shifting. I shall come tomorrow. I will smash up my moose bones and boil them. If I drink the liquor perhaps it will fatten me." The murderers said, "All right. Come tomorrow. We will wait for you to come to us."

The murderers went on ahead. The father told the son, "Look for a good place where there is plenty of firewood to put up the tent." They were planning on doing the murdering there. When they finished putting up the tent they went to sleep. The next day was a wild and awful day. It was snowing and drifting. The tracks of anyone walking would be covered up.

As soon as the starving family had gotten rid of the murderers, they took off in another direction altogether. The man knew of a large lake and made for it. At last he came to the lake with his wife and children. The lake was round. They went to the center of the lake and came back just a little way from where they had first stepped out on it. The man knew all about this lake. He knew where it always drifted up very high. So they went there and dug a hole in the snow and climbed into it, man, wife, and children. The hole was made in a high snowbank. All were under the snow and before long the hole was drifted over. They stayed in that hole.

The next day the murderers began to think the starving people were very long in coming to see them. The old man was getting cross. He decided to kill them where he had left them, so he went to see where they were. He went alone without his son. When he came to the place they had camped, he saw no signs of them; the tent was drifted over. There was not a sign of a track anywhere. The old man started to call out with all his might. When he was finished calling out he saw a very fresh-looking path. He went after the starving people. After a short distance he lost the track and could not find it. Again, he called out and his voice was something like thunder. The sound would go up— that was where he was getting his help from above. When he stopped calling, he saw two steps of the path quite plainly. Then he tried calling a third time, but it was no use and he did not see anything. So he turned and went back to see his son and his daughter-in-law.

The old man was very mad when he came back to the tent. He blamed his daughter-in-law for telling the family. He said to her, "It is you that has been telling them. That is how they found out what we were going to do." She replied, "I never told them. It is you. Your hearts are making a noise at night while you sleep." The daughter-in-law was a conjuror and knew exactly where the starving people were through her conjuring thoughts. Her scheme had always been to try to save the people she knew were to be murdered.

The next day they all went off to look for the starving family. They reached the place where the old man had given his last call before turning back. There they chopped down a small sapling and cut it into three pieces, so each had a stick to probe the snow to find where the old path was. Finally, they reached the big lake by feeling for the path under the snow. They followed the path with no trouble until they got to the center of the lake where the starving man had turned sharply and headed back to the shore. But they lost the track, and instead of returning to the shore as the starving man had done, they went straight across the lake. They saw no signs of any trail on the other shore of the lake. Then they followed the shore of the lake, feeling for the path with their sticks.

The daughter-in-law knew exactly where the starving people were lying. So at last they came to the spot where the family had stood when they returned from the center of the lake. The daughter-in-law said, "You go ahead and start probing again over there," pointing in the direction of the family. She went off in the other direction and felt for the path. The father and son walked right over the starving people under the snow. Soon they gave up looking for them, although they still thought the people must be around somewhere. They never bothered to look for the people themselves, but looked only for their tracks.

The old man wanted to continue probing to find the tracks of the people near where they were actually hiding. His daughter-in-law said, "It is no use trying any more. I have been probing all around here with my stick and have felt nothing at all." At last they all got tired of looking for them and stopped. The father said, "They must be very far away now."

The starving people stayed under the snow until the crust formed. Their tracks would not be seen on the crust. They waited until that time came, and went off and left the lake. So they saved themselves.

The murderers had a hard time after that, though they kept up their murdering job. The old man was very fond of his daughter-in-law. However, the son always had it in his mind to kill his wife and eat her in the winter. The old man never wanted to let his daughter-in-law get fat. The young husband was always watching his wife to see if she was getting fat. He would cut his wife's upper arm to see if there was any fat. The old man told his son, "You are making her cry now because you are cutting her. It is not worthwhile to eat her. She is too poor."

In the summer the woman met other people and showed them where her husband had been cutting her arm to see if she was fat. Later, the two brothers of the woman were living with their mother. The brothers often went out with their brother-in-law. One day the young man told his wife, "I cannot hold off any longer. I guess I will kill your brothers today." He went way off to a beaver lodge to work beaver. After he left, the woman told her brothers their lives were in danger and that they would be killed that day.

The old man and the woman's father were sitting in the tent with her. There was a large stone by the fire on the opposite side of the tent. The brothers went off after the husband at the beaver lodge. The old people stayed in the tent with their daughter. Her father got up and was going to throw out the stone. He said, "The stone is lying in the way." The stone was a very big one and was stuck in the sand, but finally he got hold of it and pulled it right up and threw it right out of the tent. The stone was so large that no other person could have lifted it. The old man watched the man moving such a big stone and throwing it.

The three young fellows were working at the beaver lodge during this time. They had shut the beaver in a runway in the bank, not in his lodge. The young husband told one of the brothers, "You feel for the beaver." He had decided that when the brother was feeling for the beaver he would run a chisel into the back of his neck. Just as he was about to spear the man, the other brother caught the chisel and knocked it to one side so it missed. Then the brother being attacked jumped up, took the chisel, and threw it away.

The two brothers were very strong and were in no way frightened of the young murderer. They grabbed hold of the man and wrestled with him, using only their hands. While one of the brothers wrestled with the murderer, the other ran to the lake and made a hole in the ice. Both the brother and the murderer were about the same strength, and before the ice-hole was finished they were tired out. The other brother came and started wrestling just as the murderer called out with all his might, and it sounded just like thunder. So the brother called out too, and his voice was far louder. They continued to wrestle while the other brother went to the lake and finished making a hole in the ice. When the hole was big enough to shove a person down it, they tried to throw the murderer in. At last, they got him in the hole and shoved him under the ice. The man was alive under the ice for a long time and he was singing. That is why the ice now makes a humming noise.

The two brothers never left the lake until they were sure that the young husband was not moving. Then they went back to the tent. When they came to the tent they started to sing out, "We have killed the one who was always wanting to kill us." They entered the tent and said, "We have killed the one who always wanted to kill us."

The old man was sitting inside the tent, so they said to him, "Come out. We will kill you, too. We do not want to make a mess of blood in our tent." The father was sitting bare-legged in the tent; he had been telling those in the tent about all the people he had killed, as he had expected his son to kill the two brothers.

The old man crawled out of the tent; he did not walk. The brothers were outside holding their chisels on their shoulders. As the old man came out of the tent, the brothers struck both his legs with the chisels and broke them. So when his legs were broken the marrow came out of his bones. The brothers took the marrow from the old man's bones and shoved it in his mouth. As they did that they asked him, "Is it pretty rich?" The old man answered, "Of course it is rich. I have killed so many people it is bound to be rich." The brothers gave him a good clip on the head when he said that. So that finished the murderers.

Alder-Block

◇ Y U K A G H I R ◇

There lived an old woman who had neither son nor daughter. One time after cooking her supper, she climbed to the roof of her house to stop up the chimney-hole. Then she heard from within a small child's voice. She was much frightened, but still she descended hastily and ran into the house. An infant boy was lying on the floor. She swaddled him and prepared food for him. She fed him on blood soup and minced meat, and he grew from year to year. She gave him the name Alder-Block. He was an excellent carpenter, and made fine canoes of boards and of hollowed tree-trunks.

One time he said to his foster mother, "Mother, give me permission to leave. I want to visit all the wonders of earth and sea." The woman said, "How can that be? And who will then procure food for me? You are almost full-grown. All my hope lies in you." Nevertheless, he left in the nighttime and went away across the sea. He traveled and traveled, and at last he saw an island. On the island there stood a house. In it lived the witch Yagha. She had three daughters: one, Five-Eyes Girl; another, Six-Eyes Girl; and the third, Eight-Eyes Girl. She herself had ten eyes. The witch Yagha saw the canoe and said to her daughters, "Here, girls! Get ready! A small reindeer is coming from the sea. Do try and lure it hither." The eldest daughter cooked flour-cakes. She filled a birchbark vessel as big as a man with them and put it on the shore as a decoy. She hid herself nearby in order to catch the boy as soon as he should land. The boy saw the birchbark vessel full of cakes. He came close to the shore and said aloud, "First eye, fall asleep! second eye, fall asleep! third eye, fall asleep! fourth eye, fall asleep! fifth eye, fall asleep!" The girl fell asleep. He emptied the birchbark vessel into his canoe. He threw the vessel into the water, approached the girl, and taking off his breeches he defecated upon her head. After that he struck her with the paddle and broke her back. That done, he paddled away across the sea, back to his mother.

So he brought his mother all those cakes. She was much astonished. She asked him, "O child, Alder-Block Boy! Where did you get all these cakes?"—"At such-and-such a place." The boy told her everything. The old woman was very much afraid. "Now," she said, "I will not let you go even one step from my side. The witch Yagha will devour you." That very night, as soon as the old woman had fallen asleep, Alder-Block descended toward the water, boarded his canoe, and set off again. The girls saw him, as before. They prepared a vessel with cakes and put it out on the shore. The second sister hid nearby, ready to catch him. He paddled to the shore and called out aloud, "First eye, fall asleep! second eye, fall asleep! third eye, fall asleep! fourth and fifth and sixth eyes, fall asleep!" Again, the girl fell asleep. He emptied the vessel into his canoe. Then he defecated upon the girl and broke her back with a blow of his paddle. Then he paddled back across the sea with his booty. The girl, however, came to, and crawled to her mother. The mother sprinkled her with the water of life and youth, and the girl became as sound as before.

The boy's mother took the cakes, but she reproached him: "O child, you go away secretly in the nighttime. I shall lose you and shall not know where to find you. The witch Yagha will devour you. Do stop these awful doings!" The very same night the boy went again. This time the youngest daughter tried to catch him. She also put upon the shore a vessel full of cakes and hid nearby. He paddled shoreward and counted aloud, "First eye, fall asleep! second eye, fall asleep! third eye, fall asleep! fourth and fifth and sixth and seventh and eighth, do fall asleep!" He took the cakes and defecated upon the girl. Then he struck her upon the back and paddled away. The girl could hardly crawl back to her mother.

The next day the boy came again. This time it was Yagha herself who tried to catch him. She put the vessel upon the shore and hid nearby. He counted aloud, "First eye, fall asleep! second eye, fall asleep! third and fourth, fall asleep! fifth and sixth and seventh, do fall asleep! eighth and ninth, do fall asleep!" But he forgot the tenth eye. He took the vessel and emptied it into his canoe, but the witch did not stir. He was about to take off his breeches and defecate upon her, but she caught him by the breeches and carried him home. "There, you dogs, you could not catch this small reindeer, but I have caught him." They had an oven dug in the ground. Then Yagha said, "I will call my brother; meanwhile, cook this reindeer for our meal. When brother and I come back, we will have a meal of him." She set off.

The eldest daughter brought an iron shovel and said to the boy, "Well, Alder-Block, sit down on the shovel." He spread his legs and stretched his arms. She tried to put him down into the oven, but could not do it. "Why," said she, "Alder-Block, you hold your body too clumsily. Sit down on the shovel, then draw up your legs and keep your arms together."—"How, together? I do not know how. You had better show me."—"Look here, you booby!" She took a seat on the shovel and held her body quite close. So he thrust her into the oven, snatched the shovel back, and shut the oven door. In this way he killed the eldest daughter of Yagha.

The second daughter came and asked him, "O, Alder-Block, what makes it smell so strong here of something singed?"—"It does indeed," said Alder-Block. "Your sister singed a leg of mine and also an arm, but in the end took pity on me and allowed me to live."—"I will show you what pity is! Sit down on the shovel, go your way down into the oven." He spread his legs and stretched his arms just as before. By no means could she thrust him down the oven. "O Alder-Block, you hold yourself in quite a wrong way. Draw up your legs and keep your arms together."—"How, together? I do not know how."—"Even so, you booby!" She sat down on the shovel and drew up her legs. He immediately thrust her down into the oven and shut the oven door. There she was roasted.

The third daughter came too, the youngest one. "You, there, Alder-Block! Why does it smell so here of something singed?"—"Yes, it does," said Alder-Block. "Your second sister singed a leg of mine and then also an arm. Then she took pity on me and let me live."—"Oh, I will teach you what pity is! Sit down on the shovel, go your way down into the oven." He spread his legs and stretched his arms. She could not thrust him in. "Oh, there, Alder-Block! You do not hold yourself right. You must draw up your legs and keep your arms together."—"I do not know how. You must show me." She sat down on the shovel, and he thrust her into the oven. After a while all three were done just right. He took them out of the oven and drew them up to the ground. Then he prepared the meal, cut up the meat, and laid it out on dishes and in troughs. All these he arranged on a large table. He put the table near the large bed of Yagha, where she usually took her meals, and concealed all three heads under the bed near her seat. He hid himself behind the chimney and waited for Yagha.

After a while she came back. She was driving a mortar, urging it on with a pestle, and sweeping away her tracks with a big broom. She had not found her brother at home, so she came all alone. She entered the house and saw the food all ready for a meal, so she felt gratified and exclaimed, "See there! my daughters have prepared the meal, and they themselves are gone, perhaps for a little walk." She took a seat near the table and tried to eat, but the first mouthful stuck in her throat. "Oh, oh, oh!" said the witch, "what is the matter? Why does even the first mouthful stick so in my throat? Is it possible that Alder-Block is a kinsman of mine?" She took another morsel, but could not swallow it at all. She spat it out, and looked down under the bed, and there were the three heads of her daughters. She clapped her hands and wailed aloud, "Ah, you hound, Alder-Block! You have eaten all my daughters, and none has stuck in your throat."

Yagha looked around and found the boy behind the chimney. "Ah, ah, now I have you!" She caught him by the nape of the neck and hurled him across the room and back again. After a few kicks and pushes, he felt nearly dead. Then he called aloud, "O granny! that is enough. I want to ease myself before I die."—"Go, then, and ease yourself." He ran to her storehouse. She had there two wells—one full of the water of life and youth, the other full of the water of death. He drank his fill of the water of life and youth, then he changed the places of both wells. After that he came back. He caught Yagha and threw her across the room and back again. After a few kicks, she felt very feeble and asked of him, "O Alder-Block! I want to ease myself."—"All right, you may go." She went to the storehouse and wanted to drink of the water of life and youth, but instead she drank of the water of death. After that she went back, hardly able to move. As soon as she stepped over the sill, her belly burst, and she dropped down stone-dead.

The boy gathered all her wealth—the costly furs, dried meat and fish, and all kinds of provisions—and took it to his mother. He also took along the water of life and youth. His mother drank of the water and become quite young, like a fresh berry. He became immensely rich. The end.

The Crow Story

◇ T A N A I N A   I N D I A N ◇

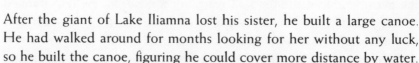

After the giant of Lake Iliamna lost his sister, he built a large canoe. He had walked around for months looking for her without any luck, so he built the canoe, figuring he could cover more distance by water.

Since he lived by himself, there was no one else around to admire his craft—that is, until old Chulyen, the crow, flew over one day.

When Chulyen saw the canoe down there on the beach he almost came to a dead stop in midair. He circled several times until a plan formed in his mind; then he flew on out of sight and landed in the woods.

Now old Chulyen had a very strong will, and whenever he needed a disguise he could change himself into a man or whatever he wanted. So now he thought real hard: "I wish I were a man. Make me a handsome prince—a rich man's son."

So he was changed into a young handsome man with fine clothes and a nice moustache, and he walked out of the forest to meet the giant. Chulyen walked right up to him and started talking. The giant seemed to like the young man, so it wasn't long before the subject swung around to the canoe.

"It sure is a fine canoe," Chulyen said politely. "Do you suppose it would be all right if I tried it out a little bit—just right here in the bay, I mean? You wouldn't mind, would you?"

"Not at all," replied the giant. He was pleased that such a nice young man admired his canoe so much.

So old Chulyen pushed the canoe out from the beach and paddled around in a circle, not very far offshore. Then he brought the canoe back and thanked the giant for the ride.

"That's quite all right. Any time," the giant said. "Any time at all."

So the next day the young man came back again, to talk with the giant and take a ride in his canoe. Only this time when he took it, Chulyen paddled quite a bit farther out in the bay, almost to the mouth, before he turned around and brought the canoe back. Again he thanked the giant for the ride.

"Any time," the giant said.

It was early in the morning of the third day when the young man showed up for another ride. By this time the giant really liked him and trusted him with the canoe. He smiled as he pushed old Chulyen out in the water and watched him paddle around in the bay, then clear out and around the point and out of sight. He stood there on the beach for quite a while waiting for the young man to bring his canoe back, before he realized that he wasn't coming back.

Meanwhile, old Chulyen was really laughing at how he had fooled the silly giant and tricked him out of such a fine canoe. He paddled around all day just enjoying himself, and when night came he camped many miles from the home of the giant.

The next morning he got up and spent the whole day just paddling by himself in the canoe. But by the end of the third afternoon he began to get lonely. He decided it wasn't much fun paddling around by himself. So he started looking for a partner. As he paddled along the beach, he began singing this song:

> *Vud sha dah' ga yu' a?*
> Who wants to come along with me for a ride?

Before long a moose heard him singing and walked out on the beach.

"How about me?" he asked. "I'd like to go along with you for a ride."

"Oh, not you!" said the young man. "Your hooves are too sharp. They might make a hole in the bottom of my canoe. No, I don't want you for a partner."

A porcupine came out next, and said, "How about me? I'd like to come out and go for a ride with you."

"No. Not you," said old Chulyen. "Your quills are too sharp. They might make holes in the sides of my canoe."

Pretty soon then a nice fat seal popped up alongside the canoe and said, "How about taking me for a partner? I'd like to ride in your canoe."

"You're just the one I want," said the crow. "Come on and get in."

As the seal climbed into the boat, he looked so fat and juicy that the old crow started thinking right away about how to kill him and eat him.

Chulyen told the seal that it was getting late and they'd better stop and make camp. He said he knew of a good spot. So they went ashore and pulled the canoe up out of the water. Then old Chulyen turned back into a crow and started walking up into the woods with the seal following along behind. He was heading for a place he remembered far inland where there wasn't any water. The crow knew that the seal couldn't survive for very long without water. Old Chulyen was pretty wise and very crooked.

When they finally reached the spot they made camp, and the crafty old crow sat down next to the fire.

"What are we going to eat?" he asked. "I'm hungry."

"I don't know," said the seal. "I'm getting hungry too."

The crow thought for a while. Then he said, "I know what we can do. I'll cut my foot off and roast it on a stick for you over the fire, and

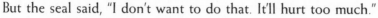

you can cut off one of your flippers and cook it for me."

But the seal said, "I don't want to do that. It'll hurt too much."

"No, no," said Chulyen, "it won't hurt. You watch. I'll make it so you won't even feel it."

And before the seal could say another word the crow grabbed an axe and chopped off one of his flippers. Then quickly he spit on the wound and rubbed it all over.

"Why, it doesn't hurt at all," said the seal.

As they watched, the seal's wound healed right over.

"See" said the crow, "I told you."

Then he whacked off his own skinny foot for the seal. Soon they were both sizzling over the fire. But the seal began to feel that he'd been cheated. As the crow's foot cooked, it shriveled up and turned hard and black, and didn't look very good to eat at all. But the seal's flipper was roasting a juicy brown and grease was just rolling off the sides, making sizzling sounds as it sputtered in the fire.

The seal remarked how dried-up and skinny the crow's foot was, while his own flipper was fat and greasy, and that the trade didn't seem quite fair. So as soon as the seal turned his back the crow smeared grease from the flipper all over his foot, which by that time looked like a burnt stick.

"Look," he said. "Grease is coming out all over my foot now."

The seal looked, and sure enough, real grease was rolling liberally down the grizzled remains of Chulyen's spindly foot. He felt a little better.

Soon the meat was done, and the two partners settled back for a feast. The seal's flipper tasted excellent and made a meal fit for a chief, but the crow's foot tasted even worse than it looked. The only thing it did was make the seal thirsty.

"I need a drink," he said. "That dried-up foot made me thirsty. Where can I find some water?"

"You wait right here," said Chulyen. "I'll go look for water. When I find some I'll bring it back here for you."

The seal thought it was nice of the crow to make such an offer and said, yes, that would be fine. So old Chulyen went off to search for water.

For the longest time, however, he didn't even leave camp. He just hung around in the bushes and watched the blubbery seal get thirstier and thirstier. Then, when the old crow did leave, he stayed away for quite a while. By the time he finally came strolling back into camp with some water, the seal thought he was going to die and ran to meet him. But just before they reached each other, the crow tripped and fell and spilled the water all over the ground. The seal almost had a heart attack.

Chulyen apologized so much the fainting seal forgave him. Then he said, "Come on with me. I'll show you where you can get some water."

So they started off, the seal so weak from thirst he could hardly walk. They went a long way before they came to three wells of water in the ground. It was all the seal could do to keep from diving right in as he lunged for the first well.

But the old crow said, "Wait! You can't drink at that well. Why the idea of it!—a seal of your prestige and dignity. That well is the one slaves drink at. You can't drink there!"

So the seal, without a word, rushed on to the second well. But before he could immerse himself, the crow said, "Hold on! You can't drink at that well. That's not for a man of your position and prominence. Only the middle-class people—the ordinary villagers—drink there. You must quench your thirst at the well of the chiefs and rich men."

At that, the seal hurled himself without comment toward the last well. He plunged his head fully beneath the surface of the water and began gorging himself. He was completely dried out. Right away old Chulyen jumped at him and began pecking a hole in him to pull his guts out from behind. Just once the seal popped his head above the water.

"Ouch!" he said. "What are you doing?"

"Why, you're so dirty," the crow said. "I'm trying to clean you up." And he went on pecking.

The seal was so thirsty he just dunked his head under the water again and kept drinking. Soon old Chulyen had pecked a hole right into the seal (for a seal's hide is tender) and pulled his guts out. The seal died then, and the crow feasted on blubber for several days.

At the end of this time, when the meat had all been eaten, Chulyen changed back into a man. Returning to the water's edge, he launched his canoe and paddled on down the shoreline to a nearby village.

As he got closer Chulyen began crying so loud that even before he'd landed people from the village were running down to the beach to see what had happened. As they helped pull the canoe out of the water, they asked him what was wrong. The poor crow explained to them through his tears how he and his partner—a seal—had been eating supper in camp and how the seal had gotten something caught in his throat and choked to death right before his eyes.

"And there was nothing I could do to help," he sniffed.

The villagers thought that was really a sad story, and they brought him up to tell it to the chief.

"Yes," Chulyen said, "it's true. I just lost my buddy. We were camped back down the shore a ways, and we were eating when he choked to death."

At the very moment he was crying and telling this sad tale, Chulyen belched and up came a chunk of seal fat.

The villagers jumped to their feet.

"You're the one," they said. "You killed him and ate him."

They tried to grab old Chulyen, but he changed himself back into a crow and flew off. He made it safely out of the village, but lost his canoe in the bargain.

Soon after that the old crow made friends with a magpie and a water ouzel.

"We can kill bears together," he told them.

"How can we do that?" they asked him.

"Simple! One of us can just fly over and land near a bear. If you sit with your tail turned toward him, he'll think you don't see him and try to grab you. When he reaches out his arm, you can fly in quickly and cut him under his arm and kill him.

"I'll try it first," said Chulyen.

The first bear he tried it on was a big brownie fishing for salmon in a stream. The old crow flew up behind him and landed on a rock. The bear didn't see him at first, and Chulyen fidgeted for several minutes right behind him. But as soon as the bear turned and spotted him, Chulyen jumped backward and flew off.

"You're scared," they told him when he came back.

"No, I'm not," he said. "But you guys make too much noise."

The magpie decided to try it next on the same bear, and he surprised the others by lasting longer than Chulyen did. But when the bear started to reach out for him, he lost his nerve and flew off.

The water ouzel was sure he could do better than his partners, so after the bear had settled back down to fishing again, the tiny black bird flew over and landed right beside him, but facing the other way. Since the little bird's tail was toward him, the bear thought he had a meal for sure. But just as he reached out to grab it, the little ouzel swooped in and cut the bear under his arm and the bear died.

After that the water ouzel killed lots of bears for the three of them to eat. In fact, there was so much meat they had to build a house to store it in.

It wasn't long, however, before they noticed that the meat and fat seemed to be disappearing from the cache-house during the night. So one evening the little water ouzel hid inside the door of the house with a stick and waited to see who was stealing their food.

After dark he heard someone walking around outside. When the door slowly pushed open, the ouzel jumped out and began hitting the thief with his stick. But before he could capture him or tell who it was, the intruder ran off.

The next morning Chulyen showed up with scars all over him.

When asked about it, he said, "I hit myself with a stick."

But the magpie and the ouzel were suspicious now, and several nights later both of them waited inside the cache for the thief. When old Chulyen showed up they knew he was the one, but they waited until he was inside and starting to eat the meat before they jumped him.

"I wasn't stealing anything," he told them after they caught him red-handed. "You guys didn't tie the meat down very good and it was falling out. I was just fixing it up."

But they knew then, and they didn't want Chulyen around any more, so they chased him away.

"I never did like you guys anyhow," he yelled back at them as he flew off.

It was a crisp and beautiful spring afternoon, so Chulyen just flew around wondering what to do next. He sure felt like settling down in a village for a while, but everybody knew him too well. No one wanted an old crook like Chulyen around.

Late that same afternoon, he flew over a village of geese. It was situated in a nice little bay, and the people seemed friendly enough, so he stopped in for the night. In fact old Chulyen liked the geese people so well that he decided to spend the summer with them.

In time he fell in love with a goose girl—the chief's daughter—and with the chief's permission they were married. (Proof of their marriage exists to this day. The Canadian brant and the Canada goose have a black head and neck, and several varieties have black feet. These are the descendants of Chulyen and his wife.)

But as fall rolled around, his brothers-in-law told him they would soon be heading south for the winter, and that he would have to stay behind and rejoin them in the spring. Old Chulyen, however, decided that he would go along.

"But it's such a long way," they insisted, "and we have to fly way out over the ocean. You'll never make it."

Chulyen knew better.

"If you fellers can make it, I can make it too," he said. "Watch. I'll show you how well I can fly."

So he swooped into the air. He shot straight up until he was almost out of sight, then he tucked in his wings and dived. He rolled and flipped and twirled until all the geese were amazed.

After that, his brothers-in-law didn't feel they had the right to keep him from going along. They still didn't think he would make it, but what could they say?

So before long the stubborn old crow found himself stretched out in an arrowhead of geese, flying south for the winter. It took only a few days, however, for Chulyen to find out that what his brothers-in-law had told him was true after all.

They were flying high, way out over the Pacific Ocean, when Chulyen began to drop back out of the formation, unable to keep up. There was no place to land, yet he couldn't keep going. The geese didn't know what to do with him. In desperation, they began taking turns packing him. When one goose got tired, another took his place, until finally the geese themselves began wearing out, and they saw that it just wasn't going to work.

So, after talking about it among themselves, they decided to drop him right where they were, or they would endanger their own chances of reaching their winter grounds. Even Chulyen's wife had to leave him and go on. If she stayed behind she'd freeze to death when it turned cold. At least this way he might make it to shore and back up the coast to home.

So, although they were sorry to do it, the geese wished him farewell, then flew right out from under him and beat their way south.

The crow pitched down, down, down. Old Chulyen's orneriness had really got him into a jam this time! But just before he hit, he went to work with that magical mind of his.

"I wish a rock would come up right under me."

And there was a rock. Right up out of the lapping waves a reef rose to meet old Chulyen, and he rested there for several days before turning homeward.

When he was ready to go, however, he had no idea which way to turn. But he took off on instinct, and flew for many hours toward the horizon.

Chulyen was just starting to get tired when he spotted a beluga floating lazily among the ocean swells. He dropped down to ask the long white whale for a ride.

"I'm lost," he said. "Will you take me to land?"

"Sure," said the beluga. "Crawl into the hole in my back and I'll dive. Then whenever you want to come up for air, just holler."

So Chulyen burrowed into the whale's blowhole, and the beluga headed for shore. After a while the old crow hollered for him to surface, and he did. Climbing out onto the whale's back, Chulyen could already see the mountains in the distance.

Now when a beluga is just floating normally on the surface of the water, his eyes are still underneath, so he can't see above the water.

This is why he asked, "Can you see land yet?"

"No," said the crow. "All I can see is water."

So the beluga dived again and raced toward shore. A while later he returned to the surface, and once more old Chulyen crawled out on his back. They were almost to the shore.

"Can you see the land yet?" the beluga asked.

"I can just barely see the mountaintops way off in the distance," Chulyen lied.

"That's funny," said the whale. "I can feel the water getting shallower under me."

"Must be a reef," replied the crow. "Dive again and swim fast so we can reach the land soon. I'm anxious to get home."

So the beluga submerged again and swam his best. He went faster, and faster, and faster—until all of a sudden they ran right up onto the beach, way out of the water. And before the surprised beluga could squirm his way back down off the land, Chulyen jumped out on the beach and started throwing rocks into his blowhole. Soon it was so filled up the beluga couldn't breathe, and he suffocated to death.

The old crow started living inside the beluga's stomach that same night, feasting on the choicest of its insides.

The next morning as he was eating around inside the rib-cage, the crow heard voices. Looking through a hole he had chewed in the beluga's side, he saw two men approaching. Chulyen didn't want them to know who he was, so he flew straight up out of the blowhole like a shot until he was almost out of sight, then he turned and plunged into the woods way inland. There he changed himself into a handsome, well-dressed *cushkaveah*, and walked over to meet the two strangers.

When they saw him they wondered where he had come from. He told them he'd been just passing by when he saw them, and thought he would come down and say hello.

"We've found a dead beluga," they said. "But a strange thing happened. Something black came out of its stomach faster than the wind, and went straight up and out of sight."

"That's a bad sign," he said. "You'd better not eat any of that meat."

They agreed with him that it didn't look good. Then after they had talked some more, they invited him back with them to spend the night.

The two strangers lived in a village just down the beach around a couple of bends, so it wasn't long before old Chulyen was sitting with the chief in his *nichithl*. A sad story had already formed in the crow's mind.

"Yes, Chief," he said. "I am a *cushkaveah*, but my family once found a beluga lying on the beach when I wasn't around. They began eating on it, and every one of them died. I'm the only one left now."

Chulyen cried a little bit at this part, and the villagers felt sorry for him and invited him to stay with them, since he had no family. Of course the old crow was more than happy to stay there with them.

So he made the village his home for a while and married up with the chief's daughter. All the people liked him, since he was so handsome, and because he was married to her. They let him do just about anything he wanted.

Meanwhile, Chulyen was slipping out of the village every night to go down and feast on the dead beluga. But because everyone liked him so well, no one suspected anything. They even let him sleep quite late in the mornings, so it was easy for him to stay out all night.

After a while people began noticing that the beluga was getting smaller, and they suspected that someone was feeding on it. But they never thought of old Chulyen.

"Naw," he said. "Nobody would eat that old stuff."

And because they liked him, everybody believed what he said. But finally the people started getting fed up with him because he slept so late all the time. So one morning several of the men came in very early to drag him out of bed to go to work. It was then they noticed that something was smeared all over his upper lip. When they looked closer they found his moustache was caked with beluga grease! Right away they knew what he'd been doing and who it was.

"You're Chulyen!" they yelled.

He came straight awake then and turned into a crow, but before he could fly off they grabbed him. They beat old Chulyen to death right there, then, after they had killed him, threw what was left out back of the village on the slop-pile with the garbage.

An old woman found him lying there and cut off his nose. She stuck it in her needlecase and threw his body back with the trash. Then she left.

After she had gone some magpies started flying around. They were screaming and hollering and defecating all over everything—including old Chulyen. It made him so mad he finally came back to life. According to legend, Chulyen is the magpies' uncle, and he thought they should have a little more respect for him. And he told them so.

But they went on chattering. "What're you doing out here?" they asked.

"Sleeping," he said.

"No, you're not," they said. "You're dead."

He told them they were crazy, then asked where his nose was. They told him the old woman had it.

"Go away now," he said, "and let me rest."

As soon as the magpies left, Chulyen changed himself into a man and ran down to the beach. He bent over and began drawing bunches of men in *vudees*. Then he spoke to them.

"When I give you guys the signal," he said, "you come paddling around the point."

Then Chulyen flashed the signal and ran back up through the village, holding his hand over his face (because he had no nose) and yelling that enemy boats were coming.

"Everybody run!" he shouted.

Someone asked him why he was holding his hand over his face, and he was just going to tell them he had a toothache, when the *vudees* charged around the point. Everyone panicked.

"Run!" Chulyen cried. "Don't take anything with you. It'll just hold you back. Leave everything—especially your sewing-boxes."

In three minutes the village was completely deserted. But the people had left everything behind, so old Chulyen changed back into a crow and started looking around for the old lady's sewing-box. Finally he found it, and when he threw it open there was his nose.

Then he heard voices again. The people were coming back. So Chulyen scooped up his nose and stuck it back on his face and flew away. But he put it on in such a hurry that it was crooked, and all his descendants even today have that same crooked nose.

Chulyen was really angry.

"What can I do," he thought, "to get even?"

Then an idea came to his mind, and he went to work and built a footbridge across a canyon between two cliffs. When it was finished he went flying off over the whole countryside.

Whenever he would see an animal of any kind, he would shout, "Hey! I built a magic bridge. Come and see it!" Then he would lead them back toward the cliffs.

Finally, when he had drawn a huge crowd of bears, moose, wolves, beavers, wolverines, caribou, lynxes, otters, minks, muskrats, and many other kinds of animals, he landed in front of them and started talking.

"This is a magic bridge," he said. "It can make you turn into a man. All you have to do is walk across it. When you step onto the other side you'll be a man. Watch!"

So old Chulyen waddled down onto the bridge and crossed over to the other side. As soon as he stepped onto the opposite cliff, he turned into a man.

The other animals were really impressed. They all wanted to try it out and started rushing for the bridge.

"Not yet," said old Chulyen. "My village is on the other side over that hill and I invite you all to a party. So everyone go home and get your families and bring them too, and we'll all go across together."

Everyone cheered for the crow and they raced each other home after their families. Chulyen just smiled.

Soon they were all back, leading hundreds of relatives, and Chulyen said, "Okay. Let's go!" And he led the way down onto the bridge and across the canyon with the rest following.

It was a long footbridge. Chulyen had barely passed the middle when the last animal stepped onto it.

When the last one was well out over the canyon, the old crow turned and said, "I told you this bridge was magical and that it could turn you into a man, but here's something I didn't tell you. Watch!" And he leaped into the air and began flying around.

"See!" he said. "This bridge also gives everyone who walks on it the ability to fly."

Once again the animals were really impressed.

"How do we do it?" they all cried.

"Just start jumping into the air," he said, "and pretty soon you'll start flying."

So the hundreds of animals began jumping up and down, up and down, until one end of the footbridge broke loose and they all fell screaming to their deaths.

Old Chulyen just flew around for a while, waiting for the groaning to stop. Then, when it was quieter, he swooped down and began eating eyes.

After that, though, he had to leave the country because everyone who was left knew about him.

As the old crow flew on up the coastline, his conscience started to bother him, and he began to feel sorry about all the tricks he had pulled. He knew that it wasn't right, so he made a vow.

"The next chance I get," he told himself, "I'm going to try to help somebody instead of always hurting people."

Then Chulyen flew on until dark, and spent the night just outside a strange village. It was wintertime now, and it snowed a little and turned cold.

When he woke up the next morning the air was chilly and it was still dark out. Chulyen knew that night should be over because he'd had a good sleep, but there was no light at all—not even the moon. So he thought he'd go over to the village and see if anyone knew what the trouble was.

The people were up already when he got there, and everyone was huddled up talking in little bunches.

"What's the matter?" asked the crow. "Why is everyone so excited?"

"A rich man has stolen the sun and the moon," said the people, "and he won't give them back. Now we don't have any light."

"Don't worry," said Chulyen. "I'll get them back for you."

So the cunning old crow put his mind to work, trying to figure out a way to get back the sun and moon for the people.

Now the rich man had a daughter who came down to the beach every morning to pack water. So the next day when she came down carrying a bucket, old Chulyen was waiting for her, and when she scooped up a dipperful of water for herself, he dropped a small crow feather in it. She lifted up the dipper and gulped down the water in huge swallows—and along with it the crow's feather. Then she packed a bucketful back up to the house and went her way.

Soon after that the rich man's daughter discovered she was pregnant. People in those days didn't understand things as well as we do today, so she wasn't really surprised. She just figured it was natural now since she was getting older that she was going to have children.

When her time came, she had a healthy baby boy. He was a little guy, but he grew fast, and soon he was old enough to talk.

"*Chada*," he said, "grandfather, let me play with the moon."

Now the old man was really jealous of the sun and the moon, because he hadn't had them very long. But since it was his grandson, and he loved him so much, the old man gave his consent and brought in the moon for the child to play with.

The little boy played and played until he got tired. Then he fell asleep and they took the moon from him.

When he woke up he cried, "*Chada! Chada!* I want to play with the sun."

So they brought him the sun, and he played with it for hours.

In the weeks that followed the little boy would often call out to his grandfather, "Can I play with the moon?" or "Can I play with the sun?"

Then one morning he awoke and cried, "*Chada! Chada!* Let me play with the sun and the moon!"

So they brought him both of the great lights and left him to play by himself. As soon as he was sure they were gone, a strange thing happened. The little boy changed into a crow. For all the time it had been old Chulyen in disguise.

He climbed out of the window and flew back to the village, carrying both the sun and the moon with him.

The mean old rich man felt so bad about losing his grandson that he really changed his ways. From then on he was kind to all his neighbors and never tried to steal the sun and moon again.

And as for Chulyen, the people were so thankful when he returned their sun and moon to the skies that they accepted him as a member of their village, and he lived there happy for quite a while.

Stingy Reindeer Owners

◇ L A M U T ◇

The short days of the year had already begun, and the cold of winter had come. Then some Lamut met to live together. They pitched their tents close to one another, played cards, and had merry talks and joyful reunions. An old shaman, who had nothing to eat, had no joy. The wealthy reindeer owners gave him nothing, so stingy were they.

One time he went to sleep without any supper, and had a hungry dream, such as the Lamut used to have. In the morning he said to the best hunter in his own family, "Let us move away! I had a dream that the wolves came and scattered the reindeer herd all over the country." So they moved away and pitched camp separately. The richest of the men had several children, and up to that time they had never known what hunger was. Still he gave nothing to the poor people.

The old shaman left him. The people in the camp played cards as usual, and laughed noisily. Then they went to sleep, the herd being quite close to the camp. In the morning, however, the reindeer were gone, and only numerous tracks of wolves were seen in the deep snow. The rich man had nothing left, not even a single riding reindeer, so he had to stay in camp with all his children and grandchildren.

The others somehow moved off in pursuit of their lost animals. His men, too, tried to search for their reindeer; but all at once a violent snowstorm came which lasted several days. It covered every trace of the reindeer in front of them, and made invisible their own tracks behind them. The great cold caused all the game to wander off. They could find nothing to feed upon, so they were starving and perishing from famine. They ate their saddles and harnesses, the covering of their tents, and even their own clothes They crouched almost naked within their tents, protected only by the wooden frame thereof. In ten days they had never a meal, and so at last they took to gnawing their own long hands.

The old father, however, set off again. He wandered the whole day long in the open country, and found nothing. Finally, he stopped in the middle of the desert and cried aloud in despair. The Master of the Desert heard his voice. He came all at once from underground, and asked him, "What do you want?"—"My wife and children have had nothing to eat for ten days, and they are starving to death. My hunting boots are full of holes, and I am unable to walk any longer."—"Do not cry!" said the Master of the Desert. "I also am the owner of reindeer. I will give you something to eat, but you must remember the ancient custom of the Lamut. When you have food, give the best morsel to your poor neighbor."—"I will," said the old man. "Is not my present trial as severe as theirs?"—"Now, go home!" said the Master of the Desert, "and go to sleep. Food shall come to your house." So the old man went home. His wife said to him, "Do come and look upon this sleeping boy! He is moving his mouth as if chewing. This presages good luck." The boy was the youngest child of their elder son. "Be of good cheer," said the old man, "the worst is over. We shall have something to eat."

They went to sleep, and in the morning they saw that a large herd of reindeer had come to their camp. All were grey, like the wild reindeer. Still, the backs of the largest bucks were worn off by saddles. These were the riding reindeer of the Master of the Desert. The people lived on these reindeer. By and by the winter passed, and the long days of the spring came back. The people broke up their tents and in due time moved away, as is customary among the Lamut reindeer herders. They came to a camp of numerous tents and pitched their

own tents close by the others. The old woman, however, had not learned her lesson. She was stingy as before and gave evil advice to her husband. Several poor people were in that camp. The old woman said again, "We are rich, but we must not feed these good-for-nothings. We never saw them, they are strangers. Let us rather move away from here."

So they moved off, and after some days they pitched camp alone, as before. In the morning, however, all the reindeer were gone, no one knew where. Only their tracks were left on the pasture ground. They may have ascended to the sky. The Master of the Reindeer grew angry with the old man and his wife because of their close hands and hard hearts. Therefore he took away his property. They walked back to camp; but the people said, "Formerly you gave us nothing. You too may go away with empty hands." They went away, and soon starved to death. That is all.

Fourteen with One Stroke

◇ C H I P P E W A ◇

Midaswe lived on the edge of a big town. He had a big family and worked in the town. Every day at quitting time he would buy a bottle and get drunk. His wife would tell him to buy grub for the kids instead of liquor, but he wouldn't listen. One day he decided not to get a bottle, and after he had worked all day, he took the money and started home. But as he passed the tavern where he usually stopped, the bartender came out and said, "Come here, I want to hire you to clear land for me. It's a good job." So he went in, and the bartender set a bottle in front of him and told him to take a drink first. At first the Indian refused, but finally he took one, then another, and then he bought a bottle, got drunk, and went home. His wife saw that he was drunk again and told him so. The next morning she told him that if he got drunk again that day, he shouldn't come home.

He went to work. That evening he got his money and started for home. As he passed the saloon, the bartender called to him, saying he had something to tell him. The Indian went in, got drunk, bought a bottle, and went home; but his wife wouldn't let him in. He sat on the doorstep and thought about how hard his wife worked and how little his kids had. Finally he got up and walked to the woods in remorse and walked around all night, not caring if he died or not.

Near morning he lay down and tried to sleep, pulling his coat over him, but there were too many mosquitoes. He struck at the mosquitoes on his face and killed a bunch of them. He counted them; there were fourteen. He struck on the other side of his face and killed some more and counted them; there were fourteen. "I killed fourteen again with one stroke," he said. Then he got up and started walking.

In the afternoon he struck the road and walked along it. Then he saw something on the road and picked it up; it was a fifty-cent piece. He walked on and saw the metal part of a scythe stuck in a stump. He pulled it out and said, "This will be my sword."

That evening he came to a lumber camp and went to the blacksmith shop. The blacksmith looked at the ragged Indian and said, "Where did you come from?" The Indian said he didn't know, but that he wanted a sword made from the scythe. The blacksmith took the scythe and made a sword out of it. The Indian said that was fine; but now he wanted the words carved on it: "Fourteen with one stroke." So the blacksmith did it. The Indian said, "Now carve the same thing on the other side." The blacksmith did that too and asked if that was all. "No, you have to make a scabbard for it." So the blacksmith made the scabbard and carved the same thing on each side of it. He charged the Indian fifty cents.

That night the Indian stayed at the camp, and the next day he started off. The next night he camped in the woods, and the next day he came to a strange town. He asked if there were any soldiers there, and they showed him the barracks. He went in. The soldiers were just sitting down to eat. The ragged Indian sat down too and ate, and then lay down on the floor and slept. The soldiers all noticed the sword with the inscription "Fourteen with one stroke." They wondered about it and went to tell the president about it. The president sent for the Indian, and the soldiers woke him up and told him that the president wanted to see him. "Why doesn't he come down here?" asked the Indian. But he got up and went over to see the president. The president asked him where he was from. The Indian said he didn't know. The president asked him about the inscription, whether it was true. The Indian said it wouldn't be there if it wasn't. The president asked him what he was doing here, and the Indian said that he was looking for a fight. The president said he had had three daughters that were eaten by a windigo, and he had only one daughter left. He said that if the Indian would kill the windigo, he would give him his daughter in marriage. The Indian said he didn't want to get married, he was just looking for a fight. The president asked, "Will you fight the windigo?" The Indian said, "Sure, but I don't want your daughter." The president told him to come back at one o'clock.

The Indian went back to the barracks and lay down on the floor and slept. At one o'clock the soldiers woke him up. He was very mad, but he went over to the president and saw the daughter crying. The president told him it was time to go and gave him directions—go north and then take the west road. The Indian took the girl and started out.

He left the girl at the crossroads and took the road to the west alone and soon came to a big oak lying across the road. He climbed over it and then walked on until he saw the windigo. The windigo had horns a foot long. When he saw the Indian, he started hollering. The Indian turned tail and ran fast. He climbed over the big oak and fell down on the other side. He heard the windigo trying to get over the fallen oak. The Indian wondered what was happening. Finally he raised his head and saw that the windigo had fallen and driven his horns into the hard, dry oak. The Indian took a rock and pounded his horns deeper into the oak. Then he walked back to the girl and told her that he couldn't haul the windigo away but had driven his horns into the tree. The girl went over and saw the windigo and believed the Indian's story.

When the president saw them returning, he was very glad. The Indian told the same story to the president, and the president took some soldiers with him and went to see the windigo stuck into the log. Then he said, "You didn't do this." The Indian said, "All right, then, I'll pull them out." He started to pull, but the president said, "No. Stop." He told the soldiers to shoot the windigo, and they did.

Then the president said, "There is one more windigo on the east road and if you kill him, you can marry my daughter." The Indian said that he didn't want to get married; he just wanted a fight. He went back to the barracks, and the soldiers wondered about him, still doubting his story. He ate his meals there and slept with the sword showing the inscription "Fourteen with one stroke."

They woke him up at one o'clock, and he was mad again, but went over to the president. This time the daughter didn't cry. He took her to the crossroads and left her and took the road to the east. He came to a bridge where there was a hole about the shape of a big iron kettle, but very deep. He crossed the bridge and walked on and then saw the windigo. He turned tail and ran. When he crossed the bridge, he fell, and the windigo, who was chasing him, fell over him and went into the hole. The Indian raised his head and saw that the windigo was trapped in the hole. He got up and looked at the windigo and saw that he couldn't get out; so he went over and got the girl and told her that he'd thrown the windigo into a hole. He took her over there and showed her the windigo in the hole, and then they went back to town.

When the president had heard the story, he took some soldiers out there, and when the president asked the Indian if he had thrown the windigo into the hole, the Indian said, "Sure I did. Watch, and I'll pull him out for you." The president said, "No, don't do that," and told the soldiers to shoot the windigo.

They all went home, and the president said, "You have done a big thing here, Indian; but there is just one more thing to do. We are at war with the president of another country, and I want you to go there and fight. If you win, you can marry my daughter." The Indian said he didn't want to get married; he just wanted a fight. The president wanted him to take the soldiers along, but the Indian said he wanted to go alone.

The next day he started off to the east, where he was told that he'd find a big house with gold plates and knives. He was supposed to ride a horse up to the big fence around the house. The Indian had never been on a horse before, and when they put the spurs on his feet he didn't know what they were for. When he got on, he tried to hold himself on by holding his feet tight on the horse, but he was spurring the horse, and the horse ran faster. They ran into the town and around the big fence that surrounded the big house. As they went by a big cross, he grabbed it to try to get off the horse, but instead he pulled it out, and they rode around the fence three times. All the people were wondering who this madman was and what he was doing. The fourth time around the fence, his horse fell down, and the Indian landed with one foot under the horse. Finally he managed to pull it loose. He got up and saw that the horse was dead and there were no people around. He saw the big cross and wondered how he could have carried it. He limped over to the gate and walked into the house from which everyone had fled. He picked up the gold keys and filled a sack with gold knives and forks and things, and then he walked back to the barracks and put down the sack and went to sleep.

At breakfast no one spoke to him, and the soldiers wondered about him. He went to sleep again. The president told the soldiers to bring the Indian to him. The Indian was mad when they woke him up, but he got up and went over to see the president. He told what had happened. The president and all the soldiers went over to check on his story and saw the deserted town and picked up all the gold they could carry. The president gave the Indian a new suit of clothes and a haircut and said that the Indian should stay there and live with him and marry his daughter because he had done so much. The Indian thought about his wife and kids, but finally he decided to marry the daughter. They got married, and the Indian was respected, because now the people believed him.

One night he dreamed and called out the names of his wife and five kids. The daughter wondered about this and went to tell her father. He told her to leave the door open that night, and he would listen. The Indian overheard their plans and made up his mind to stay awake that night. When they went to bed, his wife didn't close the door, and he noticed that. A little later he heard the president at the door. Then the Indian took down the sword and pulled it from the scabbard and started yelling, "Fight, boys!" He made believe he was in battle and started slashing around and cut off the president's ear. The president "woke" up the Indian and said, "Stop. You cut off my ear." The Indian said that he had been dreaming and asked what the president was doing in his room. The president said that he suspected that the Indian had another family because he was shouting children's names in his sleep. The Indian said, "No, I don't have any other family." The end.

PART TWO

Why Owls Die
with Wings Outspread

How Things Got to Be
the Way They Are

"THE WAY-BACK TIME of ancestors and spirits," said Sam Beulie, a Métis man, "was when we first began to *know* anything." Whether explaining a feature of the landscape, the smallest zoological particular, or the larger workings of the cosmos, origin tales are infused with a sense of revelation wonderfully invoked in the King Island Eskimo verb *qaugri*, which means the increase in curiosity and consciousness that takes place in childhood. In fact, certain Athapaskan tribes begin those tales which address the oldest of mysteries "The first time this happened . . ." How did human beings first appear on earth? Who imparted the earliest technical knowledge, such as how to build an igloo or fashion snowshoes? How did the constellations get to the sky? What is the origin of the sun and moon? By answering the hows and whys of life, such tales provide successive generations with a core of belief, uniting people in the same common knowledge. "When I tell my grandchildren how the world got this way," Mary Piwese, a Cree woman, remarked, "I am satisfied it is the same way I was educated."

Accounts of creation chronicle the inception of order out of a previously inchoate condition. Raven—or in Siberia, Big Raven—was one of the most common of creators. Yet throughout the North, accounts of humankind's appearance on earth reveal a number of creators at work. According to the Abenaki, Micmac, and other Maritime Indian tribes, the great god Kuloscap used his most potent magic to spontaneously produce human beings. He did this partly to cure his loneliness but also for the entertainment of animals, whom he had systematically shrunk from giants to the size they are today. Kuloscap then went on to defeat every malevolent demon, wizard, witch, and ice giant that threatened his beloved creatures who, like himself, walked on two feet. But finally Kuloscap could not save humankind from its own devices. In one Abenaki story, when Kuloscap first displayed human beings to his companion wolves, the wolves fell into hysterical laughter. "Kuloscap," they cried, "you have a great sense of humor!"

In the region of the Mackenzie Delta Eskimo, several cosmogonic myths maintain that the Great Beaver created two brothers: one was the ancestor of the Mackenzie Delta people, the other of all the other western Eskimos. Among the subarctic Chipewyan, the belief is that people were born from the union of a primeval woman with a dog, which for that night was transformed into a man. This ancient legend probably gave rise to the early designation of the Chipewyan and other northern Athapaskans as the "dog-ribbed" or "dog-sided" people.

The bringing of material culture is featured in many origin tales, wherein the whole narration may serve to explain the first appearance of a weapon, a basket, or an item of clothing. "Before I took my son out to shoot his bow for the first time," said Mark Edmund, a Caribou Eskimo man, "I told him how our people first got bows and arrows." Northern peoples find ongoing delight in the practical application of new implements, of new knowledge. A story about the arrival of the cooking pot may also provide a recipe. A story about the first knife may instruct people how to clean fish so as not to insult their departing spirits. In the Athapaskan tale "The First Snowshoes" it is a grouse that first shows a man and his wife how to construct snowshoes. The knowledge has a profound effect on the couple, and by extension, on the Athapaskan people. Snowshoes provide a whole new way of enriching their lives; they now can travel over deep snow to hunt caribou in faraway places.

Stories that recall the first contact with or sightings of white people traveled along the earliest whaling and trade routes, outposts established by fur trappers and later by missionaries. These myriad tales are replete with vicious satire, occasional awe, fear and caution, and often forecasts of doom. "Over in Pond Inlet," a woman from Repulse Bay in the eastern arctic related, "when the first [whaling] ship was approaching, the people were terrified. They had the shamans then, and the shamans went into trances and chanted. The Inuit thought the people on the ship had come to murder them. When the white people came to shore, no one spoke or did anything, all were so terrified."

Crews of white men navigating steamers through wilderness rivers were harbingers of colonialism and acculturation. The Hare Indian tale "The First White Men" states: "These men were monsters, really. They were white men, but also monsters." Perhaps the final word should come from Andrew Arloo, a Caribou Eskimo: "When white men first arrived, we helped them out. They stayed forever. But they are strangers."

How the Earth Was Made
and How Wood-Chips Became Walrus

◇ MARITIME CHUKCHEE ◇

Big Raven lived with his wife. Big Raven was the first living thing on earth; he and his wife created themselves. They lived on a small patch of ground. It was just floating, and they lived on it. There were no people, no animals, nothing else at all. No reindeer, no walrus, no whale, no seal, no fish, nothing. One morning, Big Raven's wife said, "This is a dull life, it's nasty living here alone. You better go out and create the rest of the earth. Make somebody we can talk with. Better get out there—now!"

Big Raven said, "I can't create the rest of the earth."

"Yes, you can," his wife said.

"I'm telling you, I can't!"

"Okay, if you say so. Since you can't create the earth, you say, I'll at least create a companion."

"Fat chance," Big Raven said.

"I'll go to sleep," his wife said.

"I won't sleep," said Ku'urkil, the Big Raven. "I'll watch you closely. I'll see if anything happens."

Big Raven's wife fell asleep. Big Raven stayed awake, watching. Nothing happens; his wife still has the body of a raven, just like himself.

Big Raven looked at her from all sides; she was still a raven.

He dozed off, just a moment, hardly at all. He woke up, looked again at his wife—what! Her feet had ten human toes, moving slowly!

"What's going on?" Big Raven said.

Big Raven stretches out his own feet. He sees the same talons as always.

He looks at his wife: her body is white and her feathers are gone!

"What's going on?" he shouts.

Now Big Raven tries to change himself. He chafes, he pulls at his feathers, he pulls at his talons, but it's hopeless. He's got the same raven feathers, raven talons.

He looks at his wife: her belly has grown big. And pretty soon, there's three of these human beings! There's his wife, and twin sons. She's given birth to twin sons! Raven now has the company of three humans, and they have the company of one Big Raven. The world was starting up!

The boys start to laugh crazily at Big Raven. They point at him. "Mama," they cry, "what's *that?*"

"That's your father!" she says.

"Our father—ha! ha! ha!" The twin boys came nearer to Raven, they kicked him, they pulled at his feathers. Big Raven flew off, crying, "Qa! Qa!"

The boys fell over laughing. "What's that sound?"

"Your father, a sound he makes when he's flying!"

"Ha! ha!—what a sound our father makes!"

They just laugh all the time.

"You children are foolish," their mother says. "Stop laughing. You have to listen and obey. You can laugh, but not all the time. Yes, it's a funny noise, but it's your father!"

By this time, Big Raven is circling overhead. He calls down, "So, you've created human beings, so now I'll go out and create the rest of the world. I might not come back. You might say, 'He's drowned.' But I'm going to try it." He flew away.

First, Big Raven visited all the benevolent Beings, to ask for advice. Turns out, nobody gave him any. He went to visit the kinds of light. He asked the Dawn—no advice. He asked Sunset, Evening, Midday, Zenith—no advice. Nothing. He traveled on. At last he came to a place where the sky and ground came together—Horizon. There he saw a tent. It was situated in a hollow. A lot of men were inside. They were making a great noise. Big Raven peeped in through a hole burned by a spark, and saw a number of naked backs. He jumped away, frightened. He stepped back slowly, trembling. In fear he forgot his ambitions, he forgot what he'd set out to do.

Then, one naked man steps out of the tent. "I thought we heard somebody out here," he says.

"It's me," Big Raven says, trembling.

"Oh—well, who are you?"

"Big Raven. I'm going to become a creator. I'm Ku'urkil, I created myself."

"Is that so?"

"And who are you?" Big Raven asked.

"Well, we've been created from the dust, from when the friction of sky and ground made dust. We're multiplying, and we'll go out and become the different peoples of the earth. The thing is, though, there is no earth yet!"

"Guess somebody has to make earth, then," Big Raven said.

"Get out there and do it," the man said. "I'll accompany you."

Big Raven and the man flew off together.

High in the sky, the man pointed down. "There," he said, "there's an empty place."

Hearing this, Big Raven let loose some feces; it flew down, it landed, and even as they watched it became a big island, and as they circled, more feces fell and became islands. The continents were born in this way, and there now was plenty of land. Big Raven spun the continents out of his belly.

"Well," Big Raven said to his companion, "let's go."

"Not enough," the man said. "There's no fresh water, and the land is too flat. No mountains yet."

"I'll do some more, then," Raven said.

Raven began pissing, but by the time it got to earth it was cleaned up, it became fresh water. So Big Raven was swirling rivers, lakes, and streams out of his belly.

"How about some mountains?" the companion said.

Big Raven strained himself, grunted, grunt, grunt, grunt, down fell hard substances, spun out of Big Raven, and that's how hills, mountains, entire ranges were born. That's how it happened.

"You've worked hard," the companion said. "There's the earth, but aren't you hungry?"

Big Raven flew off, and he found trees, all kinds of them—birch, poplar, pine, aspen, willow, stone pine, oak. He took up his hatchet and began to chop. He threw the chips into the water, and they were carried off in the current to the sea. When he hewed pine and threw pine-chips into the water, they became walrus; when he hewed oak, the oak-chips became seals. From the stone pine, the chips became polar bears; from the small creeping black birch, the chips became whales. Chips from all other trees became fish, crabs, worms, every kind of sea creature. Chips flew off, floated down, winds blew them over the land, and chips became reindeer, foxes, bears, all the game food of the land. Big Raven was chopping like mad, and animals were showing up all over. He created them. Finally, exhausted, he said, "There, now we have food!"

Out of the tents, men went off in various directions. They fashioned houses, hunted animals, procured plenty of food, they became people as we know them today. The trouble was, there were not yet any women! There were no women, so people couldn't give birth. This was a problem Big Raven hadn't dealt with yet.

"I've got to do something about this," he said.

Suddenly, a small Spider Woman drifted down on a slender thread.

"Who are you?" Big Raven asked.

"I am Spider Woman."

"Why are you here?"

"Well, I thought, How will all these people live, there being no women? I got worried. So here I am."

"What can you do about it?"

"I'll birth them—daughters."

"You're too small."

"I don't think so."

What happened next astonished Big Raven. Spider Woman's abdomen grew fat. Suddenly, she gave birth to four daughters! They grew up in front of Big Raven's eyes, and now they were young women. "Now, watch," Spider Woman told Big Raven.

A man came along, and it was the one who had flown around and created the world with Big Raven. "Hey," he said, "what sort of being is this? It looks like me, but different, too. I want a companion. I live alone. I'm unhappy. I'm dull. I want a companion."

"I don't want her to starve," Spider Woman said of her daughter.

The flying-companion said, "I've got plenty of food. We are good hunters. I'll feed her abundantly. She won't ever know hunger, I promise."

The flying-companion set out with a daughter. The next day, Big Raven visited them. He made a hole in the tent-cover, and peered in. "Oh, no," he said. "They're sleeping in opposite corners of the sleeping-room! That's bad. How can- they get children? Flying-Companion is stupid about things."

Big Raven hallood softly, "Halloo, halloo."

Flying-Companion woke. He saw it was Big Raven. "You get out here," Big Raven said, "I'll go inside." Flying-Companion stepped out, Big Raven stepped inside the tent. The young, beautiful woman lay naked there, and Raven drew nearer, and then Big Raven touched her with his sharp beak. "Oh—oh," the beautiful woman cried.

"Be quiet, sshhh!" Big Raven said, "or else Flying-Companion will hear us."

Raven opened her legs and then copulated with her. He did this again. Once more. Flying-Companion was standing outside. He felt a chill, and said, "You're mocking me!"

"Okay, come on in," Big Raven said. "It's time you learn how to do this."

Flying-Companion stepped inside the tent, then he stepped into the sleeping-room. The beautiful woman said, "It's a good thing, I wouldn't mind doing it again. Maybe once more."

"I don't know how," Flying-Companion said.

"Get closer," she said. "Right up against me."

Flying-Companion said, "That's pretty nice."

"Do this and this," she said. "Now, do that, now that."

You should understand one thing: young women understand much earlier than boys how such things work. This is a truth. This is the story about how humans became plentiful.

The First Snowshoes

◇ A T H A P A S K A N ◇

Long time ago, nobody know about snowshoes, nothing. Winter coming. That man and his wife can't do nothing. Big snow. They hunt tree squirrel, he kill some tree squirrel. They live on that kind. They see lots of caribou in the mountains, but he can't climb up there. Too deep snow. He try to put limb underneath his feet, but they don't stay long time. He try everything.

That time grouse coming, you know. Come to him. That man don't know what's the matter. That tree about that big—"Gung, gung, gung, gung," he say. He tap it.

Grouse goes to another tree. "Gung, gung, gung, gung." Another tree again. That man don't know what's the matter with that grouse. "Gung, gung."

"I guess he call you," that man say to his wife. He go ahead. It's about that deep, I guess—knee-deep—that snow. Not far, just little ways. Takes them to bear den.

"Gung, gung." Sit down on the tree. Then they got him—the bear—some way. That's their food. They pack in. Got the food now.

That's the time he start to fix them. He just do that way, "Gung, gung, gung." Showed them all the time. Showed them how to make them. If that man don't do right, he show them. Don't say nothing . . . this side . . . other side . . . he know, though, he work at it, just like he know. Put stick that way . . . go across . . . he don't say nothing . . . one right here . . . tie 'em up . . . no, this way . . . right here too.

"Gung, gung, gung, gung."

"I guess you're going to help too," he tell his wife. His wife work too.

"Gung." Stop now. That's good now, see?

"Gung, gung." He took some string now. His wife, put 'em that way.

Right here now . . . "gung, gung, gung, gung." She net it. If she don't do right, he show her, that grouse. This one too, she net it. And they're finished now!

"Gung, gung, gung," he said.

Gee, he go on top of snow now.

"Gung, gung, gung." They go on top of that mountain. That grouse go ahead. That man walk on top! He kill caribou now. On skin sleigh, he bring to his wife.

"I kill them up there."

His wife, she fixes them too. She know how, see?

That grouse did that, give them bear to live on and show them how. His wife make them, walk on top too.

See people? They walk on snowshoes. Everybody's got it. They tell them, another one, another one, another one, they teach them all. Soon baby born, they know how to make snowshoes!

Gambling Story

◇DENA'INA INDIAN◇

At one time, Dena'ina used to tell stories. In this story, two rich men met and said, "Let's play the gambling game."

One of these young man was a shaman. The other fellow followed all of the traditional beliefs.

The shaman began to win everything from the young believer. He took all his possessions, until all the young man had left were his wife and children.

"What will you bet me?" the shaman asked him. There were his wife and children, girls and a boy. He longed to keep them. But all his belongings were gone. "I will bet you: your children against them," the shaman said. The young believer wished to keep his wife and his boy. He gave the shaman his three girls. His wife and boy remained.

"Against all your things and the three girls, bet me your wife and boy," the shaman said to him. Whom did he love more, his wife or the young boy? His wife, too, he gave to the shaman.

Then he bet that boy against all his belongings and his wife and girls. The shaman took away the boy, too. The believer was left with nothing. The shaman had won all he owned, even his last gun.

The young man went out and walked far off. In the foothills, he found a ground squirrel caught in a trap he had set. It was chewed up; only a small skin lay there, for the animal had not returned to its reincarnation place. He picked it up and put it inside his shirt.

Far off he walked, until he came to a great shelter where there was life. From inside, someone spoke: "I heard you. Turn three times the way the sun goes round, and stoop down and come in." It was spacious inside. A very big old lady sat there. "I am the Mother of everything over and over," she said. "My husband is gone, but he will return to us."

Not long after, a giant man came in. "Hello," he said, "what happened that you came to me?"

The young man explained what the shaman had done to him. "The shaman took my wife, my girls, and even my last child, my boy. And somehow, I came here."

"Good," the giant said. "Well, rest, and I'll fix you up."

The young man rested well. As he sat, the little skin inside his shirt began to move and out it jumped. It formed once again into a ground squirrel and scampered across the floor. "Yes, you have come to us with our child," the giant said. "I searched all over for my lost child. And the one who gambled with you, who played with you, he is a shaman, you say. Good. I too have power. I'll prepare you to go back to him."

Animal skins were piled in the house. He cut little pieces from each of them and put them into a gutbag. With them he put in down feathers. "You will return with this. When no one is looking, sprinkle the down on it. The skins will grow into a large number of animals. These you will bet."

Then he laid out three sets of gambling-sticks and wrapped them all together. "With this first set of gambling-sticks, you will play with him, and both of you will win, back and forth. As you go on, he will increase his bet.

"When he thinks, 'I will take everything from him,' you will bounce down the second set of gambling-sticks. They will spin three times the way the sun goes round, and you will take back your belongings, your wife and girls, and the boy.

"Again the shaman will win something and he will increase his bet, trying his power. You will bounce down the third set of gambling-sticks. They will spin against the sun and you will take everything from that shaman: his property, his children, and his wife.

"Then you will tell him, 'What I have done to you, you too did to me. I went out and I went to the one they call K'luyesh. K'luyesh resupplied me and gave me three sets of gambling-sticks. With them I won everything back from you. Go to K'luyesh and tell him, Give me the gambling-sticks.'

The believer went back. Three times he gambled. He won everything from the shaman. Using the animal skins, K'luyesh blocked the shaman's power. The shaman tried to transform his spirit, but he could not make it take the form of an animal. He failed in his power. And he went out, and there was no more word of him.

K'luyesh, searching for his lost child, had walked far above us across the sky. He left his footprints on the mountains and then, disgusted that he could not find his son, he sat down hard on a summit and left the print of his hind end. His trail became the streak of light forming far above us, what we call the Milky Way.

Story While Pointing at a Constellation: A Dogrib Conversation

◇DOGRIB INDIAN◇

"Somebody's chasing it."

"Hey—no."

"It's true."

"Which?"

"That one. There. I'm pointing at it. Get behind me. Look past my hand."

"Let me see."

"See it?"

"Yes. Who's chasing it?"

"Someone always is. It's called The-One-Always-Chased."

"Who's chasing it now?"

"Some other one."

"Who?"

"The-One-Who-Chases."

"One time I was out walking. Out at night. I heard a loud flint-scrape."

"Flint-scrape?"

"Yes. And I looked up to the sky."

"The sound traveled down to you?"

"Yes. A flint-scrape."

"It was him, The-One-Who-Chases. It wasn't the other one. The other one wouldn't stop to make a fire like that. He'd be found out."

Why Owls Die with Wings Outspread
◇ S W A M P Y C R E E ◇

In a hunting camp lived Owl Old Man. He had many moods each day and did not hide them. Sometimes he threw a mood at you and at other times he took them out on the ice to throw them around, far away from people. It was also known that his moods caused various owls.

One person said he saw a mood of Owl Old Man cause a snowy owl out of a clump of snow. This happened up on a branch. The snow-clump fell, and before it hit the ground it was an owl, which flew away. That is how it went with his moods sometimes.

Another time his mood caused a decoy-mouse to scamper away! It came alive from his mood. That decoy-mouse was out inviting an owl down onto it—an owl from one of Owl Old Man's moods.

One time, also, while he was sitting in a cabin, an old woman was sweeping out the ashes from a fireplace. She swept them away down to a clean place, and there were some owl tracks under those ashes! It was at that time Owl Old Man was seen walking out the door . . .

In a nearby camp, Ohokoku the Horned Owl lived. He was a very powerful conjurer of the region. He was a very clever man, but sometimes did cruel things that were not understood by everyone. People said this was because he could not fly, for some reason. Also, in another nearby camp lived the old Woman Hermit. She lived alone now, though she had once lived in Owl Old Man's camp. She had been sent away.

Well, one morning Woman Hermit was out cutting wood and gathering twigs. She went about chopping a fallen tree and wood-chips fell onto the ground. Suddenly she saw one of these chips move aside! She looked closely under it and saw there a *mamakwasew*—a small human-being orphan! She was very happy to find him and took him back to her house. She kept him there a long time, and often said to him, "I have tied one thing to another by finding you. Now all things are connected." She said this with much happiness.

He grew up to be a small person. He could stand and put his face to Woman Hermit's knee, which he liked to do. He was a very small person. He often went to visit Owl Old Man, but no one in his camp really wished to see this orphan. He always visited, but in that village they chased him around and hit him with sticks, and he cried often. Owl Old Man's daughter was the one who disliked the orphan most, she said. She would run to scare him even before he reached the village, though no one knew how she always knew he was about to visit.

The old woman told the orphan, "You must watch that daughter very closely. When she pees on the ground, you do the same on that very spot!" This he did.

After some time passed, the daughter found she was pregnant! Her family did not understand this. They watched her closely and listened in her sleep for someone's name. They knew she had found a man to marry, but this man lived far away. When she found that her daughter was pregnant, Owl Old Man's wife said to him, "Did any of your mood-owls have the face of the man our daughter chose to marry? I thought I saw an owl fly into her room one night!"

"No," he said.

When it was time, the baby was born. No one could tell who the father was, and this caused some anger. It is lucky that everyone in that village could not cause owls from their bad moods, or else they would be on every branch, everywhere. All over. The mother's anger made her forget things. She only kneaded bread with her thumbs some days. Her father's anger again caused some owls, some of which flew crookedly or upside down.

It was then they sent for all the men in the region. Ohokoku the Horned Owl arrived among them. He walked there. Everyone sat down to talk. But no one had asked the orphan to sit down and talk.

The old woman said to him, "Go and sit with them. You should be there too. Don't worry what insults they throw at you. Go and sit with them." The orphan arrived there too and sat down. One other man said, "What is he doing here? He better get out!"

But then Owl Old Man said, "No, he lives close by. He had a better chance than many of us to sleep with my daughter." The daughter said, "Get him out of here!" Then Owl Old Man said, "He will sit quietly."

Then Owl Old Man picked up the baby and said, "Here is a grandchild. I will pass him around. This child will pee on the man who is his father." So with this the baby was passed around. Everyone watched carefully. Then the baby reached the Horned Owl. The owl rocked it back and forth and held it tightly. Suddenly the owl cried out, "It has peed on my chest!"

With this, the daughter looked as if she was shouting, but only a whisper came out. "I don't know this owl," she said.

It was then that Owl Old Man said, "I saw the owl spitting all over his own chest! That is your owl-spit!" Then he took the baby from the owl. Then he said, "It is still not known who the father is!"

"What about the orphan?" a man called out.

"He is only a child," Horned Owl said.

"Yes, but he lives nearby," the man said again.

Owl Old Man handed the child onto the orphan's lap, and it was then the baby peed there. The orphan said, "Yes, this is the truth of it. This is my child. He knows it is true."

Then the orphan ran out of the house with the baby in his arms. The family and the others all chased him, but he had disappeared into the woods—two small people could hide well there. When they returned from their search, everyone gathered up their belongings to leave. But before they left they stood around the daughter and said to her, "How can this be, how could you seduce a child?" They took off her clothes and burned them, and left her there with little to eat. The orphan and the baby and Woman Hermit watched all this together from their hiding-place.

Quickly then the old woman went back and got some clothes. Then she said to the orphan, "Here, take these things to her. And bring her back to live with us." He went to the abandoned village and saw the daughter lying on the ground, howling and sobbing. He said, "My grandmother invites you to live with us." Then he led her back to their house.

On their way back they passed the Horned Owl, who was sitting on a tree-stump. "I'll tell you something about your child," he said.

"You are known to be cruel," the girl said. "Why should we listen to you?" They also knew the owl had a few ways to tell the future. "I'll say it out loud, then. You don't have to believe me," said the owl.

They listened. The owl said, "One day you will help me. And then you won't see me for a long time. Then your son will be out walking and he will find me."

That's what the owl said. Then he flew away. The others walked on. They kept walking. When they arrived home, the old woman said to the orphan, "Now, turn right around and go back to the abandoned village and see if anything is there now. If anything is there, toss it into the air!"

The orphan returned to the abandoned village, and there found a few things. He found a piece of cloth and a length of thread. He tossed them into the air. The cloth became a moose hide, and the thread became a satchel for carrying things. With this, the orphan returned home, where the old woman made a coat from the moose hide. She sewed the satchel to it. Then she gave all this to the girl.

The next day the orphan said to the old woman, "I'm going to sleep. While I'm sleeping, kindly make a hut for me to sweat in." He slept. When he woke, the sweat-hut was completed. The orphan then said to the old woman, "Now I'm going to take the baby inside and sit." Then he said, "I'll be singing in there. When you hear me sing, don't look in at me. I won't harm the baby. He's got to be in there with me right now."

They went inside the hut, and right away he began to sing. The old woman and the daughter stood leaning to hear inside. It was then they heard two voices inside. The singing had stopped, but talking had begun now.

There were two voices talking inside. One was lower than the other, but both got louder.

Then they grew louder still.

The girl was frightened and began to reach to pull aside the hut-door blanket because she was worried about the baby's ears. "Cover his ears! Who's in there with you?" she shouted into the hut.

"Don't look inside yet!" a voice shouted out.

Now it happened that the voices were getting to resemble each other more and more. They seemed to be coming from the same place in each throat. Then the girl heard, "Now is the time to uncover us!"

She threw aside the blanket. There she saw two young men standing in front of her!

"Which is my husband?" she asked. "Which is my son?" She could not tell!

They were nearly twins, they were both tall and very good to look at. The girl hugged them both. One of these men pointed to the other and said, "He is your husband." It was then the orphan-husband stripped some bark from a nearby birch tree and walked with it to the shore of a lake. He laid it down there and said, "Be a canoe. Now!" It was a canoe then.

"You see, this is what I dreamed I could make happen when I was asleep a while ago," he said.

Then he said to the girl, "If you are to be my wife, we must find some gifts for your parents." They went hunting and killed a ptarmigan, and also they caught some fish. They made some fat and brought it all to the canoe. Then the orphan and his son got into the canoe and rowed to the new camp of the girl's parents.

When they landed there, they saw the owl was visiting. They saw owl tracks on the ground he had walked over to get there. The old people did not recognize the two men, but the owl did. Because of his conjuring powers, he could see who they were, yes. The owl pointed and said, "That one there is the orphan!"

"No!" the others said. "It can't be true! This is a full-grown man in front of us, not a small person."

"It's true, this is the orphan. He has changed and arrived here with his son," the owl said.

"His son!" the parents cried out. "Our grandson, you mean?" Owl Old Man got ready to throw moods around, but he waited. He at first thought this was all lies.

"Yes," said the owl.

It was then the orphan said to his son, "Bring your grandparents the gifts." The son carried the gifts over and said, "These are sent by the old Woman Hermit and my mother whom you did not want any more." Then he said, "Come back with us to our camp. We have all you need back there."

The owl watched this, then he spoke up: "Before you leave, let's test this orphan. After all, he was once a *mamakwasew,* and who knows how he will act in this world now?"

The orphan agreed before anyone could argue. "It must be a test of my own choosing," he said.

The owl agreed to this.

The orphan pointed to a particular spot on the ground and said, "Sit here. Be ready with your bow. When you see a deer pass by, aim and try to shoot one for food. They will pass by soon."

Then the orphan stepped into the woods and disappeared. Everyone waited there, and the owl had his bow ready. Soon the deer appeared; one by one they showed themselves. The owl pulled on his bow. He then chose one deer to shoot at. This deer he chose was really the orphan in a deer-disguise he conjured himself into. He knew the owl would still be able to recognize him, though no one else could. So by this he knew the owl was trying to kill him! He finally learned what he had suspected of the owl.

The owl shot four times and each time missed the deer.

Now the orphan was back again. He said to the owl, "It's your turn now."

With this the owl disappeared. The orphan stood waiting. Soon the deer came by, all in a herd. And the owl, who was then also dressed as a deer, hid in the middle thinking that the orphan would not recognize him in there. But the orphan picked him out right away and shot him. The owl went off wounded in the disguise of a deer. The orphan followed, but the owl-deer was gone!

Some days later, when everyone was back in the camp of Woman Hermit, the grandson went walking. He came upon the owl with his wings spread out stiff on the ground. He was nearly dead.

The owl said, "I flew here to die."

When Musk Oxen Spoke Like Humans

◇ I G L U L I K   E S K I M O ◇

Two musk oxen—both bulls. They were chewing food at the top of an icy hill. They were talking, but it wasn't human speech. They didn't have human speech yet.

Some hunters came along and saw the musk oxen. They whispered, "They can't speak like us, so if they hide in fog, we can't find them. We have to teach them human speech."

First, a hunter jumped on some small ice puddles, and the musk oxen saw this and did the same. They jumped on some ice puddles.

Then a second hunter sharpened a knife on a rock, and the musk oxen bent down and sharpened their horns on a rock.

Then a third hunter snorted, and both musk oxen snorted.

Then a fourth hunter shouted, "We are small round hills, our grasses ruffled in the wind. No one is interested in killing hills! We are safe."

With this, the musk oxen spoke up, "We are small round hills, our grasses ruffled in the wind . . ." But before they could finish, the hunters sent their dogs ahead.

When the musk oxen saw the dogs approaching, they felt danger and they stood back to back and lowered their horns. Then fog began to issue from their nostrils. But it was too late to hide them. The hunters saw where the musk oxen stood, and even though the dogs were gored in the fog, the hunters were able to kill the musk oxen.

This was the first time musk oxen spoke human speech, and how it gave them away in the fog.

Why the Path Between Fish-Camps Is Always Worn Down, and No One Walks It Any More

◇ HARE INDIAN ◇

Indian people know things by dreams. Old people say, "Bad dreams come true lots of times." This story is like that. It came true. It's my grandfather's—his story. It's about how a path got worn down between Ónkaifʷe tl'á, summer fish-camps. Because of a bushman.

Bushman gets you when you're alone. Then either kills you or knocks you out. If you are out alone, hunting. Then suddenly you wake up. Crazy—as drunk. Wobble-headed. Think you have been to the other world. Like that. It's a bushman.

Two things dogs will bark at and won't stop. You have to kill them to make them stop. Ewén—ghost. And bushman.

So if you have to go out alone, take dogs. Take dogs along. Bushman stinks to dogs before—even a whole day before—it stinks to men.

Going back: the dream he had, Grandfather's. He was flying and he looked down. He saw a man. Grandfather lowered. He saw a cap he recognized. A shirt. Shoes. Grandfather called out, "Hey, William!" It was a man he had gone hunting with that year, a few times. He knew the cap. He knew the shoes. "William!—William!" This was up near Fort Franklin, along a river up there.

This man, William, was a neighbor. He kept walking. Then he stopped and set a trap. He walked away. Then he crawled to the trap and snapped it shut! He snapped it shut on his own ankle.

He howled. He rolled around. Grandfather stayed up in the air, watching.

Then the man hobbled away. He was dragging the trap. Then he tore it right off.

The man arrives at a fish-camp. He left his own fish-camp behind, now arrives at another. And right away he kills the dogs. He ambushes them. He tears the fur off the dogs and dresses in a coat of that. Now he's in the fish-camp. It's nighttime and everybody's asleep. He flings the dog carcasses so far.

Now Grandfather knows William is a bushman. Something's gone wrong, and Grandfather has watched it. He knows he must kill this man. He knows it, but he doesn't want to do it yet.

It's hard. Because this is a man he knows. He looks close again at the cap. He looks close at the shoes. But then he thinks, "This isn't an Indian man. He doesn't smell like any man I know." So Grandfather lowers, then he kills this man.

Now the dream is over, but a man has been killed. This news arrives to Grandfather at a fish-camp. Up near Fort Franklin. Grandfather is there with some others—families. This news arrives, and Grandfather goes out to have a look. He arrives at another fish-camp. Right away the fish-stink is everywhere. Grandfather says, "What's gone on here?" They tell him. They show him the dead man.

Grandfather says, "Give me his cap, shirt, shoes." They give him those.

Grandfather takes home the clothes. But his dogs won't let the house rest. The dogs Grandfather owns are snapping and like that. Grandfather wants to kill these dogs, but others say no. He shouldn't, they say. Grandfather has nailed the clothes up. The others say for Grandfather to burn these clothes. Grandfather gets very drunk and puts on the cap. The dogs snap at his face. Some men force Grandfather down on the ground. They shove him inside a room. They tie his dogs outside. They keep Grandfather inside. Then these other men take all the clothes somewhere and burn them. Grandfather stays drunk, but then he came out of that. He was a young man when this happened. He had a family, and he knew the cap, shirt, and shoes belonged to a white man he had gone hunting with.

Now the path between those two fish-camps is always bare. Worn-down. That's because a bushman traveled it. That's all he told me. He said, "No one walks it any more. They go another way."

What Is the Earth?

◇GREENLAND ESKIMO◇

Three friends were curious about the size and shape of the earth. They were so curious that they decided to go exploring. They had traveled for three days and two nights when they came to an enormous ice-house. "Let's go in," one of the friends said. And so they went into the house, which seemed to be without end. They followed the walls in order not to get lost. Where was the passage through which they'd entered? They walked for days, for months, for years. At last they grew very weary. It was all they could do to crawl now. Then two of the friends could no longer crawl and they sat down and died. The third friend managed to find the exit-passage. His kayak was exactly where he'd left it. He came back to his people as a very old man. And he told them, "The earth is simply a very big ice-house."

Then he died too.

How the Narwhal Got Its Tusk

◇GREENLAND ESKIMO◇

A very long time ago, an old woman lived with her grandson and granddaughter in an isolated village. One day they just picked up and left on a journey, and soon they were caught in a snowstorm. The storm held them for a number of days. They got hungry. Then they began to starve. The oldest grandchild, the boy, had been blind from birth, and now he was pacing around the igloo.

They waited and waited. Then, one day, a fat bear came right up to the *igalaaq*, the window, and stood swaying in front of it. His face appeared, then disappeared, then it was there again. Then the bear stood still, looking in, sniffing.

"It's a bear," the woman said to her grandson. "You try and shoot it. I'll bend the bow and aim, and you let the string go."

She aimed. He shot. They heard a thud.

"You missed the bear!" she said. "The arrow has stuck into the wall by the window. What a shame."

But the blind grandson knew that his grandmother was lying. And he was right, because the bear had been struck straight in the center of its chest.

"Too bad, too bad that you didn't shoot straight," she said. Then she whispered to her granddaughter, "We won't give him any part of the bear to eat. Let's push and drag the bear away, and we'll eat bear meat in secret."

The blind grandson knew what was going on. He heard them boil up the meat. He smelled it boiling.

The grandmother and granddaughter fell to gorging. But as the granddaughter ate, she let little bits of meat roll down her neck, inside her collar, and they stuck to her chest. She did this a few times. "I'm amazed at how hungry you are!" her grandmother said. "You've been gorging and you aren't stuffed yet!"

"I'm hungry, all right," she said to her grandmother. "I'm hungrier than I've ever been. I'm gorging, I'm eating sloppy, and I'm gnashing my food loudly, all because I'm so hungry, hungrier than ever!" Then she let some bigger pieces fall down her collar. Her grandmother didn't notice.

The grandmother fell asleep. And right away, the granddaughter fed her brother. She reached down her collar and got out the bits of meat, and he ate them quickly. "I'm terribly thirsty," he said. "Lead me to some open water so I can drink."

She took him there, crying all the way. When they arrived, the blind boy begged his sister to leave him and go back to their grandmother, but not to forget to lay stones, big stones he could knock his ankles against to feel his way, in a path back to the igloo. And she did this, crying all the way.

Sitting on the shore of the lake, the boy realized that in spite of his great thirst he was unable to drink. He couldn't figure out why. He simply couldn't gulp down any water. Suddenly he heard a terrible whistling. A bird had landed beside him. "Hang on to my neck," the bird said. Which the boy did, and the bird took him underwater. They surfaced, dove again—this went on four times. Each time they stayed under a longer time, and each time the boy had more trouble breathing. But something else was happening, too.

"How do you feel?" the bird asked.

"Better, better! I'm actually beginning to see!"

After the fourth dive, the boy said, "I can see everything!"

"You are all right now," the bird said. "When I can, I'll come back with food."

The boy saw the path-stones and followed them.

"Look there," he said, "a big bearskin near the igloo, a stretched skin."

He walked into the igloo. "Oh, *that!*" the grandmother said. "That bearskin was given to us as a present. Some people happened by, they gave us some bear meat and left this skin stretched out for us. Good luck, eh?"

"Well, well," the boy said, knowing it was a lie he'd heard. He knew it was a lie.

The three of them stayed camped there for a few days.

One morning, they were out near a sea-break, and they saw some white whales offshore. The boy prepared to harpoon them. He tied the end of the harpoon line to his sister's leg; in this way, according to tradition, it became his "whale's tail," and when he'd killed an animal she would be given the same amount of meat as he would. She was his partner in the hunt.

"Tie me too," the grandmother said. This was done. A small whale was harpooned. The grandmother shouted, "Hurry, one more, one more!" So quickly the boy harpooned another white whale, a beluga. This was a big whale, and it was swimming farther out.

This big white whale was wounded, and it pulled hard on the line. The grandmother was connected to this one, and she tried to hold on, to keep her balance, but she was being yanked toward the water. She couldn't fight for long. She desperately grabbed onto her granddaughter's boot. The whale yanked, then pulled, and her hand slid off the boot. She was dragged across the shore ice, into the water, far off, down toward the bottom. They surfaced—the grandmother gave off a loud gasp, loud as a whale spouting. They went down, came up again. "Toss me my ulu, my knife!" she yelled. "My ulu, my ulu, my ulu!" She hoped to cut herself free.

At that moment—just then—from the spin of things, the whirlpool, her hair was being braided into a tight, thick pigtail. Then, when the braiding was done, and there was a type of braid that had never been before, the whale dragged her down to the bottom once and for all.

There she was transformed into a narwhal, a black male narwhal with a long, twisted tusk sticking out of its mouth, a white tusk that glints if the sun hits it right, and this was the first narwhal. That's what happened. It happened way back then. That is how the narwhal got its tusk.

Ayas˙e and the Origin of Bats
◇TIMAGAMI OJIBWA◇

The Ayas˙e were a large family. They lived in a camp. Very often they used to go picking berries, for their country was a rocky country where berries abounded. Very often some of the berry pickers would get lost and never be found again. It was thought that some creature made a prey of them and ate them.

One time one of the Ayas˙e men was traveling. On his way he came across a kind of cabin of rock, from the top of which smoke was rising and in front of which a number of human skulls hung in the opening. Now this Ayas˙e managed to enter. By being very careful and not touching the skulls, he gained the inside of the rock-house without making any noise. These skulls were put there to rattle when anybody tried to pass.

When Ayas˙e got inside, he beheld two old blind women. As soon as they became aware of his presence, one of them said, "We had better begin to cook something and we will find out if Ayas˙e is passing here." Now these old women had some grease in a bark dish, and one of them put some of the grease in a cooking pail. When she did this, Ayas˙e pulled it out with his hand and ate it. Then she took the spoon to taste her grease, but found it gone. So she put another lump in the dish. Ayas˙e took this, and when she started to dip it up, it too was gone. This happened three or four times.

At last the old woman said, "Ayas˙e must have passed; somebody told us that Ayas˙e was going to pass. He must have passed now." Then she took a stick which she used to poke the fire with and began feeling all around, poking in the corners of the wigwam to find if Ayas˙e were there. Every time she came near poking him, he moved to another part of the wigwam, so she could not reach him. Pretty soon she touched him with the poker, and then he took off his coat of fisher skins which he was wearing and threw it into the doorway. The old women jumped up, and when they felt the fur coat they thought it was Ayas´e trying to escape through the door. Now these old women had a sharp pointed bone at each elbow. With these pointed bones they began stabbing the fur coat in their haste to kill Ayas´e, and pretty soon in their blind fury they fell to stabbing each other, each one thinking she was stabbing Ayas´e. They killed each other. One of the old women said before she died, "I believe you hit me by mistake." It was too late; they both died.

Now Ayas´e sat down in the wigwam and looked at them a long time. Then he dragged them outside and looked at them a long time. All around the wigwam he saw men's and women's bones, the bones of the victims of these two old blind women. Then he knew that all of his lost people had been killed by the old women and eaten. They were cannibals in the shape of monster bats, large enough to kill and eat people. Then Ayas´e took their bodies and cut them up into small pieces. These he threw into the air and they sailed off, transformed into small bats as we see them today.

The Loon and the Raven
◇REPULSE BAY ESKIMO◇

Way back, the loon and the raven were tattooing one another. The raven went first. He made some nice patterns, some nice colors, and then he finished. "There," he said. Now it was the loon's turn. He wanted to tattoo the raven. The raven said, "All right, go ahead." But when the loon began tattooing, the raven kept hollering "Ouch!" The raven became extremely skittish, shying, fluttering up. The loon really got mad and said, "Stop it!" The loon was proud of his tattooing skills and didn't like his work interrupted, and the raven kept saying "Ouch! Ouch!" The loon was getting madder and madder. "I'm going to fly off the handle," he said, "if you say ouch or get skittish." With that the raven, getting tattoed, said "Ouch!" And the loon flew off the handle. He picked up the drip-pot from under the oil lamp and poured it over the raven, and tore out of the house. The loon got out of there fast. But just as the loon was about to bend down through the doorway, the raven hurled the drip-pot at him. The drip-pot hit the loon violently, right in the legs. Because of these events, loons can never walk and ravens are black, and it will be this way forever.

The Giant Skunk and His Offspring

◇ A T T I K A M E K I N D I A N ◇

Aniw ˙ye was a giant skunk, a monster. He traveled all over. He searched and searched for people, the Ojibwa. If people hid in the ground, he rooted them up. If people hid in a cave, he stayed by the cave-mouth, and when they came out, there he was, waiting. He turned around. He sprayed them. They died. That was called "sickness," his spray. It was the only sickness around. That was long ago. The skunk's spray was the only sickness to worry about. Not like today—today, in a hospital, hardly anyone is in a bed there because Monster Skunk sprayed them. It still happens, though. It can happen.

How did skunks get smaller? I'll tell you. It was a long time ago. As usual, Aniw ˙ye was looking for Ojibwa. He had been finding them all along. But some days passed and he hadn't found any. He had built up a lot of spray inside him. So, he was moving slowly.

Far away, there was a camp. A camp of people. They were going out for a hunt. "Let's watch out for Aniw ˙ye," one said. This was always said. It was good to say this: "Let's watch out for Aniw ˙ye, because he's out there, and we know he's looking." They set out. But almost right away they found Aniw ˙ye's tracks. "These are empty ponds," one said. "No, those are Aniw ˙ye's tracks—yes, they're big."

"Let's go in every direction," one said.

It was agreed, right away. It was agreed: "Let's go in every direction. That way, we might lead Aniw ˙ye away from our camp, and maybe some of us will escape, too."

They went in every direction. "We'll meet at Fisher Lake," one said. "No matter where you go, meet there. Fisher Lake."

Fisher Lake was where Giant Fisher lived. He lived there, people had seen him there and knew how large he was. They knew Giant Fisher and Aniw ˙ye were enemies.

"What about her?" one said. He pointed to a whittled-up woman. An old woman, the oldest, who looked like a whittled stick. Frail as that. She sat there. "What about her? We can't hurry in every direction, not if we have to take her!"

This old woman couldn't walk alone, she fell. She couldn't see, she fell and couldn't even see where she'd fallen. She was hobbled, blind.

One of the people yelled in her ear, "We're going. We're running from Aniw ˙ye. He's nearby. He'll kill us. We're going."

But the old one said, "I'm sitting here."

The rest left her. She was left, sitting by herself. She was inside a hut.

Pretty soon Aniw ˙ye found her. He bit off the top of the hut. He looked there. He saw the old woman. She had built a small fire. "Where's the rest of your people?" Aniw ˙ye said. The old woman didn't hear whose voice it was. She thought it was a young man speaking to her. She answered. "They've left," she said. "They saw Aniw ˙ye's tracks, and fled. They're gone. I'm old, can't see, I'm hobbled, so they left me."

"I'll cure you," said Aniw ˙ye. He turned around. He bent forward and raised his tail. He sprayed on the hut, and it blew to pieces and the old woman disappeared. She—*pssaaattt!* Gone!

Aniw ˙ye followed a trail, a trail of tracks. He followed a trail of footprints. When he stopped, he looked and saw Fisher Lake. He grew angry, knowing Giant Fisher was there. But he wanted those people. He chose to get them.

The people had arrived. They said to Giant Fisher, "Aniw ˙ye is on the way. We know this. He's coming. He wants to kill us."

Giant Fisher said, "I know what to do. I can do it with your help. Listen: when Aniw ˙ye gets near enough to spray, I'll be hiding behind you. I'll be hidden. Just when he turns his back, flee. I'll know what to do. First, I'll practice."

Giant Fisher pinched off some trees. He squeezed them tightly with his hands—the juices stayed inside, though. He did this a few times.

"It's time," Giant Fisher said.

"Yes—okay," the people said.

They went out to meet Aniw ˙ye. Giant Skunk was out there, he had crossed the lake. He stood there. The people approached.

Suddenly, Aniw ˙ye spun around, his back toward the people. But the people fled. Giant Fisher leapt forward and pinched closed Aniw ˙ye's hole! He kept the juices inside. He kept the spray in. "Let go! Ayu! Ayu! Ayu! Ayu!" Aniw ˙ye screamed. But Giant Fisher held fast. He held on.

Aniw ˙ye clawed the air, he tumbled, but Giant Fisher stayed pinched onto him until Aniw ˙ye was dead. His own juices poisoned him.

"Build up a fire," Giant Fisher said.

The people built a huge fire. They kept tossing branches on. It was sparking up. They tossed Aniw ˙ye on it, and he burned. His ashes floated up, and when they landed, each became a small skunk. A skunk like we find today. That day, the winds were strong and ashes were drifted far. That's why skunks live in so many places. There's plenty of them.

A Yukaghir Tale of the Origin of the Chukchee

◇ Y U K A G H I R ◇

There were two orphans, a boy and a girl. They lived on the tundra. Suddenly the sky became dark. There was no food and they were starving. While they walked groping in the darkness, young ptarmigans happened to come into their hands. The boy said, "Something is moving in my hand." The girl answered, "In mine, too, but men eat this. Let us also eat, or else we will die of hunger."

One of the young ptarmigans spoke to the boy and said, "Do not kill me. At my father's and mother's place is much food. If you do not kill me, I will also find light for you." The girl listened and said, "Do not let it go, whatever it says. People eat it and we will eat it." The ptarmigan begged again for its life: "Do not kill me, I will let snow fall for you, I will walk on it, and you may follow my tracks and you will reach my parents."

While the boy was still holding the ptarmigan, snow began to fall. It continued to snow. Much snow fell.

"Now," said the ptarmigan, "let me go, I will go and you follow me. Now my tracks on the white snow will be visible."

The orphans let go of the ptarmigan and followed its tracks. Suddenly they saw the young ptarmigan sitting with two old ones, its father and mother. The ptarmigans said to the orphans, "We will give you food: willow leaves and larch cones. Men eat them."

The orphans tried eating leaves of willows, and they were pleasing to them. Then the old he-ptarmigan said, "Now you have food, so I will go to find the hidden light. Stay here, but even if I do not return for a long while, do not eat my wife and children."

The ptarmigan flew off upward towards the sky. It flew a long time. Suddenly it felt something firm. It scratched with its claws. It was hard. Then it picked with its beak. It picked a great while. At last it picked through the firmament, and light appeared as if through a window. Its entire beak was rubbed off, but light set in. The ptarmigan looked down and saw a bright day on earth. The ptarmigan flew down. After reaching the earth it asked the orphans, "Well, now is it light on earth?"

"Yes," answered the orphans, "light has set in."

"And you did not suffer hunger in my absence?"

"No," answered the orphans. "We were eating willow leaves and larch cones, and we have grown fat."

"Well," said the ptarmigan, "now live here as you like, but I will not remain with you. I will fly towards the white world."

The ptarmigan flew off with its family, and the orphans remained and lived on willow leaves and larch cones. They married, and from them the Chukchee originated.

That is why the Chukchee at present like to eat fresh willow leaves and larch-tree cones.

Which Animals Are on the Moon
◇ N O A T A G M I U T   E S K I M O ◇

About one mile downriver from Noatak village, at Napaktusuguruk, a few families lived.

A family with only one daughter lived at Napaktusuguruk. This family made an *ibruluk*, a moss cabin. Afterwards their girl always wanted to get water. Even when she was sewing, she would put down her work and go for water. In the afternoons she went to get firewood.

One night it was freezing and it began to snow lightly. When it snowed, the girl always went out. She was like a child who can't stay indoors, one who goes out whenever it rains or snows. Her mother and father asked her why she always wanted to go out, but she never told them.

Just because men always wanted to have this girl, her parents let her stay where there were no people.

And when it was getting dark, while people were traveling by, this girl would go to the river to get water. And she would come home late.

That night it was snowing lightly. She went out and didn't come back. The father told the mother to go look for her. The mother went to the well and found the girl's footprints. Her bucket was frozen in the ice. There weren't any tracks going from the well.

The father and mother couldn't find that girl anywhere. They made torches from sticks with oily moss on the end, and they used these for light. They looked for their daughter all night at places where she used to get wood. They couldn't find her, not even her tracks.

The father got tired. He told his wife he wanted to rest. He said he would go downriver to Napaktusuguruk to look for her when it was daylight. Early in the morning the father went to look for her. He never even ate his breakfast.

Nobody had seen this man's daughter. He came back home. Then he went upriver about thirty-five or forty miles to Kugrurak, a Noatagmiut camp. The people there hadn't seen his daughter either.

Then the father went home and stayed alone (because people couldn't be with them—you know how it is when someone dies). The

father and mother put the girl's clothes in a bag on an elevated platform—a cache. They didn't know what to do. Then the father went
down to Kivalina to look for his daughter. He asked there. The Kivalina
people knew that the girl was lost but they didn't know where she was.

When spring came, the parents moved to the coast to hunt seals.
They left things at the cache.

This couple couldn't stay with people anywhere. The husband
hunted, he got *ugruk*, seal, everything at the coast. The wife fixed food.
She put *ugruk* and seal meat with oil in pokes. The man made ropes
of walrus and *ugruk* skin. He hunted everything and they stayed away
from people. Then they went with their skin boat. When the other
people were leaving, they were ready to go. They started alone, a little
way from Sealing Point.

They got to Sisualik camp. They traded their seal oil and rawhide
rope for Kobuk people's dried fish. They camped here at Sisualik, at
the Noatak camp. They made different kinds of food. After they traded
oil for dried fish, they put away the fish in oil, in pokes. Then before
it got dark (it begins to get dark at night in the last part of July) they
traveled near people, but still they had to live alone.

When they got home, above Noatak village, they left their things,
took just a little food, and went to hunt caribou. They went with people
but still they camped alone. They got caribou. They went home when
the other people went downriver. They went by Kugrurak, and when
it was beginning to freeze they stopped at their home.

They caught salmon with a fish spear. At that time there were no
nets. From other people the Napaktomiut bought sinew nets. That's
the way the Napaktomiut always fished, never trying to catch fish as
they do now. The fish harpoon they used had a rope to hold the
harpoon to its handle. So this man got quite a few salmon. Then they
began fishing with hooks through the ice. Their fishing lines were made
of baleen. They made hook shanks out of beluga teeth or elephant—
fossil mammoth—teeth.

It was about the same time of year, one year after that girl disappeared. When it was moonlight, when it was freezing, a dog team came. The mother went outside. She saw a sled and harness. The harnesses were moving, but she couldn't see the dogs. The sled was loaded. She saw two persons and she saw them tie up the dogs, but she still couldn't see the dogs. It was snowing.

The father didn't come out to meet these people. He told his wife to touch their sled-load. He told her these ones you can't see—*atalbis*—they act like people, but they're invisible.

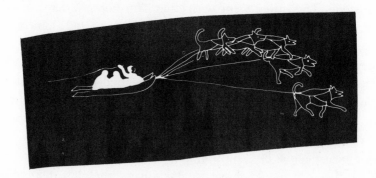

When the wife got inside she shut the door. Then that woman visitor opened the door and called her name, "Aka." She told her mother that her husband said to put a seal-gut curtain in front of their sleeping-place. She said they wouldn't stay if they didn't put up a curtain.

Then the mother called, saying to them that she had already put up a gut curtain. They brought their things and threw them inside. Then the couple brought in some caribou meat, then caribou skins. Even their ropes were made from caribou hide. They brought in everything. The two old folks took some of their things out.

The girl told her mother to work on the skins. There were wolverine and wolf skins with snow on them. The two people had snow between their inner and outer clothes. They took off their clothes and the mother beat out the snow from their clothes. The weather was too snowy and stormy, they said.

The mother asked them what they wanted to eat. The daughter wanted dried meat in seal oil. The mother gave her frozen and dried fish—anything they had gathered in the past year. The daughter's husband would eat oil, as well. When they were eating, the mother asked the girl why she had got lost. The mother told how they had looked for her for a whole year. She wanted to know how the girl got away. The daughter and her husband were eating behind the gut curtain. The old folks were eating too. They were eating what their daughter brought, things like dried caribou meat with tallow.

Now the daughter started to tell her mother of the things she asked about. She said she hadn't wanted to leave without telling her parents, but that the man didn't want her to tell them. She knew they would look for her, but he wouldn't let her tell them.

The mother knew now why her daughter was always outside. And the man was from the moon. It was so stormy he carried her on his back, that time last year. The father thanked the man. He told him to come again.

The mother made a sealskin parka, sealskin pants, getting ready for the couple to leave. They stayed one year. The parents could see their daughter, but they could only see the man's shadow against the curtain.

One time, another man came to them. That person would always come to see what they were doing. He came while the couple stayed there. That man came in and ate. He couldn't see those two from the moon, but they talked and he heard their voices. After they ate, that man went outside. He looked to see what kind of sled these visitors had. Their dogs' harnesses and lines were made of caribou hides. Their sled was made of wood; its runners had no shoes. But the father made them a new sled with whalebone shoes.

That man who came stayed overnight for the first time. He went home when it was daylight. When he got back to his home, he told about the two people who were staying with the old folks. He told about everything these visitors had: their dogs' chains were made of wood and the lines of caribou skin; the dogs' chains turned around the posts but he couldn't see the dogs. These dogs even ate; still he couldn't see them.

After one year, when it was becoming spring, the couple wanted to go home. They wanted to take home some *ugruk* oil, dried skins, and skin rope but no things of caribou. They loaded their sled. They started. They went on the ground for a while, then they went in the air, up in the air. Then the parents couldn't see them.

This couple used to tell them that the moon had lots of arctic hares and caribou but no sea animals, no oil.

They went back and forth from the moon to the parents' home from that time on.

Why Rattlesnakes Don't Cross the River

◇ T H O M P S O N   I N D I A N ◇

Rattlesnake-of-the-North had a house in Okanogan country, British Columbia, where he lived with his wife, Bow-Snake, and his brothers, Wasp and Bee. He had a set of new teeth and two old teeth. He kept the new teeth and gave the old teeth to his brothers, saying, "These will be your fangs. When you sting people, it will cause soreness and swelling, but those you bite will not die. With me, it will be different. When I bite any living thing, it will die. But I will never bite anyone without first warning him with my rattle, which I will always carry with me. A person who treats me respectfully and says, 'Pass on, friend,' I will not harm; but those who laugh at me or mock me, I will kill." Turning to his wife, he said, "You are a woman. It would not be right for you to have the power of killing anyone." This is why today the bite of a rattlesnake is deadly, while that of the bow-snake is harmless; also, why wasps and bees have stings that cause pain and swelling.

Rattlesnake-of-the-North had many children, most of them sons. Rattlesnake-of-the-South also had many children. He lived across the river in eastern Washington. Between the homes of these people lay a flat tract of country, consisting of clay, mud, and small lakes. This was the home of Mesai, who had two daughters. One of them she sent to marry the son of Rattlesnake-of-the-North, and the other to marry the son of Rattlesnake-of-the-South. But both girls were refused, the mother Rattlesnakes saying they would not have daughters-in-law who smelled so bad. When they returned, Mesai felt indignant and insulted, and went to the houses of both the Rattlesnakes, asking why they had insulted her and refused her daughters. The Rattlesnakes answered, "We do not care to have our sons married to women who smell as bad as yourself and your daughters."

Mesai replied, "Since you have insulted me, no Rattlesnake will from now on enter my country. If you swim across the river to it, soon after you touch the shore you will die." This is the reason why no rattlesnakes are found in that tract of country to the present day. The place is called Smelta'us, and mesai roots are very plentiful there. North and south of Smelta'us, rattlesnakes are abundant.

The First White Men

◇ H A R E I N D I A N ◇

In old times, there were no white men around. Then a few boats arrived. The white men were on the boats. The boats moored a ways out, never touching land. When the fog lifted, the boats would be there. They must've been eating fish, fishing from the other side of the boat where the Indians couldn't see them.

These men were monsters, really. They were white men, but also monsters. They sharpened their teeth on the wood-burning stove made of iron. The Indian people could hear this at night. They figured out what the sound was.

So what was going to happen? Because the white men were on their boat for part of a year, fishing from the invisible side and sharpening their teeth. No Indians sent a boat out to visit.

Then one night the sound of their teeth stopped. The Indian people noticed this.

The white men swam to shore, and walked until they were at the edge of the Indian town. The dogs got nervous, they barked and snapped like they had lice. All the dogs.

Then the white men started barking and snapping with those sharp teeth sharpened on the iron stove. They rolled on the ground, snapping like they had lice. They thought what the Indian dogs were doing was an Indian greeting.

A few of the white men bit themselves almost to death and had to return to the boat. They swam back out.

These men were truly monsters, big and merciless, but that time they didn't get past the dogs who greeted them. Finally, they returned to the boat. Out in the fog, Indian people heard their teeth against the iron stove. The white men continued to fish for a number of days off the far side of their boat.

Then one day, when the fog lifted, the boat was gone. The few boats were gone. By the time I grew up into a man, white men were all over that Indian town, and every one of their houses had an iron stove in it.

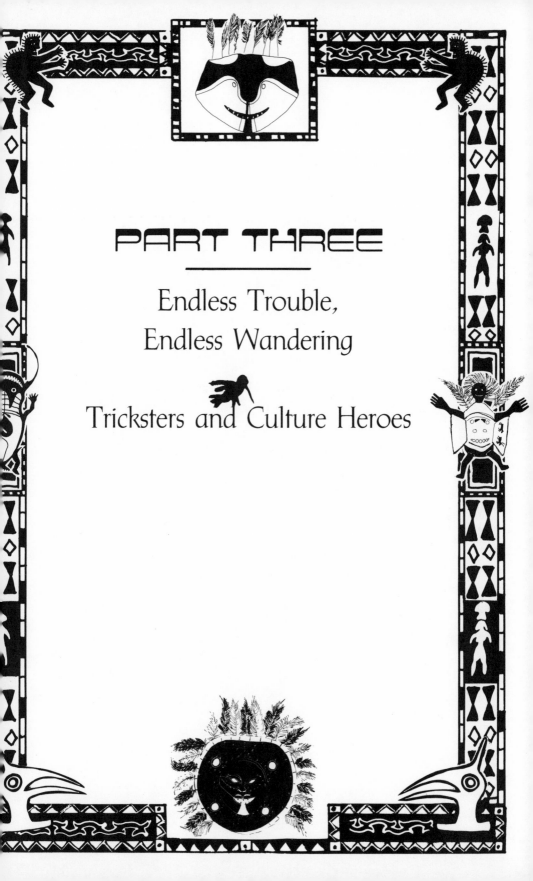

PART THREE

Endless Trouble,
Endless Wandering

Tricksters and Culture Heroes

FOR CENTURIES TRICKSTER STORIES have enjoyed tremendous popularity in the North. Trickster delights every audience with his infinite capacity for troublemaking, his bawdy, outrageous, often violating, and always wildly humorous behavior. The arrival of Beaver-Trickster to an Athapaskan village or the great Creator-Trickster Kuloscap to a foggy Maritime fishing community is in itself an adventure: it is all but impossible to predict what will happen next.

Trickster's many mythological vocations—clown, explorer, teacher, magician, raconteur, lover, thief—are as complex and as generous as time itself. They offer a tale-teller a vast repertoire, sometimes a cycle of stories, as with the "Smart Beaver Cycle" in this section. As a buffoon, Trickster might fall flat on his face, then blame everyone but himself. As a lover, with spontaneous and insatiable lusts, he might mate with every human and animal in sight and yet remain without a family. As a jester, he might juggle his eyes, therefore juggling reality. As a protector, Trickster may be heroic. Kuloscap, for instance, announces, "I will have to kill the Ice Giants. Whoever eats people, I will do away with." Yet even the greatest of culture heroes is capable of chicanery: "Kuloscap tricked people all the time. He tricked witches and evil spirits, too—he was out for fun," says one Micmac tale. As the bringer of news, Trickster might lie repeatedly, exaggerate the most commonplace event, brag about triumphs not his own.

It is well documented that almost every tribal people in the world has a trickster central to its oral literature. Raven, Crow, Coyote, Beaver, and Wolverine are some of the northern tricksters. In addition, there are "humanlike" figures, such as Nanabusho among the Ojibwa and Wesukechak among the Cree. They are idiosyncratic in that each trickster was born out of a quite different tribal sensibility, geographical locale, and language.

But what does a trickster look like?

We hear, for instance, a Tagish woman, Mrs. Angela Sidney, say,

"This Beaver is a person, but he can turn into Beaver when he's in a tight spot. Most times he looks like a man." Kuloscap is described as follows: "He was a great giant and could swim with immense strokes." Whatever insights we are given into a trickster's personality, we know one thing for certain: if we follow him long enough we will see him turn into various forms. We will witness metamorphosis.

Trickster can never fully belong to any one village or family. Like a magical hermit, he must live outside civilization, even though his life-lessons, his mesmerizing tricks, nurture the human imagination, make people laugh, and animate life itself. Trickster can never fully marry into human life, just as he can never truly become physically human. Likewise, he cannot inherit our human past, nor does he long for any future. He is the perfect embodiment of the present tense. In tales, this is substantiated by the fact that whenever Trickster appears, people and animals tend to drop everything and pay full attention to him. He is expert at manipulating time in this manner. As the writer-philosopher Elias Canetti notes: "The effect [in Trickster] of a command and the effect of transformation meet within him, and the essence of freedom can be gleaned from him."

In turn benevolent, malevolent, and indifferent to the human condition, Trickster nonetheless has an immediate effect on whomever he comes in contact with. He shakes things up. He can turn the most sacred and long-established institutions into a scattered jigsaw puzzle in the wink of an eye. He makes people fine-tune their sensibilities, be on the alert. By the sheer force of his personality, Trickster is the precise opposite of Everyman, or at least the most accepted notions of what that is.

And yet, Trickster does mirror human foibles—greed, envy, jealousy, lust, hypocrisy, spiritual and even moral confusion—a considerable talent indeed! However, whereas humankind has cultivated and exploited such traits even, one fears, to the brink of self-destruction, Trickster never goes that far. His presence demands, cries out for, compassion and generosity toward existence itself. Trickster is a celebrator of life, a celebration of life, because by rallying against him a community discovers its own resilience and protective skills. The result, alas, is that Trickster is exiled, kicked out, sent on his way.

Once in a while, though, Trickster will live among people, partaking as best he can of village life, even enhancing it insofar as humans do.

Yet even in human disguise, Trickster is not safe from himself. He may prove to be the village loudmouth, the inept hunter, the outlandish Romeo, the hypochondriac posing as a healer. At some point, his old self will emerge. He will break a taboo, anger a spirit, trespass on a chief's hunting territory—*something* will go wrong. And in the natural order of things, Trickster will be better off for leaving. He will continue his endless wandering. The more he wanders the North, the better someone's chances of running into him—and that is how trickster stories have always proliferated.

Smart Beaver Cycle

◇ T A G I S H   I N D I A N ◇

This cycle recounts how Smart Beaver, or Beaver Man, made a heroic voyage down what was possibly the Yukon River, "cleaning out" all the giant men and animals that terrorized people. He killed the giant men and reduced the animals to their present size, taught them to eat nonhuman food, and made it safe for people to live there again. The stories reflect the uneasy balance existing between certain animals and humans and the close relationship, even interchangeability, between them.

◇◇◇

This is a story about Beaver Man. Sometimes called Smart Beaver 'cause he's smart. Sometimes called Little Beaver 'cause he's youngest of five brothers. Sometimes called Beaver Brother.

This Beaver is a person, but he can turn into Beaver when he's in a tight spot. Most times he looks like a man. He's got lots of clothes, piled on top of each other. He's got all those shirts because he will be away so long. When wear out, he takes off, throws away because he's long time gone. Those shirts help him in tight spot, too. You'll see. That's why he's smart.

This is about how Beaver clean up the river, maybe Yukon River. That's after people all left the river. All leave one way—go out hunting and never come back. All his brothers killed that time. He's trying to get even for them and for others. He wants to find why all people left that river and where they go. Move away and never came back.

◇ LITTLE BEAVER MAN MEETS GIANT ◇

Little Beaver Man starts out. He come to valley and he rest near a mountain. He sees trail there that people go out on, never come back.

He sees Giant coming toward him. Giant sit just above Beaver on that mountain. So Beaver climbs around and he stop and rest just above

Giant. They keep doing this until they get to the very top of that mountain. The last time Beaver is above the Giant, he jump on him, squeeze his muscles. They roll down to the bottom. Little Beaver stays on top till that Giant has no more strength.

"You might as well kill me now," Giant says. "Poke in middle of my hand. That's where my strength is. You made me weak. I am no good for nothing now."

So Beaver Man pokes him in the hand and he bleeds to death.

Then Beaver Man cuts up that Giant in pieces. He throws these pieces, and wherever those pieces drop he tells them to turn into rock rabbit—those little tiny white rabbits. Every time he throws a piece he tell him, "Turn into rock rabbit."

"Thut." He make noise like that. People not supposed to make that noise or it brings on cold weather.

After he kills that Giant, he start down trail again. He's trying to find out more about why people left that river.

◇ BEAVER MAN MEETS MINK LADY ◇

Next place he comes to, sees that Mink Woman. She's smoking skin. He sees that she tans human being's skin—long arms, long legs. When he comes up she put that skin away quick. But he already see it and know what it was.

"Oh, my husband," she say. "I'm just going to look for you." She tries to fool him.

"Since when I'm your husband?" Beaver ask.

"I'll go get water, cook for you," she tell him. When she comes back she wants to sleep with him right away. He looks at her and he sees animals—mink—live inside her.

"I want to eat first," he says, smart like that. "I'll get water."

He went out to get water and when he's there he pick up long thin rock. He throw it in fire. He fool around till that rock gets hot. As soon as it's hot he says, "I'm ready now." Stuck that rock in her. Her breath stop. She die.

He calls out those animals. "I want you to be weasel, you to be mink, you to be mice," he tells them. He sets those animals free.

After all the animals came out, she came back to life again.

She says she wants to marry him. "You kill all those animals that I use to kill people. I'm pure now."

"No," he say. "I'm not going to marry you."

She's mad so she run off to try to chew up his boat. Somehow he fix up his boat and go. She start to swim after that boat just like mink.

"When you row, that wave behind your boat will catch you," she say.

He lose her somehow in the dark. When it's dark he row to the islands.

He lost her, I guess. He went to bed on some kind of island.

◇ BEAVER MAN MEETS OTTER MAN ◇

Early morning Little Beaver took off in boat. He went quite a ways before he saw anything. He saw tree fallen in water. Saw someone standing on that tree, hollering.

"Where is dog barking, brother?" ask that person.

"I don't know," said Little Beaver.

"Land here and I'll find out," he tell Little Beaver.

He land there. That's why he came there, to check why people are gone. He has to stop. He make little fire.

He hear "uh, uh, uh," sounds like something heavy being pull up. It's that person, Otter Man. He's got big rope he's pulling. "Help me, my brother, help me."

So Beaver helped. Here it was otter on that rope. That man starts skinning otter. "I'll feed you," he tells Little Beaver.

Beaver say, "Don't worry. I don't eat that kind. I've got my own food."

His brother put otter on plate and gave him. They changed plates.

"I don't eat otter," said Beaver Man. "People don't," he tell him again. He gave that man his food, gave him fish. He said, "Don't eat otter." He teach that man that lesson.

◇ BEAVER MAN MEETS WOLVERINE ◇

By now it's winter. Beaver Man has his little boat. He pull up at head of trail, starts walking again.

He go along. Still have to clean up river. He follows trail, comes to hill. See spear sticking up. Just like someone sliding downhill on that spear. There's fresh blood.

Looks like trouble. Little Beaver take off one shirt, stuff with willow branches, make padding. Then roll shirt down hill. It gets stuck on that spear. Then he makes nose bleed. Puts blood on that spear. He put shirt back on. Pretend he crawl out of that sharp spear. Pretend he's dead. Beaver Man is smart.

He pretend he die. Lay there. Pretty soon along comes Giant Wolverine. Wolverine run that trapline every day.

"Ha! Got somebody," he says. "Thought I wasn't going to catch you." He ties that Beaver's hands together, feet together.

"Wish he pack me backwards," think Beaver. Comes true. Wolverine pack him backwards. Pack him to under leaning tree. Gets caught on limb. *Pfzf!* Drops him.

Then Wolverine pack him home. Lay him outside. "My daddy kill something. Game this time." Those kids are happy. Wolverine sharpen knife. Kids lick Beaver.

"Stop lick off that fat. That's for your mama," Wolverine say.

Those kids see Beaver open one eye. "Hey, he's alive, this one," they say.

"You crazy? You think he live when knife go through his body? I saw blood on that spear."

There's special knife to cut that Beaver. But that knife is under him. His doctor—power—bring it to him, so it's under him.

All of a sudden he jump up, grab stick. He club that daddy, that mother. "I'm going to look after you kids." He cut open that mom.

She's giant too. How big Wolverine is now is that size, size of those baby pups inside her.

Those older kids cry. He build fire. "Blow on it," he tell those two older kids, the ones that lick him. They do that and while they blow, he drops logs on their heads. Kills them.

Those two little ones inside mother, he lets live. He tells them, "Don't want you to eat people."

"Ha, ha," they laugh at him. "When we're big we'll steal cache from you." Then run up tree. He try to smoke them down but those kids pee on fire, mess it up.

He try to shoot them but they tell those arrows, "Go different way, go other way." So he never kill them. "Don't grow any bigger," he tell them. "Eat rabbits, gophers. Don't eat what your mother and father eat." That's the time he give them rabbits, gophers.

"We'll steal your food, mess up your cache." Those kids laugh.

◇ BEAVER MAN MEETS GIANT BEAR ◇

Next Beaver follows along, comes to Giant Bear on a hill.

Sees bearskin hanging on that hill. "What's that?" he asks.

"Oh, that's just my daughter. She's just become young lady. I hide her. She's sewing now," Bear tell him.

"Me, I've got hole in my moccasins," Beaver say.

"Give it to me, I'll take to my daughter," Bear say. Beaver sneaked after Bear to see what he does with it. Bear ran over to that place, but he sewed up himself with his left hand. Big stitches.

"My daughter can't sew good today, has headache," he tell Beaver. He's trying to slow Beaver down. Try to keep him from kill giant animals.

Beaver look at moccasins. "Could do better myself," he say. Unrip moccasins. Sew up himself.

Beaver knows something wrong. Knows these bears kill people. Wants to see that daughter.

"You're going to marry my daughter," Bear tell him, "but you can't see her until you kill animals that bother us." He wants those animals to kill Beaver Man.

"I need bow and arrow fixed," Beaver say.

"You fix bow and arrow. Then you see her."

◇ BEAVER MAN FACES FOUR TRIALS ◇

"First I need bow," Beaver say.

Bear tell him, "Go chop tree down." Beaver size up. Sees tree would splinter and fall on him if he chop it. It's a giant tree. His power tells him it's set up. So his power helps him poke that tree somehow. He gets his bow. Comes back.

Bear sees him coming. "He's coming again. *Yan a'goot.*" They're surprised, that Bear and his wife. Bear thought he killed him.

"I've got bow, but no sinew," Beaver tells him.

"Lots of sinew up on that hill," Bear tells him. "Find grizzly for sinew."

Beaver goes up there. Giant Grizzly lying in the meadow. He knows Grizzly will see him. First he finds mice.

"Grandma," he say, "help me." So those mice help him. "Dig hole— tunnel—to where Grizzly is sleeping. Take fur off so I can poke him with spear." Has two copper arrowheads for his spear. Hides those arrowheads in his hair and pulls them out when needs them.

Those mice come up just under that Grizzly arm. Mice pull away at that hair, clean hair off under that arm.

"What do that?" Grizzly ask.

"Need hair for my little ones, they're cold," that mice tell Grizzly. "They all die off."

"Then take from my tail," he tell them, "not from under my arm!"

Mice run back and tell Beaver, "Now!"

Then Beaver Man shoot Grizzly with spear through that hole mouse dig.

Grizzly is mad. Walk around mad. Shake. They crawl back out of hole. Sure enough, it's laying there.

"I want fat and meat for my kids," mice say to him.

"Okay, but don't waste any," say Beaver Man. "Live on it for a long time."

Little Beaver took that sinew. When he brought it back, Bear sure was surprised. "He's coming again," Bear say, surprised.

He expect Grizzly kill Beaver Man. He wants that to happen.

Next Beaver Man wants paint for arrow.

"Get from Frog," Bear tell him. "Giant Frog lives in a hole in the middle of the mountain."

That Frog lives near swampy place. Spring water there. Where that spring run down, see blue mud. When they burn that mud, those ashes make blue. You can use for paint.

"Son-in-law," that Bear tells him, "that hole in there was blue mud. Get it."

When Beaver get to that hole, spring water coming out. It's like that spring halfway to Carcross, across from Tagish. Beaver Man take top shirt off. He throw it right in front of mudhole. Sure enough, out comes Giant Frog. He kill that one too, I don't remember how. He come home. Got that paint too.

"He's coming again. *Yan a'goot*," wife tells Bear.

"Now I need feather for my arrow," said Beaver. Bear thinks. He tells him:

"Look up there. Eagle up high. Get feathers there." He thinks Eagle will finish off Beaver.

Two little Eagles are in the nest when Beaver comes. Beaver go to them.

"Which of you two is tattletale?"

That littlest one say, "Her." She point at her sister.

So he kill off that sister. Then he give that little one gopher to eat.

"How do you know when your mother come, your father come?" he asks her.

"When my mother come, there's warm and sunshine. When my father come, there's hailstorm."

That little one helps him—helps him to dig hole in nest. Little Beaver tell her, "It's no good what your mother and father eat." He sees people-bones around. "Shouldn't eat people," he tell her.

"My mother comes, my mother comes," that little Eagle say. It's warm and sunny. Beaver Man hides, holds that spear ready under nest.

That mother comes. "I smell fresh meat." She brings back front part of person's body. Just half a body.

"Ooo, ooo, makes my head ache," says little one.

"Where's your sister?" mother asks her.

"She flew down to creek because she has headache."

Then through that hole underneath, Little Beaver poke her with spear. Kill her. Little Beaver threw that body away.

Next come hailstorm. "My daddy comes, my daddy comes," little one say.

Beaver hides. Eagle brings hind part of man's body.

"Where's your mom, your sister?" he ask.

"They've got headache. Go to water."

He step over hole and Little Beaver spear him. He throw that body down.

"You stay here and I'll get you something to eat," he tell little one. "Don't eat people. Don't grow big. Stay the same size as you are."

You know the size eagle is now? That's the same size that baby Eagle was. Beaver look for louse in baby's head. Scratch, find louse. He put louse in little Eagle's ear: "Stay same size." That's how he medicine that little Eagle, with that louse.

Beaver bring gopher, ptarmigan, rabbit only for that one. "Don't eat people. What are you going to say when you cry?" he ask her.

"Gluk, gluk, gluk."

"Good," Little Beaver tell her.

"I don't want to leave you before you can get along by yourself," he tell her. "Get grouse."

She does. So he knows she's okay and he leaves. Before he go he burn bodies up.

He brings back feather. "He's coming again," Bear say.

◇ BEAVER MAN FIGHTS BEARS ◇

When he's coming back, Bear gets mad. "Makes me sick. He kill off all my animals," Bear say. Bear decides to kill Beaver himself. "You kill him too," he says to wife.

Before he comes back to camp Beaver spots Bear. Knows Bear is mad. Beaver goes up that hill first, to see if he had daughter. He went up. Sure enough, he really had daughter. He kill that daughter, that Bear daughter.

"He kill our daughter," Bear say. "Let's kill him ourselves." Starts chasing him. Chase to Little Lake. Bears run to the narrows. That lake has narrows just like Tagish Lake.

Beaver Man turns into Beaver. He's in tight spot. Beaver dive and go through narrows. Bear turn to wife: "Run, get your skirt. Let's fix it for beaver net." She went home to get her skirt for net. Beaver hear them.

Anyway, he got ashore. Take big tree-stumps. Went in water again. By that time, net is ready. Beaver put stump in net. They pull and pull. Riverbank hangs over water. Beaver pull and pull. Then all of a sudden let go.

Those Bears fall in water. Beaver slits their throats. That's how he get rid of Giant Bears. No more bears eat people.

◇ BEAVER MAN MEETS SHEEP ◇

After that Beaver Man goes along, meets Sheep. Giant Sheep. That one's got sheepskin on stick hanging way up there.

"What's that?" says Beaver Man.

"My dog's stuck up there, barking, throat getting dry."

"Where?" ask Little Beaver. "I can't see."

"I'll show you."

So they go up that mountain to peak. He look over edge of hill at that skin. He knows it's just a skin, knows that Sheep wants to kill him. That Sheep wants to shove Beaver Man over, down other side. Sheep looks over hill, to show Beaver where to go. Beaver push him.

That Sheep's wife waits there with an axe. She thought it's Beaver Man, so she killed him. When Beaver Man came down, she's crying.

"Can't help it, grandma. He goes to show me something and he falls over." He lies.

He tells her, "Don't eat people. Eat grass, stuff like that. Don't get too big. Just stay that big, like you are." So he left her too. That's the end.

So that's how Little Beaver cleaned up that river. Maybe that's Yukon River.

Kuloscap Tales

◇ M I C M A C ◇

◇ HOW KULOSCAP DEALT WITH ICE GIANTS ◇

There once lived a man with his two sons and a daughter. All were great wizards. They lived for a while in Maine, but traveled to Nova Scotia, Newfoundland, all through the Maritimes, whenever they chose. They just said, "Let's go," and off they went.

They were wizards. They were Kiwa'kws—Ice Giants who ate people, men, women, children. Everything they did was cruel. They did horrible things. And the people living in the villages were tired of the Ice Giants. They had a way of sighing which, without a word, meant "Ice Giant," and everyone sighed all the time.

Kuloscap arrived and heard about the Ice Giants. He said, "I knew them when they were young! They were my family back then! But now I must find out the truth myself. If what I have heard is true, I will have to kill the Ice Giants. Whoever eats people, I will do away with. It makes no difference who they are."

The Ice Giants had moved up to the rough coastline of Maine, across from Nova Scotia, across the Bay of Fundy. They lived on the sandy field in the bed of the river Saco at Elnoebit, or Ogyagwch, between Kearsarge and the big rock where the mermaids basked and ate seaweed.

The old man, the father of the Ice Giants, was one-eyed and half grey. So Kuloscap made himself look exactly like that! He entered their hut and sat down next to the old man.

A few Ice Giant brothers overheard someone talking. Slyly, they looked in and saw this newcomer who looked so much like their father that they could hardly tell the difference.

One Ice Giant sister then took up a whale's tail; she cooked it for the stranger. She placed it on newly peeled birchbark. Then an Ice Giant brother entered the hut; he held up the birchbark and said, "You are eating too well!" Then the Ice Giant brother ran off with the whale's tail.

Kuloscap says, "The Ice Giant first offered me a meal, then he took it back! Now I will get it for myself!"

But Kuloscap doesn't leave the hut. He sits still. He closes his eyes.

He thinks hard. He *wishes* the whale's tail to him. And back it comes, on the newly peeled birchbark, right into Kuloscap's hands.

The Ice Giants huddle and say, "This, truly, is a great wizard in our midst. But he has to be tested further."

The Ice Giants fetch a great whale's jaw. The oldest Ice Giant tries to break it with both his hands, but it bends only a little. He then gives it to Kuloscap. Kuloscap snaps it in half. He uses only his thumb to snap it like a pipestem!

Again the Ice Giants say, "He is a very great wizard, but he must be tested further!"

They fetch a great pipe filled with strong tobacco. Anyone who is not a wizard cannot smoke it. They pass it around. Everyone smokes. The Ice Giants swallow the smoke. Kuloscap fills the pipe, then burns out all the tobacco with a single puff!

Again the Ice Giants say, "He is a very great wizard, but once more he must be tested." They try to smoke with him again. The hut is closed; the Ice Giants want to smother Kuloscap with smoke. Kulscap puffs away. The Ice Giants cannot bear this any longer. They say, "This is not worthwhile for us; let us play a game of ball."

Kuloscap says, "So, my being in the smoke-hut isn't enough for you! Okay, I'll provide the ball." He goes over to a tree near the river, breaks off a bough, and turns it into a skull much more hideous than anything the Ice Giants have ever seen. The Ice Giants flee. The Ice Giants are completely defeated.

Then Kuloscap stomps on the ground. Foaming water rushes down from the mountains. All the earth rings with the roar. Then Kuloscap sings a song which changes how everyone looks. The Ice Giants become fish. These fish are each as long as a man. They flop into the rapids. They swim to the sea, where they live forever. Every once in a while they surface, just to have a look at Kuloscap on shore, smoking, picking his teeth with a giant whale bone.

◇ HOW KULOSCAP SAVED HIS UNCLE TURTLE'S LIFE ◇

Kuloscap was canoeing from Newfoundland to Pictou when he happened upon an Indian village. There he found Turtle. Turtle was very lazy. He moved slowly. The only way he wasn't lazy was in his blinking.

He blinked all the time. He blinked rapidly. But everyone said, "No matter, he's Kuloscap's uncle."

Turtle, the blinker, was Kuloscap's uncle.

So, Kuloscap, on Pictou, takes a liking to Turtle. He decides to make Turtle powerful, a powerful man.

At Pictou, there are more than a hundred wigwams. There, all the women love Kuloscap. They all want him but Kuloscap refuses to see any of them. He stays with his uncle Turtle. Turtle, the strange one. Turtle's telling him stories all the time, about long ago.

There are great feasts and games, but Kuloscap doesn't care to attend them. He doesn't even wish to watch. He asks Turtle, "Will you attend?"

Turtle says, "No, all the girls will be there."

Kuloscap says, "Why don't you marry?"

"I'm so poor," says Turtle, "that I don't have one garment which is suitable for a feast. I'll stay home and smoke my pipe."

"If that's all you want," says Kuloscap, "don't worry. I can easily change over your outside."

"Yes," says Turtle, "but can you change over the inside of a person?"

"Now, that's hard to do," says Kuloscap, "but I promise you that before I leave, I'll do just that. But first you have to put on my belt."

Turtle puts on Kuloscap's belt, and immediately he becomes young and handsome; no one has ever seen the likes of him! Kuloscap dresses him in the most beautiful clothes. He says, "Till the end of your days, you'll be a most beautiful man."

Turtle goes to the feast.

Now, the chief of Pictou has three young beautiful daughters. The youngest is the first that Turtle sees. Right away he returns to Kuloscap and says, "That youngest, she's the one I desire!"

"Well," says Kuloscap, "all the men on Pictou desire her! They'll kill whoever wins her."

Kuloscap fetches fine gifts, then proposes on behalf of Turtle. The mother consents; she approves of Turtle. The young woman spreads out new fir boughs; she covers the bed with a great white bear's skin. She goes to Turtle, and they eat dried meat for supper. Then they are married.

Turtle still is very lazy; when the others go hunting, he stays at home. One day his wife says to him, "Now, if you don't go hunting, we'll starve to death."

So, Turtle puts on his snowshoes. His wife follows him as he goes out hunting. She wants to see what he'll do. He hasn't gone far when he stumbles. He falls down and hurts himself. His wife returns home; she says to her mother, "Turtle is not worth anything!" Her mother says, "Be patient, in time he'll do something."

One day Kuloscap says to Turtle, "Tomorrow will be a big ball game, and you must take part in it. All the young men are your enemies, and during the game they'll try to kill you."

"If I just don't play," says Turtle, "they can't kill me."

"No, they'll just move the game right over you and kill you there," says Kuloscap.

"I see what you mean," says Turtle.

"They'll try to crowd you and trample you," says Kuloscap. "When they do, it will be near your father-in-law's wigwam. I'll give you magic powers so that you can jump over that wigwam twice and escape them. Now I warn you: the third time you jump, it will go terribly."

Then Kuloscap says, "It has to be that way."

And everything happened as Kuloscap said it would. The young men tried to kill Turtle, and in order to evade them he had to jump over his father-in-law's wigwam as if he were a flying bird. Once, it went well. Twice, it went well. The third time, Turtle was caught on the top of the wigwam poles. He hung there, dangling, smoke-blackened by the fire below.

Now Kuloscap, sitting in the wigwam, says to him, "Turtle, my uncle, I'm going to mark you so that you'll be recognized as a great chief, the chief of the turtles. You can carry great nations." So, he sent smoke up at Turtle. Turtle's skin got hard. Marks formed on Turtle, so you see how he looks today. Then Kuloscap disembowels Turtle, except for one thing: the greater intestine is left.

Turtle calls out to him, "My nephew, you're killing me!"

"No, I'm not," says Kuloscap. "I'm giving you great life. From now on, you'll be able to roll through flame. You can live in land or water. Even if they behead you, you will still live for nine days. Your heart will keep beating for that long."

Hearing this, Turtle rejoices.

But the next day, the village men go hunting. Kuloscap warns Turtle, "They'll try to kill you."

The men are out hunting. Turtle waits.

Suddenly, he makes a magic leap and flies over their heads. He lands in the distant woods. There, he kills a moose. He drags it to the snowshoe road. When the hunters arrive, he is sitting on the moose, smoking, waiting for them.

Now Kuloscap arrives. He tells them, "Turtle will be ahead of you all day. He'll get all the animals to eat."

The hunters are all angry. They decide to kill Turtle and Kuloscap.

Kuloscap goes and says to Turtle, "First, they'll kindle a great fire, then they'll throw you in it. But you won't suffer, uncle, because of my power. Then they'll try to drown you."

So, the hunters seize Turtle and throw him in the fire, and he rolls over and goes to sleep. When the fire burns down, he wakes up. He says, "Can I have some more wood for this fire? It's getting to be a cold night."

Again the hunters seize Turtle. They try to drown him. Turtle, as if he is fearful, says, "Please don't drown me!" He screams and fights, he tears up trees, he rips up rocks and roots like a madman. They put him in a canoe and paddle out to the middle of the water. They throw him in, and they watch Turtle sink down.

The next day they see something beginning to crawl on a great rock, far away as their eyes can see. Two young men take out a canoe and paddle out to see what this could be. On a great rock island, Turtle is sunning himself. He sees them coming; he knows they're coming to seize him. He plunges into the water. He still lives there. Even now, when turtles see someone, they plunge into the water.

Now Turtle lives with his wife and children. Sometime later, Kuloscap comes for a visit and begins to talk. One turtle child cries. "Does anyone know what the child is saying?" asks Kuloscap.

"No," Turtle replies. "Perhaps he is speaking some other Indian language now, maybe Mosigisw! Who can understand it?"

"I can," says Kuloscap. "He's saying, 'Eggs! Eggs!'" Then everyone laughs. Kuloscap says, "Yes, eggs."

"Where are any?" says Turtle.

Kuloscap directs him to dig in the sand. "You'll find many there," he says.

Still, to this day, to commemorate what Kuloscap did for the turtles, the turtles lay eggs.

WHY LOONS DON'T GET STUCK ANY MORE IN BOTTOM WEEDS

One day, Kuloscap decides to travel to Newfoundland, and he sees a loon flying out over the water. The loon circles the lake twice, low near the shore where men and animals are, as if he was looking for something.

Kuloscap calls out, "What are you doing?"

Loon says, "I was looking for you. I'll be your servant."

So right away, Kuloscap teaches Loon a strange cry. Loon tries it out. "What is that echoing cry?" Loon says.

"That's you," says Kuloscap.

"How can it be from me, but still sound like it's in the distance?" says Loon.

"That's the way I made it," says Kuloscap. "Whenever you want to summon me, use your call."

Now Kuloscap arrives in Newfoundland. He travels awhile and comes to an Indian village. People there are happy to see him; they give him gifts, they sing, they show Kuloscap a good time, they celebrate. Kuloscap is pleased, so he makes them all loons, who to this day are always faithful to Kuloscap—that's what happened. So even today it is said, "The loon is calling Kuloscap," or, "It is looning to Kuloscap," or, "The bird is in need of Kuloscap," or, "Kuloscap is riding in on the loon's call," or, "There's no mistaking, Kuloscap and the loon are talking."

Now one day Loon, who is the best of divers, got stuck in some weeds at the bottom of a lake. He called out but could not be heard, because his voice did not break the surface. Loon was stuck and soon would drown. But it happened, too, that Kuloscap was wandering and said to himself, "I haven't heard Loon in quite some time!" Kuloscap listened hard, but heard no Loon. He stood by the lake, listening. No Loon.

It started to thunder. "Shut up!" cried Kuloscap. "I'm trying to hear Loon."

"Don't be angry," Thunder said. "I'm trying to say that Loon is stuck at the bottom, in the weeds!"

Kuloscap dove right in, and there at the bottom he found Loon, nearly drowned. Kuloscap swam up with Loon, who flew into the air. Landing on the far side of the lake, Loon again called out.

Kuloscap answered, "From now on, you can dive almost to the bottom, but not into the weeds."

So today you also hear, "That's the loon, telling Kuloscap it didn't go into the bottom weeds."

◇ KULOSCAP AND THE WITCH ◇

There was once a village of Indians. Every one was a black cat. One, the cleverest and bravest, went off every day with his bow and arrows, axe and knife. His name was Pogumk, and he was the chief. He killed moose and bear. He handed food around to everyone. Whenever he returned to the village, everyone ran up and said, "What do you have for us?"

He would tell them, "Over there, I've left a bear. Over there, I've left a moose." Wherever he would point, an animal would be waiting for them. The black cats would scatter out and find food. They went with their toboggans.

Pogumk's father was a bear.

In the village there also lived Pukjinskwes, the witch. She was a black she-cat. But she could become a human man or woman whenever she wished. In the days I'm talking about, she was a man.

Pukjinskwes hated Pogumk. She was always plotting to take his place as chief.

One day, they prepared to travel. Pukjinskwes says to the chief, "Come with me, we'll go together. We'll gather eggs." So they set out in a canoe. They paddle a long ways. Finally, they come to an island. When they land, Pogumk starts to gather eggs. Gathering eggs, he turns into—Kuloscap! The great giant. He's still chief, but he's also Kuloscap.

Now Kuloscap is off gathering eggs. Pukjinskwes sneaks off, gets into the canoe, and paddles away. She is singing, "I leave the island. Now I am chief!"

She paddles back to the village. She walks into the village and says, "I'm here. Pogumk is not here. I am chief."

In the morning, everyone goes into the woods. They camp there. Every day, for many days, they expect Pogumk to return. But he doesn't return. Pukjinskwes is chief.

On the thirteenth day, Pogumk—Kuloscap, as we know—remembers his friend Fox, who is a magician. His friend is a wizard. Pogumk begins to sing. He sings in a way that his friend Fox will understand. Fox is far away but still hears the song. He sets out for the island.

When Fox finds the island, he realizes that Pogumk cannot swim very well. He says, "I will take you by water myself. Close your eyes and seize my tail; don't fear, we'll quickly be on land again."

Fox starts to tow Pogumk. Pogumk is also paddling, moving his arms this way and that, and he is growing tired. He opens his eyes a little, but he doesn't have much confidence, and he says, "We'll never get to land."

"Don't believe that," says Fox.

Still, Pogumk thinks it is very far to go. He is trying hard, but he is very weary. He looks out on the horizon, and where his eye settles there is a storm! Now the water they are swimming in is stormy. The waves are high. "Pukjinskwes has caused this storm!" says Pogumk.

They swim all day. Just after dusk, they arrive on land.

"My good friend," says Fox, "now you can go home."

Pogumk hurries to the black cats' camp. When he arrives, all he finds are ashes, and he feels cold air all around. The people are all gone. He looks for tracks and, finding them, begins to follow. He travels all night, and in the morning he overtakes his mother carrying his younger brother, Sable, on her back. His mother is looking ahead, but his brother Sable is looking backward.

As Pogumk comes out from the leaves, Sable sees him. "My elder brother is following us!" he says. But when his mother turns to look, she does not see anyone. Pogumk has hidden in a tree. The mother and brother Sable continue on. She is looking ahead, but he is looking back. Again, Sable calls out, "Certainly it was my elder brother I saw!" Suddenly the mother turns around; she catches Pogumk. They rejoice! They laugh! Then she throws Sable down on the leaves like a piece of wood.

Kuloscap—Pogumk—instructs Sable: "Run to camp. When you arrive there, make a big fire, a hemlock-bark fire, and throw it at Pukjinskwes's child. Then get out of there fast and return to me."

Sable runs off. He builds a fire, and when it's good and hot, he throws it on Pukjinskwes's child! The child burns up. Pukjinskwes is terribly angry! Angry! She is screaming and chasing after Sable.

Sable, who is very frightened, calls out, "My elder brother, my elder brother!"

Pukjinskwes shouts, "Sable, you must go as far as the island where Pogumk is to save yourself!"

Just as this is said, Pogumk steps right out from hiding. Pukjinskwes sees him! Now it is she who is frightened! She laughs loudly and says, "Oh ha, oh ha! I was only chasing Sable as a joke, because I like him!"

Pogumk answers her, "I know you, and I know what you have done, and I know what you are capable of, witch!" Then magic arrives, and Pogumk knows how to use it properly. He places Pukjinskwes with her back to a tree. She sticks to it; she can't get away.

Sable and Kuloscap go back to the camp. But Pukjinskwes has a stone hatchet, and with great difficulty she cuts herself loose and escapes! In the distance, Pogumk hears her pounding the earth and screaming all night.

In the morning she arrives in the camp; when they look up, they see she is carrying a piece of the tree on her back. They yell scorn at her. They sing, "That one, there, left a chief on an island; now the chief has stuck her fast to a tree!"

Now Pukjinskwes is terribly mad again, with shame and insult. She leaves the humans, running away like a crazy wolf. She arrives at Mount Desert; she sits on a log. She says, "Now I'll change myself into something to try and drive people crazy!" She cries out, "A mosquito! Yes, that's it." So that is what Pukjinskwes became. The witch was gone, but mosquitos arrived.

Now it is said that much later, out by Mount Desert, Pukjinskwes returned to her witch-self. There, mating with giants and monsters, she had many children. Her children were all ugly. She raised more and more of them. She stole a lot of pretty children from humans, too. She raised them as if they were her own!

One time, she stole a boy. Later someone asked him, "Haven't you noticed that many of your brothers and sisters are ugly? Why is that, since you are so handsome?"

"What does it mean?" he says.

"It means you were born in the day and those others were born in the night." Today, that is why Pukjinskwes sleeps all day and prowls by night, stealing children sometimes, and why, if an Indian child is to be born at night, the parents make sure there is plenty of light around! Kuloscap chased Pukjinskwes away, but she can still come around at night.

◇ HOW KULOSCAP SANG THROUGH RAPIDS AND ◇ RETURNED HIS FAMILY HOME

Long ago, Kuloscap had seven neighbors, all different animals. One day, the neighbors steal Kuloscap's family! He follows them, all the way to Newfoundland. He finds their camp at night. But no one is there, except for Sable. So he takes Sable out in the woods and teaches him to hunt. He gives Sable magic powers, and now Sable gathers a lot of food.

The next morning Crow sees Sable drying meat near his house. Crow flies off, shouting, "Sable has learned to hunt well. Kuloscap must have arrived!"

With this, all the animals return, go into their houses, and wait to die. Overhead Crow is shouting, "Kuloscap has arrived! Kuloscap has arrived!"

Then Kuloscap does arrive at the camp. He looks into the houses, and in one he says, "Are you rabbits shivering because a bobcat is near?"

"No," they say, "it is because you are here, Kuloscap!"

Well, being good-natured, Kuloscap takes pity on them and forgives them.

The animals were hungry, for when Kuloscap arrived they had no luck in hunting. "Give them some meat," Kuloscap instructed Sable. "And here's some venison."

"Hey, what's that there?" the animals shouted.

"That's sorrow going away from here," says Kuloscap.

And he was right; sorrow went away because people had food.

Now Kuloscap leaves the camp. Before, when they did not know Kuloscap, they would leave him to die on an island somewhere. Now that they know him, they are themselves afraid to die. They call out, "Don't leave us, we'll die!"

"No you won't," Kuloscap says.

Now Kuloscap makes a canoe. Along with Sable and She-Bear, they travel to a great river. It is broad and beautiful at first, so they sail down to the mouth. Then they come to great cliffs. The cliffs close in. The river runs far below, into ravines. They slide forward, going deeper and deeper, until they crash into rocks and tumble into ravines so horrible that all they can think of is death! The canoe jumps, then it falls. The river gets more narrow, and more terrible.

Sable and She-Bear are filled with great fear; they almost die of fright, but there's Kuloscap, sitting silently, then singing magic songs. He closes his eyes and sings, and everything suddenly passes on into the night and through, and suddenly the sun is shining. There is a single house near a river. And there, too, are Sable and Woodchuck and She-Bear, his grandmother.

Kuloscap says, "My grandmother, Woodchuck, Sable, you weren't sleeping!"

From this adventure, Kuloscap gained even more power.

The river runs underground in darkness.

The Wenebojo Myth

◇ C H I P P E W A ◇

These episodes are taken from the Wenebojo origin myth
from Lac du Flambeau, Wisconsin.

◇ THE SUN IMPREGNATES A GIRL ◇

The story that I'm going to tell you won't be about this earth. It will be about a different world. There were only two people living in this other world: an old lady and her daughter.

Look how this world looks around us—trees, flowers, and everything. In this other world there was only grass and bushes, no timber.

The old lady's daughter used to go every day into the woods to find something that she could use for food. This was in the summer. She got those early berries that come in the spring. That was their food. She went into the woods to pick the ripe berries all day long, picking here and there.

Then one day somebody saw her traveling all alone by herself in the woods. That person seemed to take a liking to her. He even wanted to marry her. He knew what to do. When she was out berrying one nice hot day, when there was no wind, at noontime, she heard a noise like a gust of wind. She looked around in the direction of the noise and saw a wind coming. When the wind reached her, she couldn't pull her dress down for some time, until the gust of wind went by. She didn't think anything of it, because no one was there to see her. She started picking berries again.

Shortly after that, the woman's mother had a queer feeling about her daughter. One day the old lady asked her daughter, "When you go out every day to gather berries, do you ever see anybody out there?"

The girl said, "No, I never see anybody. I'm all by myself all day." But the old lady had a feeling that there was something wrong with her daughter, and she didn't like it. She kept asking about her trips picking berries and whether she ever met anyone. But the girl said she never saw anyone in the woods. The woman's mother didn't like to see her daughter's condition. "There's something wrong," she said. She asked her again; but she said that she saw no one.

Finally the girl got to thinking, "I wonder what's wrong with me?" She began to feel that something must be wrong with her. The only thing she could remember about was that gust of wind. So she told her mother about the time that happened. Then the old lady knew right away who had done it. It was the Sun.

◇ THE GIRL GIVES BIRTH TO TRIPLETS ◇

It wasn't long afterwards that the girl found out that something else was going to happen. She left that place where she and her mother had been living and went into the woods. There she gave birth to some children—three of them. The first looked just like a human baby boy. After it was born, she held him in her arms. Then she heard a voice from somewhere telling her to put her baby on the ground. She didn't do it. After the person whose voice she heard got tired of waiting for her to put her baby down, he spoke to her again: "You don't want to do what I told you to do—put your baby on the ground. If you had done that, your baby would have got up and walked. But since you don't want to do that, it will be a year from the time that he is born that he will be able to walk." That's the way that people of this earth would have done from the time that they were born. They would have walked right away, just like animals. The Indian could have done that too.

Then the next baby was born. This one didn't have human features exactly, but he looked like a human baby to some extent. Just a little while later another one was born. This one didn't look like a human child. This one was stone, *Maskásaswàbik*. Sometimes when I go into the woods I see this stone. It's a very hard stone. I'm just telling you what I heard. It doesn't say that this woman took her babies home. I'm just telling what I heard.

These three boys didn't take long to grow up. They were *manidog*, spirits. Their mother always managed to get something to make bows and arrows for them when they were ready to use them.

◇ WENEBOJO KILLS HIS STONE BROTHER ◇

Wenebojo, the oldest boy, killed everything he could kill, even the little birds. He brought them to his mother to show her. Wenebojo's mother told him not to kill any little birds. He even tried to kill both big and little *manidog* when he saw them. Wenebojo didn't listen to his mother. He killed everything that he could see.

His little brother, the stone, never went anywhere. He stayed right by the camp where they were living. But the other two boys went together all the time. They traveled just as far as they could go, but they never left their youngest brother alone overnight. They came home every evening.

They were very happy traveling through the woods, but they always came back to camp. At that time the three boys were the only persons living. Well, their grandmother was somewhere, but I'll tell you about her later. Those boys knew all the country round about, but they couldn't go any further.

One day Wenebojo asked his brother if he would do what he was going to ask him. He said, "We can't go any further. We know the country round about now. But it would be very nice if we could go further."

The other boy said, "What is it you want to ask me?"

Wenebojo said, "If you think it's all right, I will kill our brother, and then we won't have to stay in this one place any more."

The other one didn't say anything. They were walking home to where their youngest brother was waiting. They didn't know how far away he was, but their brother at camp was listening to every word they were saying. While they were walking home through the woods, Wenebojo got tired of waiting for his brother to give him an answer. So he asked him again, "Why don't you say something about what I'm asking you?"

Then his brother answered him, "You're the one that's thinking of what you're going to do."

Wenebojo said, "Yes, I will do what I said."

When the two boys got home, it was just before nightfall. The brother who was at camp spoke to Wenebojo: "Why don't you do what you were talking about? If you can do it, go ahead and start right now."

Wenebojo said, "Yes, I will."

He went to borrow his grandmother's pole-axe. His grandmother lent it to him, and Wenebojo tried to kill his brother with it; but he couldn't even scratch him. He wore the pole-axe out.

Then his brother spoke to him: "You can't do what you're trying to do, unless I tell you how to go about it."

Wenebojo spoke to his brother whom he was trying to kill: "All right, tell me what to do. I'll do whatever you tell me."

"Build a fire, put me in that fire, and when I get to look like a red-hot coal, throw some water on me."

Wenebojo said, "All right. That's what I'll do." So he made a fire and put his brother into it. Wenebojo looked at his brother. He was getting to look like a red-hot coal. He asked him, "Is it time now?"

"No, not yet."

He built a bigger fire. A little while later, he looked at his brother again. He looked just like a red-hot coal. "Is it time now?" he asked.

"Yes, I think it is," said his brother.

Wenebojo poured the water on his brother. Then his brother looked different. The stone cracked in different places. Then there were only two brothers left. When Wenebojo killed his brother, that was the first time that anybody ever died on the earth.

After that, Wenebojo and his other brother left that place. They traveled here and there, far and near. Whenever night came, they lay down and went to sleep. They had no special place to come back to now. They traveled all the time.

WENEBOJO CAUSES HIS SECOND ◇ BROTHER'S DEATH

After a while Wenebojo's brother began to get tired. He stayed behind sometimes. He walked slowly, because he was tired and always lagging behind Wenebojo. Wenebojo always waited for his brother to catch up with him. One time Wenebojo wondered how long it would take his brother to catch up. Finally, when he arrived, Wenebojo spoke to him: "Brother, can't you wait for me here a few days? After four days I'll come back."

His brother answered, "All right, you're the one that is thinking of what you are going to do."

"Then I'll leave you here to wait for me."

Wenebojo made a place to put his brother in. He made a hole in the ground. When his brother was inside, Wenebojo covered the place up so that no one would know that he was there. He put a stone at the head of it to let him know where the hole was. Then Wenebojo went away.

He traveled and traveled and traveled. He went just as fast as he could, because there was no one to hold him back now. He was all by himself. Wenebojo was happy, because he could see how the earth looked. He looked all about him. He kept traveling all the time.

Wenebojo forgot that after four days he was supposed to go back to his brother, because he was too busy looking around at the earth and traveling here and there. Long after the four days were over, he happened to remember his brother whom he had left behind.

He went back to look for him. When Wenebojo got there, he couldn't find his brother any more. He saw his brother's tracks, so he knew that his brother had left. Wenebojo sat down and tried to cry. But he couldn't cry. He tried and tried and tried. Finally he suc-ceeded. I don't know where he was, but his brother heard him. His brother said, "I wonder what is wrong with that fellow." He told Wenebojo not to cry. "I'm here," he said. Wenebojo spoke to his brother. "What did you come back for? Why don't you go back to where you were? The *manidog* have heard me crying already."

Wenebojo's brother said, "You are going to make it hard for the people, your parents, because of what you are saying. I will make a road for the people to travel along when this thing—death—happens to them."

Wenebojo and his brother had only one dish. They ate out of the same dish. The only time they ate was when they were both in the same place. The one couldn't eat unless the other was there too, so they had to eat at the same time. Wenebojo's brother said to him, "I'm leaving you our dish, and this is what the people will do when this thing happens to them. I want you to look at me when I go." He went. He went toward the sunset.

◇ WENEBOJO'S BROTHER MAKES THE ◇
ROAD TO THE OTHER WORLD

As he went along, he made four signs of places. He put four *manidog* along the way. At the first place he put an otter on the right-hand side of the road. He went along the road, traveled a long distance, and then put another sign at the left-hand side of the road. This was an owl. The Indians say that the owl's eyes are like a looking glass, and he looks just awful. When he speaks of the owl at the last supper with a dead person, sitting next to the coffin, the Mide priest says, "When you see your grandfather's eyes shining like glass, don't be afraid of him. Just go up and offer him your tobacco. He'll take it." They don't say "the owl." They speak of him as "your grandfather."

After he had put the owl on the left-hand side of the road, Wenebojo's brother went along the road some more for a long distance, and then he made another sign, on both sides of the road this time. He made it look like two hills when they meet together. They're right on the road there. They're not real hills. They're two snakes with their heads together. When those snakes breathe, fire shoots across the road from their mouths. The road runs between them.

Then Wenebojo's brother kept going along the road for a long ways, and then he put up a fourth sign. He made a river. It wasn't very big or very wide. A man can jump across it, if he's a good jumper. He put a log across the river. It wasn't really a log. It's really a snake. They don't tell this in the story. When it's referred to, it's spoken of as a log; but the Indians know it's a snake.

The water is swift there. The log bobs up and down all the time. On the right-hand side of the log, the water is clear. Where the river flows, it's as dark as it can be. You can't see the bottom of it. On the left-hand side of the log, the water is black.

Wenebojo's brother kept on along the road. He went up a hill. Later on a strawberry was put there. Wenebojo's brother didn't put it there. The Devil put it there. Near the top of the hill, the road forks in two directions. The strawberry is right there in between the two roads, where they branch off. There's a spoon in the strawberry. When you see it, you hear a voice saying, "Eat this first." If you eat it, you'll go along the road that branches to the left. That is the road built by the Devil, not by Wenebojo's brother. That road doesn't go far, just a little ways. If you follow it, you won't be able to get a new suit of clothes when the ones that you've got on wear out. The only food you can get there are roots which you have to grub out of the ground with your hands, rooting like a pig. Your fingernails wear out, and your skin wears out too. People who get there always stay there all the time; they can't come back. Once you get there, you stay forever.

Wenebojo's brother kept going along the road. He went up a hill and down the other side. Then he spoke to his brother, Wenebojo. He asked, "Do you see me?"

Wenebojo said, "Yes, I see you."

"Well, I'll tell you what the Indians will call me. They'll call me Nekajíwegìžik." Then he disappeared. Wenebojo couldn't see him any more. That name means "someone who goes down behind the sky, behind the sunset." Wenebojo's brother never had a name before then. He named himself.

Now Wenebojo was all alone by himself. He'd killed his brothers. He was the one who committed the first murders on earth. His brother made a trail for people to go along when they die. His first brother, Maskásaswàbik, never went along that trail. He's still on earth, because he's just a stone.

Wenebojo had that dish that he and his brother ate out of. Now when a child or husband or wife dies, we give the person who is left a dish to keep for the one who has died. The Indian does that, because Wenebojo's brother left him that dish. We call them mourning dishes, *bepagwéčinùnk*, "something to take your mind off it."

Now that Wenebojo was all alone, he traveled wherever he wanted to go.

◇ WENEBOJO ASSUMES THE FORM ◇
OF A BEAVER

Wenebojo started walking again. He went noplace in particular, just kept going on. Then he came to a river. There was a lot of water in that river. He went around the water's edge. After a while he found a beaver dam. He saw a great big beaver house. He hid somewhere nearby and found out who was living there. Wenebojo saw the beavers coming out of their house. Then he came out of his hiding-place and spoke to them: "Brothers, so this is where you are! I've been looking all over for you! I heard that you were somewhere here. Come here, brothers! I heard that you were here someplace!"

Then he got those beavers to come near. Wenebojo said, "When I last saw you, you were little babies. You wouldn't remember me. That was a long time ago." Then he asked them if they couldn't make him look the way they did. "No, I can't do that," said one of the beavers. Wenebojo didn't leave them alone. He kept on begging and begging them to make him look like them. Those beaver-people got tired of him after a while. Finally one of them said, "Well, I'll try." Wenebojo said, "If you can make me look like you, I want a big wide tail, bigger than I am."

They told Wenebojo to throw himself into the water. So he did so. The story doesn't say how far he went in the water, but when he came out, he was just like a beaver. Wenebojo looked at himself. He had a great big tail, bigger than himself. That's what he had wanted. Wenebojo said, "I knew that you could make me look like a beaver!" He had the biggest tail of all the beavers.

Wenebojo started to work now. He made the beaver dam bigger, and he put a big door in it, so that he could get in and out. He stayed there and worked along with the other beavers. In the fall they gathered their food for the winter. It turned cold. The water froze to ice. They were underneath the water then. They had to stay there, because it was winter.

Later on, some people came around, and one of the Indians saw the place where the beaver dam was. When he saw it, he was surprised to see the work of those beavers. This man told the others that he'd seen a big beaver dam. So they decided to go and catch some of them. When they got there, they saw a little nest hanging in the beaver house. One of the Indians said, "What's this little nest hanging here for?" The beavers down below could hear what those Indians were saying. The little nest in the middle was the house of the king, *ógima*. That's why it was up on top there.

The Indians started to break up the beaver house. The beavers down below could hear them. After chopping away for some time, they got it thinned down. There was a lot of mud there, and the Indians cleaned it out. Meanwhile the beavers in the bottom could see the axe coming through the top of the beaver house. They all started to swim away. But in all the excitement, Wenebojo forgot to go out through his own big door. He tried to get through all the other doors, but they were all too small. He just had to stay there. The people outside were working all the time to break open the beaver house. After they'd broken it down, they saw that big beaver tail sticking out. One of the Indians said, "Here's one!" They dragged Wenebojo out of there and put him on top of the ice. They killed him there.

They were there all day, trying to catch the other beavers too. But while Wenebojo was lying there dead, he was watching those Indians. Toward evening they were through killing beavers. When they killed the biggest beaver, his nose bled. They tied him up in a pack and carried him home. But where that blood fell, Wenebojo rose up again. He came out of that pool of blood.

◇ HOODWINKED DANCERS ◇

Then Wenebojo went along. I don't know where he went, but he kept on going all the time. Finally he came to another lake. He approached the shore. The lake was full of ducks and geese of all kinds, playing in the water. Wenebojo stopped to figure out how he could catch those ducks. He knew what he was going to do. Along the way he'd come, Wenebojo had seen some grass and hay. He thought, I'll get that hay. He went to get it, cut it up, and put it in a bundle. Then he walked back to the lake. Wenebojo walked along the edge of the water. One of the birds saw him and said, "Look! There's Wenebojo. What is Wenebojo packing?"

Wenebojo paid no attention. He kept right on going.

Then another one spoke up: "Wenebush'! What are you carrying?"

He paid no attention, as if he didn't hear them at all.

Another one spoke out loud: "Wenebush'! They're asking you. What are you carrying?"

Then he turned around, looked toward the woods, looked around again, and pretended that he didn't see anybody. He kept on going.

Then another bird spoke up very loudly: "Wenebush'! What are you carrying?"

He looked in that direction. Wenebojo pretended he hadn't seen those birds before. Then he said, "Brothers, I am carrying songs. I will make a place where you and I can dance. When I'm finished making our dancing-place, I'll come and tell you, so that we can dance and have a good time."

It took quite a while for Wenebojo to build a long wigwam. He made it good and strong, with one door in the front. When he was all through and had covered all of the holes in the structure, Wenebojo made a rattle. Then he called the ducks and geese to come and have their dance.

All the bird-people came, every last one of them. They filled up that long dance-lodge. When the birds were all inside, Wenebojo started to talk to them. He said, "I want you all to close your eyes. Anybody that opens his eyes will have funny-looking red eyes forever." The duck people did just what he told them. He shook his rattle, and they danced. He told those people to holler all they wanted to. Then he sang a song: "Brothers, all of you, close your eyes. If you open them, they'll be red forever." He just kept on singing that over and over.

The last birds that came into the hall were the helldiver and the loon. The helldiver stood on one side of the door; the loon stood on the other. Wenebojo kept going around among the birds while he was singing that song. He came up to the geese and started wringing their necks. They made a noise, but everyone else was making a noise too. But the goose whose neck was being wrung made a different kind of sound from the others. Wenebojo was afraid that maybe some of the birds would guess what he was doing, so he told them all to make any kind of noise they wanted to—all kinds of noises.

Those two people were still standing at each side of the door. The helldiver said to the loon, "Those people are making an awfully funny kind of noise. It sounds queer to me. Do you hear it? You know, Wenebojo does anything and everything. Let's open our eyes. What does it matter if we have red eyes the rest of our lives?" So they both opened their eyes just a little bit. This is what they saw: they saw a pile of dead geese stretched along the dance-lodge. The loon and the helldiver hollered, "Wenebojo is killing us!"

Some birds with sharp beaks were there, and the loon and the helldiver shouted at them, "Peck him! peck him!" Wenebojo tried to get out of that hall, but he couldn't because he'd made the walls so strong, and he'd made only one door. He was caught there. The birds kept pecking Wenebojo.

The helldiver and the loon were stepped on and crushed by the other birds. That's why they have flat backs. And they have red eyes, too, because they opened them to see what Wenebojo was doing.

After all the birds had left the lodge, Wenebojo finally got out of there. He picked up the birds he'd killed and looked for a place where he could build a fire. He went to the bank of a river and made a big long fire. Then he dug holes all around the fire-place and stuck a bird in each hole with its feet sticking out. After he'd done that, he sat down and waited for them to get all cooked.

◇ WENEBOJO BECOMES DEPRESSED AND THREATENS ◇ ALL THE SPIRITS

One day, when he was walking along by the ocean, he happened to remember the time when those *manidog* made him angry. Then Wenebojo just sat down by the beach with his feet nearly in the water, and he hollered and cried. He sat there crying, remembering the *manidog* who made him angry, and thought of what he would like to do to those *manidog*. He spoke to the earth and said, "Whoever is underneath the earth down there, I will pull them out and bring them up on top here. I can play with them and do whatever I want with them, because I own this earth where I am now."

The Indians say that this earth has four layers. The bottom layer does not look like the one we are in now. It is night there all the time.

That is where the *manido* is who is the boss that rules the bottom of the earth. He rules all four layers. There is no special name for him or for the different layers.

When Wenebojo spoke that time, the *manido*, the boss, heard him. Wenebojo spoke again. This time he spoke to the sky: "Whoever is up there, those *manidog* up there, I will get them and pull them down. I will play with them here and do just as I please with them. I will even knock down the sky." Then Wenebojo took a deep breath, and the earth shrank up. When he sniffed from crying, the sky made a loud noise like the cracking of ice.

◇ THE SPIRITS TRY TO APPEASE WENEBOJO ◇

The sky has four layers too. In the top layer of the sky there was a *manido* who is equal in power to the *manido* at the bottom of the earth. It is always day there. It is never night. This *manido* has no name, but you can call him Gičimánido, Great Spirit. There is no name for the top layer. We're right in the middle in between the four earth layers and the four sky layers.

The first *manido* at the bottom of the earth spoke to his runner, *škabéwis*, and told him to go and ask Gičimánido if he had heard what Wenebojo had said. He went there. He asked the Great Spirit if he'd heard what Wenebojo had said.

Gičimánido said, "Yes, I heard him. He will do just what he said. I told you never to make him angry in any way."

The runner went back to the *manido* who had sent him and said, "The *manido* says that Wenebojo will do just as he said."

Wenebojo thought to himself, "When I get up, I'm going to do what I said I'd do."

Those *manidog* had no right to this earth that we are living on. Wenebojo owned this earth. The *manido* of the last layer of the earth had no right to this earth that we are living on. The only world that he owned was the old country, the earth that Wenebojo had lived on before. I don't know what layer Wenebojo lived on then; one of the bottom ones, I suppose.

The *manido* from the last layer of the earth in the middle of the old world came up to the old country. After he got to the old country, he spoke to Gičimánido, asking him to come down to where he was. Gičimánido took his runner with him, so that there were two *manidog* and two runners—four of them—down there. The *manido* from the bottom spoke to Gičimánido and asked him, "Are you willing to give Wenebojo what we are going to give him?"

Gičimánido said, "Yes, I am willing to give Wenebojo this thing, if he is willing to accept it."

The *manido* from the bottom said, "We will call him, then."

Gičimánido said, "We will call him if he is willing to come, and if he will listen to us."

The two *manidog* were in a hurry. They didn't know when Wenebojo might get up and start to do what he had said he was going to do.

They sent one of the runners to go and get Wenebojo where he was sitting; and this runner said to Wenebojo, "Your grandfathers want you to come." Wenebojo didn't even move his head or his eyes or anything. He just sat there. All of the *manidog* were afraid that if Wenebojo got up, he would do just what he said he'd do. They sent everybody that they could get hold of, but still Wenebojo wouldn't listen to any of them. After all of these people had tried and failed, all of the *manidog* were very scared. They got to talking. Who would Wenebojo listen to? They looked around for somebody.

Somewhere up in the North, where the ocean is, there is an animal that is called an otter. He is white; he isn't the kind of otter that's around here. He's a white otter. He has no arms—just little parts like wings. I've seen them in the museum in Milwaukee, but not white ones. I haven't seen any around here. We call them *misá ˙kik*.

The *manidog* looked around and saw the *misá ˙kik* playing around in the water. Then they sent the runner to him. He went and brought the *misá ˙kik* back with him to where the *manidog* were waiting. The two *manidog* talked to the white otter. They told him that everyone whom they'd sent to Wenebojo had failed. The otter spoke and said, "I will bring him. He will listen to me." So the otter went to look for Wenebojo.

The otter hollered, and the echo of his voice was heard in the sky. Where Wenebojo was sitting, he heard someone. He didn't know who it was. When the otter came to the middle of the ocean he hollered again. The otter came up to the top of a hill and hollered again. Then he went into the other ocean. There's another ocean there. He went into the water, and when he was halfway across the ocean, the otter hollered again. Wenebojo was sitting on the shore of that ocean. That otter hollered again. The water made a sound just like the sound that the otter made. Wenebojo looked in the direction where that sound was coming from and wondered who it was. He couldn't see the otter. A long time later he heard a sound like a waterfall. After a while he finally saw the otter coming. He didn't recognize him until he came close up to him. When the otter came close by, Wenebojo looked at him, and he saw that he was all white, and his eyes were black. The otter spoke to Wenebojo and said, "*Nitáowis*, my cousin, I have come after you. Your grandfathers want you to come."

Wenebojo answered, "Huh! You shouldn't do what they tell you. I suppose that's why they sent you to come and get me, because they know that you and I are related to each other. Well, all right, I will go with you. But I was going to do what I said I would do."

THE SPIRITS GIVE WENEBOJO SOME
◇ PARENTS AND ESTABLISH ◇
THE MEDICINE DANCE

The otter took him to where the two *manidog* were waiting. When they got there, the *manidog* pointed to the place where Wenebojo should sit. When he had sat down where they told him to sit, the *manido* from the bottom of the earth spoke to Wenebojo. He said, "You will see what we are going to give you, and if you will accept it, this is what your parents, the people who come after you, will do."

Wenebojo had no mother or father.

Wenebojo just sat there and didn't say anything. The *manido* from the bottom spoke to Wenebojo. He built up some clay the size of a human being in length and about one foot high, and placed it in front of him. After he had done that, he placed a shell, *mígis*, on top of the earth-heap. After he had done that, he took his rattle and shook it.

Then he talked and shook his rattle as he talked. At one point he stopped shaking his rattle, and the heap of clay in front of him began to take the form of a person. He shook his rattle some more, and kept on talking. When he stopped again, you could see that it was a person there. Wenebojo sat there and looked at what the *manido* had done. Then the *manido* shook his rattle some more and kept on talking. When he stopped this time, the person was breathing. He started shaking his rattle and talked some more. Then he stopped. The person—it was an Indian—got up to a sitting position. They saw that it was a woman.

The *manido* from the bottom of the earth stopped shaking his rattle and talking then. He spoke to Gičimánido and said, "Now it's your turn to make the thing that we are going to give to Wenebojo." Giči-mánido started to do the same thing. He heaped up some clay, made it like a figure, and placed the shell on top. Then Gičimánido took the last rib of the woman and put it into the clay figure. Then he started to shake his rattle and talk. Finally he stopped. It looked still more like a person. Then he shook his rattle and talked again. When he stopped, the person was breathing. He started shaking his rattle and talking again. When he stopped, the person got up from there. It was a man.

Now there was a pair of them, a man and a woman. Then the *manido* from the bottom of the earth spoke to Wenebojo and said, "You see what we have done. This is the thing we are going to give you, if you will take it." These people that the *manidog* had created, they were the ones that Wenebojo was going to call his parents. They were not really his parents, but he was going to call them that. They looked the way Wenebojo's parents had looked—the Sun and that woman. They had no names. Wenebojo didn't call his parents "mother" and "father." He called them "my uncle" and "my aunt"; but when he spoke of both of them together, he said "my parents."

Then the *manidog* started to talk to Wenebojo. They told him all about the *midewiwin*, the medicine dance. They said, "This is what the Indians will do." Then they told him all about it. All of the *manidog* in existence were there then; I don't know how many of them.

Those first people, the ones that the *manidog* created then, were made hard, like a shell. They were meant to live forever. They would live for a hundred years; then go into a trance for four days, and then go on for another hundred years. This was decided on by the council of the *manidog*. They all agreed to it. All of the *manidog* from all over the universe were there. They were all invited except for one—Nekají-wegìžik, Wenebojo's brother, who was way down in the bottom of the earth somewhere.

This is where Gičimánido made his mistake. He should have seen to it that Nekajíwegìžik was present at the council too. Although Nekajíwegìžik wasn't there, he could hear everything that was going on. He said, "It's no use to make your plans that way. I've already made that road to the other world, and everyone who lives on the earth will have to follow that road."

Nothing could be done about it. Man had to die, in spite of what the *manidog* decided. That was where God made his mistake—in not inviting Wenebojo's brother to the council.

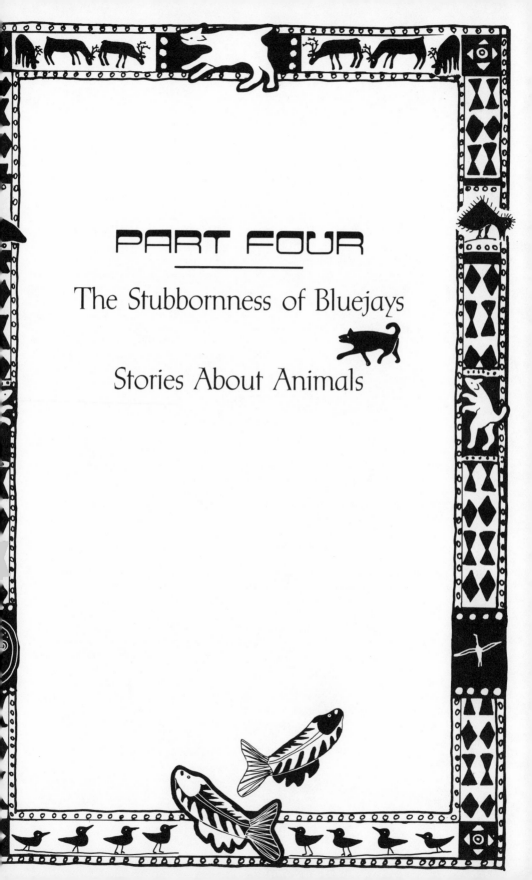

PART FOUR

The Stubbornness of Bluejays

Stories About Animals

NORTHERN TALES ABOUND WITH ANIMAL LIFE —not only the waterfowl, mammals of land and sea, and fish taken for food, but the snake, snow-flea, turtle, and mosquito as well. Each one has its distinct personality and is regarded by native peoples accordingly. Tribes in different regions may view the same species in opposite ways: certain Algonquian groups know Bear to be a benevolent grandparent, whereas over in the Gwich'in region, Bear is a masterful antagonist. In parts of Siberia, Fox is a creator and transformer, while in some Chipewyan traditions Fox may hoard duck eggs and be a thief who leaves lice as a calling card—and there is a Caribou Eskimo tale in which Fox forages each night in a polar bear's anus, the ultimate sort of scavenging.

In the earliest known tales, as in those told about contemporary times, human kinship with animals is recognized; oftentimes an animal is referred to as "grandmother," "brother," or "brother-in-law." In the beginning, animal and human cultures overlapped; animals differed from people only in form, not in essential nature. It could be said that the North was "peopled with animals." Many tales begin with statements such as "Long ago, when all the animals lived like humans" (for example, the Gwich'in tale "The Wolverine Loses His Shoes").

Throughout history people have learned from animals, mimed them in dances, echoed their voices in songs, created an array of ritual homages to them, maintained communication with them through a common language—or through intermediaries such as shamans. "In the old times, people and animals talked with each other, just like I talk with my family every day," said Samson Autao, a Cree Indian. "There are still people who can do that, but not many. The way to do it is still here, but not many know it." People loved, admired, often feared animals—the whole range of human emotions and ritual was necessary to attend to their importance in day-to-day life, as well as their vanity. In tales we find animals as tricksters (Raven, Coyote, Crow, Turtle, Beaver), messengers, guides, spirit overseers, givers of medicine, deities, paramours, portents of good or evil, grudge-holders, husbands, wives.

Stories such as those in this part allow us to look out over a stretch of sea or a snow-hushed forest or an icy swampland and recognize the visible and invisible world of animals. The beaver dam contains the beaver's family life; the freshly fallen snow covers the vole's network of tunnels. Every animal has its hiding skills.

All northern cultures were hunting cultures; most carried on the tradition of giving place-names associated with animals, especially in hunting territories. "I know their favorite paths," said Moses Sandy, a Cree hunter. "I know the dams and muskrat push-ups. I know the land I walk on and know the names where things happened to my father out there, and his father. I continue to name such places." The ethnographer Knud Rasmussen mapped out many Netsilik place-names in his travels, and the few mentioned here give precise examples of how animals entered the language and local history: "Place-Where-There-Are-Many-Trout-of-the-Species-Il'q"; "Lake-in-the-Land-of-Caribou-Bulls"; "The-One-Stocked-with-Fjord-Seals"; "The-Place-Where-Bones-Were-Left." Or these, from Caribou Eskimo: "Mastodon-Horn-Scrape" and "Blowhole-Spray-Drifted-Out-There-All-Day."

Throughout the North children, too, were and are given animal names or names derived from particular sorts of animal behavior—Big Billy Salmon, Michael Fish-Eagle, Charlotte Runs-Fox, and so on. In a number of northern languages, the zoological vocabulary contains not only an inventory of indigenous species, the stages of their lives, their uses to humans, but anthropomorphic and supernatural forms as well.

Artwork such as quill baskets and zoomorphic masks are made from the bones, fur, and sinew of animals and therefore contain animal power. The ritual forehead mask of an Alaskan tribe depicts a bird carrying a fish in its beak; this illustrates a specific predator-prey relationship, a cycle in nature full of power. And in recent decades we have innumerable soapstone carvings as well as paintings and prints that pay visual homage to animals.

Tales about animals celebrate the diversity of life in the North. In recent centuries, our bond with animals has fallen into severe disrepair. From Dogrib Indian hunters to the presidents of wildlife conservation groups, thousands have testified to this in different ways. John Iniuq, a Caribou Eskimo man, put it like this: "Now-days, look around. Animals are insulted. They might go away forever. This can happen. It is not like when I was a child. People don't understand animals any more. People who have to go among animals, out on the land, they still understand. Animals are people like us. They can die out. And not come back."

Knowledge and empathy go hand-in-hand in northern tales whose central characters are animals. Perhaps no story better shows this than the following one told by a Netsilik man, Qaqortingneq:

> There was once a great shaman who wanted to see what it was like to live the life of all animals, so he let himself be reborn in all kinds of animals. For a time he was a bear. That was a tiring life; they were always walking, the bears, even in the dark they roamed about, always on the wander.
>
> Then he became a fjord seal, and he relates that the seals were always in the humor for playing. They are ever full of merry jests, and they leap about among the waves, frolicsome and agile, till the sea begins to move; their high spirits set the sea in motion.
>
> There was not much difference between humans and seals, for the seals could suddenly turn themselves into human shape; when in that form they were skillfull with the bow and amused themselves by setting up targets of snow, just as men make them.
>
> Once the shaman was a wolf, but then he almost starved to death until one of the wolves took compassion on him and said, "Get a good hold of the ground with your claws and try to keep up with us when we run." This is how he learned to run and catch caribou.
>
> Then he turned into a musk ox, and it was warm in the middle of the big herd. Afterward, he became a caribou. They were strangely restless animals, always timid; in the middle of their sleep they would spring up and gallop away. They became scared over the slightest thing, so there was no fun being a caribou.
>
> In this way the shaman lived the life of all the animals.

The Bear Goes on His Long, Solitary Journey
◇ G R E E N L A N D   E S K I M O ◇

A young male bear loved a young Eskimo woman very much. He used
to go see her in her igloo every day.

Her husband would be out hunting—bear, to be exact.

And while he was gone, the little woman and Nanoq embraced each
other in the warm igloo.

The bear said, "Listen, little woman, I live up there. You go that
way, keep going that way, then you turn right, you walk for two hours:
and you are there. I would love to have a little wife like you." Then,
in a loud voice, he said, "But don't ever tell Inuk where I live. Remember
that even from very far away, I will hear you."

"Ieh . . . ieh," the little woman answered, hiding in her lover's warm,
tufted armpit.

The days went by. The Inuk had still not killed a bear.

This put him in a bad humor every night. Sometimes he sniffed the
air and said, "Tipi! That's strange. It smells very bad in here, like—
you'd almost say like bear."

"No, no, of course not," his wife would answer. "It must be your
kamiks, which I'm mending."

Soon the Inuk became so peevish that he no longer cared about
anything. Yet his *qulitsaq* was well sewn, his house was clean, a supply
of snow for water was always within reach, and the floor was regularly
swept and covered with fresh snow every morning.

"Oh, I don't care about all that," he grumbled. "All I know is, I haven't
killed a bear! Hmm!"

Then one night, when once again he had pushed his little wife away
to the other end of the bed on the *illeq*, she put her mouth close, close
to his ear and whispered into it as softly as she could, "Nanoq."

The man started up and leaped for his harpoon.

"Nanoq! Naa! Where is it? Where?"

"Laaaa, laaa . . ." she said to calm him, and again she whispered in
his ear: "Up there, high up in the mountain . . . you go this way, that

way, keep going that way, then you turn right, you walk for two hours, and there it is. In a hollow full of snow—yes, that one."

The man ran from the igloo. Quickly, quickly, he flew up into the mountain with his harpoon and his dogs.

But up there the bear's den was already empty. Nanoq had heard.

Back home, the woman had crawled beneath the *illeq*, trembling so hard that her fingernails dug into the snow.

A kind of thunder poured down the mountain.

It was he—can you hear him? Panting, he ran down and went straight to the igloo. He was about to crush it; he raised his enormous paw . . . No.

Betrayed and grieving, the bear limped away on his long, solitary journey.

Bluejay's Revenge

◇ S H U S W A P   I N D I A N ◇

Bluejay was the greatest warrior and war chief among the ancient people. No one dared to disobey him. For many years he had carried on wars with the Hoary Marmots and the Antelopes; but then for a number of years there had been peace, and Bluejay almost forgot to look on them as enemies.

One day he said to his people, "My heart feels soft toward the Marmots and Antelopes. I want a final peace between us. This peace will be carried out by a marriage. Woodpecker, who is the greatest of my people, will marry one of the Marmot or Antelope daughters. Antelopes and Marmots have wealthy chiefs, and they have beautiful daughters. So, Woodpecker, go ahead and find a wife. Flicker, Red-Breasted Woodpecker, and Sapsucker will travel with you."

The four birds set out, and soon they arrived at a village of old people. One old man asked them, "Where are you going?" The birds answered, "Nowhere in particular. We're just seeing the country." The old man said, "Young men generally don't travel around just to look at the country. They look for women. I know that you're going to ask for a chief's daughter. Well, you might just get one, because the chiefs are saving their daughters for rich strangers."

The birds set out again, and soon came to a great open plain, where Antelope lived in an underground house. Nearby, on a knoll, was the house of Hoary Marmot. The birds believed that Hoary Marmot was the richer, so they went to his house first. Marmot welcomed them and entertained them, and when night came he spread marmot robes on the ground, where his guests could sleep. They lay there together. When everyone else seemed to be asleep, Woodpecker got up and crawled over to the chief's daughter. He said to her, "Will you marry me?" She said yes.

The next morning, the chief's daughter said, "Woodpecker lay on my robe last night."

Her parents agreed to the marriage, saying that they were happy to become relatives of the great Bluejay.

Marmot gave them a lot of wedding presents. Four days later, Woodpecker and his three companions, along with his new bride, left the village, lugging the presents with them.

When they neared home, Coyote saw them approaching. Coyote called out, "Four men are coming with one woman!" Hearing this, Bluejay prepared a place for the bride, and he welcomed her as a father-in-law.

Some time passed, and Bluejay said, "Why not visit the Marmot village?" He sent along many bodyguards, and the bride and bridegroom set out. Everyone carried presents for the Marmot people. Woodpecker lived with Marmot until his wife gave birth to two children. Then they returned to Bluejay's village. When he saw them approach, Coyote called, "I see a man, a woman, and two children!" Bluejay was delighted to see them, and welcomed the children, caressing them as a grandfather. They all stayed many years with Bluejay, and the children grew large.

Finally, the Marmot-wife said, "I'd like to visit my people again." Once more, Bluejay sent an entourage along to escort them, and he sent many presents for the Marmots. He said, "You may stay some time with the Marmots and Antelopes, play games with them, talk with them—but none of you must marry their women."

The visitors stayed with the Marmots a long time, and when they were about to leave, Flicker suddenly married an Antelope daughter!

When Coyote saw the party approaching, he called out, "I see men coming, and two women and two children are with them." When Bluejay heard this, he took to his bed, covered himself with his robe, and wouldn't speak. When the party arrived, Woodpecker's children ran to play with their grandfather, but he ignored them.

At last Bluejay got up and said to his people, "Flicker disobeyed me, and I've been crying. When my tears rolled down, I remembered my enemies, and my heart grew hard again. Tomorrow, we'll attack them." Bluejay painted and dressed himself for war, and all his men went with him, including Woodpecker and Flicker. They didn't dare refuse. They attacked the Marmot and Antelope people, and killed almost all of them.

"Now," Bluejay said, "I wipe away my tears."

The Wolverine Loses His Shoes

◇ G W I C H ' I N   I N D I A N ◇

Long ago all the animals lived like humans, they say. Wolverine was going around hunting when he met a man.

"Brother-in-law," he said to the man (Wolverine called all creatures "brother-in-law"), "where are you going?"

"I've been looking for food to feed my children," the man said.

"Spend the night with me," Wolverine said.

All night the man was looking at Wolverine, and he didn't sleep. He didn't trust Wolverine enough to sleep. In the morning, when it was still dark, Wolverine got up barefoot. The man was peeking at him. And what did Wolverine do? He exchanged his own moccasins for the man's moccasins. As soon as Wolverine fell back asleep, the man got up and put the moccasins back where they belonged. After a short while, Wolverine got up again, stirred the fire, and took his own moccasins—which he thought were the man's—and tossed them into the fire!

When the man got up and started to put on his moccasins, Wolverine said to him, "Brother-in-law, what are you doing with *my* moccasins? Those are the only shoes I have. They are all ragged, but I make do with them." The man put on his moccasins, and Wolverine kept arguing with him. The man started to leave, and Wolverine said, "My brother-in-law, it looks like I'll starve. Send somebody to me quickly." But the man paid no attention to Wolverine. He slipped into his snowshoes and set out.

Wolverine stood in front of the smoldering fire in the cold. Soon after that, the man returned to have a look at Wolverine, but he was gone, and only his tracks were to be found. Wolverine had tied spruce boughs under his feet and walked away, so people say. From that time on, the tracks of the wolverine look as if someone has tied something under his feet and is walking around, so they say.

Skunk's Tears

◇ T H O M P S O N   I N D I A N ◇

Skunk pretended to be sad, and wept. He said to his wife, "I'm so full of sorrow, let's have some guests over. Cook lots of roots and fish—a feast!" He then asked all his neighbors over. Grizzly Bear, Marten, Fisher, Wolf, Wolverine, all dropped in. When they all had arrived, Skunk said to them, "I've been thinking of our dead parents, and how they were killed by our enemies. And my heart is sad. I think that we ought to go to war with the Shuswap Indians, who killed them."

The animals agreed and pretty soon started out on the warpath. Skunk was their chief and guide. After traveling many days, they got to the edge of some steep hills looking down on a valley filled with smoke. Skunk said, "That's enemy country. The smoke is from their fires, because there's many lodges. It wouldn't be wise to attack them all at once. You stay here. I'll go and reconnoiter."

Leaving his companions, Skunk snuck down into the valley and was soon camouflaged by smoke. He went to the bank of a river that flowed through the valley, and there he picked up a lot of dead dog salmon. He cut off their heads and placed them in a row. Then he opened their mouths and said, "Bark like dogs!"

Skunk backed away from the dog salmon, and they barked.

Back up on the hill, Grizzly Bear said to the others, "Oh, no! Our enemy's dogs have detected Skunk!"

But when Skunk returned, he said, "No—but there are many Shuswap down there. It's best to wait until daybreak."

Now there was a large pit that the Shuswap had used for trapping, and Skunk said, "Let's all hide in this pit until daybreak. You may all sleep. I'll keep watch." So all the animals went to sleep in the pit, the big animals on the bottom, the smaller ones on top. Just before dawn, Skunk let loose his obnoxious fluid all over them and thought he'd killed them. He went home.

When he got near the village, he defecated, then turned his excrement into a boy. "Who are you?" he said.

"I am Skunk!" the boy answered.

His answer really annoyed Skunk.

"No," said Skunk, "you're my slave."

"No," said the boy, "I am the shit of Skunk."

Skunk argued a long time with the boy. Finally, the boy said, "Okay, I'm your slave."

Skunk set out with the boy, and they reached the village. The people there wondered where the rest of the animals were. They wanted to hear the news. Skunk told them, "I'm the only one who survived a big war. We attacked the Shuswap and had a fierce fight with them. I'm the only one who got away. As I was leaving, I saw this boy and made a slave of him."

Then Skunk called the animals' wives together, to tell them more about the battle. He said, "Your husbands are all dead. So now you'll become my wives, all of you. I'm your husband!" Then he called each of the wives forward and pointed out the parts of the body on which each of their former husbands was wounded. "Your husband was hit here," he'd say, first placing his finger on the woman's brow, then on her mouth, her chin, her throat. He touched each part of her body, until he got to her most private parts, saying, "He was hit here! Oh, my finger went in!" Feeling ashamed, the woman went to sit in a corner. Skunk did this with all the animal wives. They were his wives now.

But a lot of people were suspicious of Skunk. They asked the boy, "Who are you?" "I am skunk-shit," he said, which made the people more suspicious. A few said, "Skunk lies! He's somehow disposed of his friends, and this boy is really made of skunk-shit."

Skunk was pleased with himself, now that he had all these wives. But his pleasure didn't last too long. Because a few days later, all his warrior animals arrived! Skunk's odor had drifted off and the warriors were revived. Here they came, down the hillside! When they got to the village, they said, "Has Skunk come back?"

"Yes," some people told them. "He said that you'd been killed in battle. He's taken all of your wives for his own!"

Now, when Skunk heard that the warriors had returned, he got nervous and told his wives to get back to their own houses, but some wouldn't go. "You've shamed us," they said. "And why should we go back, when our husbands are dead?"

The warriors were furious with Skunk. They attacked his house. They killed the women inside and killed the shit-boy. Skunk was badly wounded, too, stabbed all over his body. "You might as well kill me outright!" he pleaded. "Put me in a basket with a lid, and throw me into the river." The warriors did just that. They put him in the basket and tossed it into the river. "From now on," they shouted, "you'll never be a chief, you'll never be able to betray your friends or steal their wives. You'll be shunned by all men and animals because you stink!"

Skunk floated down the river in the basket, and finally he scrambled ashore in the Shuswap country, where he remained. So: skunks are plentiful around there, even today.

The Duck Whose Grandmother Was Out of Her Wits

◇ C H U V A N T Z I ◇

There was a duck who called herself White-Cap. She asked her grand-daughter to louse her. "Oh, grandma, there are no lice on your forehead, but plenty on the back of your head."

"Gete, gete!" said the old woman in duck language. "There are none on the back of the head, but quite a good many on the forehead, gete, gete, gete."

"Oh, grandma, why do you talk like that? You never used to."

"Gete, gete, I always talked like the grey geese that pass high above me. They made me lose my wits, gete, gete, gete!"

The girl was frightened and ran away.

For some time she remained alone; then she felt lonely and sat down on a high stone. A snow bunting perched on a cranberry bush. The girl asked it, "What do you want?"

"Pititi, do you feel warm?"

"I do feel warm."

"Pititi, why do you not bathe in the river?"

"I am afraid I might drown."

"Pititi, why do you not hold on to a willow?"

"I am afraid to get a splinter in my palm."

"Pitititi, why don't you put on mittens?"

"I'm afraid they'll get torn."

"Pitititi, why don't you just mend them?"

"I'm afraid the needle might break."

"Pitititi, why don't you sharpen it?"

"I am afraid the whetstone might split, and my brother would blame me."

"What is your bed?"

"A dogskin."

"What is your pillow?"

"A dog's neck."

"What are your spoons?"

"Dog's paws."

"What are your forks?"
"Dog's claws."
"What is your kettle?"
"Dog's skull."
"What is your sledge?"
"Dog's cheekbones."
"What are your ladles?"
"Dog's shoulder-blades."
"What are your tidbits?"
"Dog's tongue."
"What are your cups?"
"Dog's teeth."
"And where is your fire?"
"A jay passed by and extinguished it."
"And where is the jay?"
"It flew away to the mountain to pick larch-gum."
The end.

The Helldiver and the Spirit of Winter

◇ C H I P P E W A ◇

Every winter the birds went south. One time a helldiver volunteered to stay for the winter to take care of two birds, an injured whooping crane and a wounded mallard duck, both of whom had broken wings. He got fish for them by diving through a hole in the ice. Now Gabibonike, the Spirit of Winter, was jealous of his success at fishing and froze up the water at the hole after the helldiver had gone below the ice. But the helldiver swam to shore where there were a lot of bulrushes and pulled one of them down through the ice with his bill. This made a hole, and the helldiver got out and flew home to his wigwam. Then he saw that someone was peeking in through the door. It was Gabibonike, who was trying to freeze him out. The helldiver got a warm fire going, but it was still cold in the wigwam. Still, he tried to fool Gabibonike by mopping his face with a handkerchief and saying, "It's hot in here!" Afraid of the heat, Gabibonike went away.

One day the helldiver decided to have a feast. He got some wild rice and sent a duck to invite Gabibonike, but the duck froze to death before he got there. Then he sent a partridge, and she set out. She got very cold, too, but she dived under the snow to warm up and then went on again. She got to Gabibonike and said, "You're invited to the helldiver's feast."

When Gabibonike arrived at the feast, it was like a blizzard coming into the wigwam. He had icicles on his nose and face. Helldiver kept on making the fire blaze up, and it began to get warm. The icicles began melting on Gabibonike's face. He was getting too warm, but he liked wild rice and wanted to go on eating it.

Helldiver said, "It's warm in here. It must be spring already."

Then Gabibonike grabbed his blanket and ran out.

Helldiver had brought the spring, and now there were just patches of snow left here and there. Gabibonike had a hard time getting back to his home in the North, where there is always snow.

The Stubbornness of Bluejays

◇ C R E E ◇

You know the robber jays? There were some living in a tree. They were loud. As always, they were loud. There was a girl who often went to see them. Her name at the time was—"She-Tears-Things-Up." Each time she saw the jays, she asked them, "You jays, you ever see me tear things up?"

Well, each time they heard this those jays began arguing in the air. One would say, "Yes, I saw you tear up a tree-stump!"

"No, I never did that!" she would call up.

"Then how come you got that name? Skee-wah-chay-chay!" one jay mocked her with his call.

Then another jay would scream, "I saw you bite up a feather robe and spit it out! Skee-skee-wah-tch-tch-chay!"

Then the girl said, "No, I never did that. I hate to hear that. You see any feathers stuck in my teeth?"

"Just look," one jay would say. With this, the girl would look, and each time she found some feathers stuck in her teeth.

"These feathers weren't there when I arrived!" she'd say. "One of you conjured them between my teeth. Who did it?"

But the jays, all together, made the whole tree seem to argue.

This made her angry, for she knew they threw lies down at her. She shouted at them, "I'm going to argue louder than all of you!" Then they all made their noises down at her again. They made so much noise they couldn't hear her, and it looked to them as if she was just moving her mouth. And no words coming out!

One time she said, "There are more of you than I can see!" It must have seemed this way to her, standing under that jay-tree.

After talking loud a long time, she would arrive home with a sore throat. She talked in an old voice then. Her parents warned her, and her throat warned her, "Don't go argue with those jays."

Don't go argue with those jays.

One morning, she said to her parents, "I want a new name."

Her father said, "Why is that?"

She told him, "Because I no longer tear things up, is why."

Then she said, "I want the name Able-to-Carry-On-Many-Arguments-at-Once. It will help me against those jays."

Again, both her parents said, "Find another name. That one will only get your throat in more trouble."

Right away she went back and stood under that tree! She argued at the jays. She went on doing this. There was a stubbornness there which made her like one of the jays. So she was given the new name Who-Caught-Stubbornness-from-Jays.

Coyote and Fox

◇ S H U S W A P   I N D I A N ◇

Coyote, while traveling about, came to an underground house which was inhabited by very small, short people. They were the rock rabbits. He said to himself, "They are too short for people. I will kill them all and eat them." After slaughtering them, he tied all their bodies on a string and carried them over his shoulder. It was very hot, clear weather, so he sought the shade of a large yellow-pine tree, where he heated stones and, digging an earth oven, put all the rock rabbits in to bake. Then he lay down in the shade to sleep until they should be cooked. Meanwhile Fox came along, and seeing Coyote asleep, he dug up and took out the rock rabbits from the oven and began to eat. He had eaten about half the rock rabbits when Coyote awoke, but feeling too lazy and overcome by the heat to get up, he said, "Spare me ten." Fox didn't pay any attention and went on eating. When Coyote saw there were only ten left and Fox continued to eat, he said, "Spare me nine." But Fox paid no attention, and although Coyote continued to ask him to spare the rest, Fox continued to eat until there was only one rock rabbit left. Coyote was still too lazy to rise, so he said, "Spare me half a one." But Fox ate the last one up and then crawled away, having eaten so much that he could hardly walk.

At last Coyote rose up. Saying to himself, "I will kill that fellow!" he set out to follow Fox's tracks. Soon he came upon Fox sleeping in the shade of a very thick fir tree. Coyote, by his magic, made the tree fall on Fox; then he laughed loudly, saying, "I told the tree to fall on him, and now he is dead." The tree was so branchy, however, that it had fallen over Fox without the trunk touching him, for the many branches had hindered the trunk from reaching the ground. Soon Fox crawled out from underneath the tree and walked away.

Reaching a place where the wild redtop or ryegrass was very thick and tall, he went into the middle of it and lay down to sleep again. Coyote followed him and set fire to the grass all around; but Fox, waking up, set counterfires around himself, and thus made Coyote's fire harmless.

When the fires had died out, Fox went on, and entered a piece of country overgrown with reeds, where hares were very numerous. Coyote, following, set fire to the reeds, saying, "They will burst, and then Fox's eyes will burst also." When the fire spread, the hares ran out in large numbers, and Coyote was so intent on clubbing them that Fox escaped and was some distance away before Coyote noticed him. Coyote said, "Fox, you may go."

Then Coyote traveled on, and came to a place where magpies were very numerous. Here he set snares, and catching many of these birds, he made a robe of their skins. He put his robe on and admired it very much, saying, "What a beautiful robe I have and how the feathers shine!" Soon afterwards he met Fox, who was wearing a robe thickly covered with tail-feathers of the golden eagle. Coyote said to himself, "His robe looks better than mine and is much more valuable." So he offered to exchange robes; but Fox said, "How can you expect me to exchange a valuable robe like mine for yours, which is made only of magpie skins?" Just as they were about to separate, Coyote seized Fox, and tearing his robe off, went away with it.

Fox sat down and watched Coyote until he was out of sight. Coyote, arriving at a lake, took off his magpie-skin robe, and tearing it to pieces, threw it into the water. Then, donning the robe of eagle feathers, he strutted around, admiring himself and saying, "If a wind would only come, so that I could see and admire these feathers as they flutter!" Just then Fox caused a great wind to come, which blew the robe off Coyote's back and carried it back to himself. Then Coyote went back to the lake to see if he could find his old magpie robe; but the wind had scattered all the pieces and the feathers, so that only here and there on the surface of the lake could one be seen. Coyote was now worse off than at first and had to travel along naked.

The Owl Woman

◇ D O G R I B   I N D I A N ◇

An owl-place. Owls were around. One night an owl landed in a village of Indians. When this owl landed, it looked around. Then it decided to become a human. Now it was a woman. She married an Indian man, who already had a daughter.

One day they were cleaning fish. The men had brought in some fish and set them down. The daughter then noticed that her new mother picked up fish differently than anyone else. Her mother stuck her fingernails into a fish and carried it that way to the fish-cleaning place.

"What village are you from?" the daughter asked.

"It's a village where fish are picked up the way I pick up fish," the old woman answered.

While they were cleaning fish, they saw a man come back to the village. Now, the old woman thought that this handsome man was her son-in-law, who'd been away a long time hunting. She decided to get rid of her daughter and have this man for herself. "Climb that tree over there!" she instructed her daughter. "There's an old owl-house up there. Get some owl feathers for me."

"No!" the girl said, and then said no again. She was afraid that if she entered an owl's house, that high up, she might turn into an owl. She knew that could happen.

"I'd get the feathers myself," the old woman said, "but I'm too old to climb."

But the daughter said no. She stood back and watched the old woman suspiciously. Now the old woman shook her head back and forth, tsk tsk tsk. She picked up a fish with her open hand and said, "Oh, I don't know why I ever carried fish any other way. It was just something from the other village I once lived in. It was how things were done there. Your way, daughter, is much better!"

Hearing this, the daughter joined the old woman again in cleaning fish. But the old woman kept after the daughter: "Go up the owl-tree, there's no danger. Go up the owl-tree, there's no danger."

Finally, the daughter gave in. She began to climb the tree. And nothing happened until she looked down and saw the old woman's head for the first time. What she saw greatly disturbed her. It frightened her. She saw old owl feathers growing there. But—it was too late. The daughter's clothes fell to the ground, and soon, when she'd reached the top, she'd grown owl feathers! And by the time she was in the owl-house, she was an owl.

The old woman abandoned the fish and walked to the pile of clothes. She put them on and fixed up her face and hair to look youthful. She covered the top of her head. She waited. Soon the handsome man, who had been resting in his house, walked over. The old woman was yanking meat off a bone with her teeth. "See how young I am!" she said. "My teeth are sharp and strong." The young man looked at her. Then the old woman stood up. It took a long time. "See how quickly I can stand?" she said. But the man saw it had taken a long time, the time it would take an old woman. She was stooped, too.

The man grew suspicious. He pulled off her hair and rubbed her face with a cloth. He saw it was an old woman. "You are the mother-in-law I heard about while I was away hunting," he said. "You've killed my wife and taken her clothes!" He killed the old woman.

He set out for his own camp. On the way he passed the tree where his wife was, in the owl's house. She was an owl still. He saw her up there. He called up, "She's turned you into an owl! I beg you, fly down."

He stood there waiting. She didn't come down.

"Come down!" he cried.

"No!" she called down. "You have killed my mother. I'll remain an owl."

Crow and Camp Robber

◇DENA'INA INDIAN◇

That Crow was hungry.

So was Camp Robber. He walked around humans, eating scraps.

Crow called, "Camp Robber! You're a little too stupid. You'll stick your head in a kid's toy, a snare, or a little trap."

Camp Robber laughed. "You're a little too scared. I'm not the hungry one."

At dawn Crow stole fish from the fish-rack. A boy came out and saw him. He shot Crow with his toy arrow and dumped his body on the beach. Crow drifted until his body washed ashore.

Camp Robber came along and saw him lying there, half rotten and full of maggots. He blew into his friend's nose, saying, "Come back as a new animal."

Crow came back to life. He was itchy. "Here I was just sleeping," he said to Camp Robber. "You woke me up!"

Camp Robber told him, "You were stealing fish, and that boy put an arrow into you. You were destroyed. You drifted ashore and got maggoty. That's why you needed new life. I fixed you up."

He told Crow how he had dipped water and said, "Let it turn to medicine." He spilled it on his friend. "Shake yourself," he told Crow, and Crow shook himself. The maggots fell off and he was healed.

And, "Ggagh!" Crow cawed.

Why Brown Bears Are Hostile Towards Men

◇ C H U G A C H   E S K I M O ◇

A man and his wife were living at Nunaq, in Orca Bay. He liked to hunt and used to stay away for days and days. His name was Aktying-kuq. Then he fell sick and told his wife, "When I die, put my hunting boat and all of my hunting implements on top of my grave." So when he died, his wife buried him and carried out his request. She would visit the grave every day. On one visit, she discovered that all of her husband's possessions were gone! And his grave was open! After that, she'd go down to the grave and weep.

One day, she heard a little bird singing:

> Tyik tyik,
> Aktyingkuq behind the Qilagat mountain
> is sleeping hard,
> is sleeping with a woman,
> tyik tyik.

The old woman said, "If you are telling the truth, I wish you would fly to where my husband is." So the little bird flew towards Nuchek. The woman got ready and started to follow the bird. When she got to the narrows, she took a rotten drift-tree, made a canoe out of it, and crossed to Nuchek. She walked over the mountains and went towards the village. When she got to the top of Qilagat she looked down into the bay—Constantine Harbor—and there she saw her husband's boat amongst all the animals he had killed. She then went down to the sandspit and saw the bark smokehouses, and two women in them.

Aktyingkuq's wife said to these women, "I am hungry for some seaweed. I wish you'd heat some water to cook some seaweed in." The women looked surprised. "Come on!" Aktyingkuq's wife said. "That's the way my people eat!"

Now a whole basketful of seaweed was boiling. She was jealous of these women. They all stooped down to eat. She was sitting on one side of the basket and the two women were on the other side. Suddenly, she took them by their necks and put their faces into the water and drowned them in boiling seaweed. "I wish one of these women would come up with a smiling face and one with a sad face," she said. Then she took both drowned women out of the smokehouse. She made two spits to roast meat on, and poked them through their stomachs, and set them on the path with the smiling one in front and the sour-faced one behind. Then she hid behind a stump.

Aktyingkuq climbed from his boat, and thought he saw the two women coming down to meet him. He didn't know that his wife was there. She had a sewing-bag made of a brown bear's snout. She soaked it and made it soft while she was hiding. Then she put it on over her nose and said, "I'll fix that fellow."

Aktyingkuq saw the two women then and said to them, "Don't worry. Here's a white sea otter. You can clean it. I've got a black one too." He just thought that the two women had been fighting!

Suddenly, his own wife turned into a bear. "I'll fix you!" she cried. "You fooled me, pretending to die that way. But you had two wives here!"

"No, no!" he said. "I was going home tomorrow."

But the old woman started to chew up his boat, beginning with the bow, and when she'd finished she chewed up her husband.

The sun was shining. She let her hair down and spread it out, turning her back to the sun. Then she heard a voice: "We are coming, looking for you." It was two boats carrying four men. They took the old woman far out to sea, she didn't recognize the place. The men said, "Jump overboard. We're going to jump in after you."

The four men were really fur seals.

The old woman put her nose on again and turned into a bear. The seals all jumped into the water and swam away as fast as they could.

The old woman started swimming too, and when she looked up she saw land just ahead of her. It was Shukluq—Montague Island. She was still swimming, but she grew very tired. Then she met some seaweed floating on the water. She kicked at it and spit at it, saying, "I wish you'd turn into land." The seaweed became Qutyuaq—Middleton Island. She rested on Middleton Island and finally went on to Montague, where, even today, brown bears are so wild.

The Wolverine Grudge

◇WOODLAND CREE◇

One time, there were three brothers living with their wives and children. The families were camped near the Wolverine River. They were living there for a while.

Now, one brother did things wrong all the time. Sometimes it was funny, but other times they had to throw him out.

It went that way. They'd throw him out. In a few days he'd show up again, and they'd take him back.

One day he said, "Might be I'll eat some of this wolverine." He shouldn't have eaten any, because he didn't kill it. But he went ahead and ate it.

Now, when a wolverine is killed it leaves a place open. So that another wolverine will soon arrive. That's how it goes. No one actually sees this.

So, since a wolverine was killed, sure enough, another soon came along.

Now the people ate and ate. And after the meal, they were drumming. Passing the drum around. He sang, and passed it around. The other sang. The other sang. Until everyone except the singers fell asleep.

Then the singers fell asleep, too.

Now, the new wolverine's got a grudge, because the wrongdoing brother ate the first wolverine. When it got dark, the new wolverine snuck around near the lodge.

No people are awake. But still an argument starts up! Usually these people don't argue. Everything goes okay. But now they start to talk in their sleep. They start to say bad things about each other.

A wolverine sneaks around; such things can happen.

In his sleep, one man says, "The song that you sang will bring bad luck. You sang it wrong."

Another man says, "No, it's your fault if bad luck arrives. Your song— you sang it wrong."

The third man says, "It wasn't my fault!"

"It was you! Your fault! You, you, you!"

Outside, the wolverine is pleased by what he hears.

Now the families wake up. But the arguing men remain asleep. They go on arguing. Their families sit there watching them.

The oldest wife says, "I've seen this kind of thing before. It means a wolverine is nearby, and he's carrying out a grudge. I knew this would happen. That brother there, who ate the wolverine when he shouldn't have, his song is the one that brought bad luck. We have to wake these men up. It won't be easy."

Everyone tried to jostle the men awake, but it didn't work.

They shook the men, they kicked the men, they shouted into their ears, they pulled their hair. Nothing worked.

The families were exhausted.

The sleeping men kept on arguing: "You! You! You!"

Now the wolverine got busy outside. He was chewing on canoes. He chewed through them. He got busy again. He found the meat cache. He tore it up. He ate the meat.

Then he went along the trapline, not too far away. He found all the traps. Hare in one. Lynx in one. Hare in another. The wolverine chewed those down.

He went back to the lodge. Pretty soon it's snowing. Snowing hard, all night long.

The wolverine hides under the snow, just his snout showing.

"We can't sleep with all this loud arguing!" the old wife says. "I've seen this before. When people fall asleep and start arguing, it's a wolverine's fault. And it won't stop unless the wolverine lets it. This once happened to my own father, a long time ago. It won't stop. So, let's throw these arguers outside, where they can argue. Hurry up, let's dress them."

Now the families dress the men. While they were being dressed, they stopped arguing. Then: "You! You! You!"

The old wife pushed them out. The men fell down, all around the wolverine's snout. They lay there asleep, arguing. The wolverine's under the snow.

Now the old wife says, "We have to worry two ways. The wolverine grudge is going on. And the men are outside asleep in the snow, and they are arguing. I know something. I know something from the old times. If you want to get that wolverine away, for the argument to stop, you have to do one thing. One thing. You have to pour hot tallow on its snout! That's it."

They heated up some tallow. They went outside, searching for the snout. The snow's falling and they can't find it. But they can hear the men arguing. The old wife says, "I know where the snout is! It's right in the middle of the men!"

She got down to crawl, and crawled to the voices she heard in the snow. "You! You! You insulted the wolverine. You brought bad luck!" she heard.

She went about pulling the men's hair so they'd shut up. Suddenly the arguing stopped. It was quiet, except for the snout breathing. The old woman heard the snout. She poured hot tallow on it!

And that wolverine sank away—way down, making a tunnel, fast. Fast out of there. The old woman said this was how to get rid of a wolverine, and she was right.

She woke the men up. They went back to the lodge.

It's said that hot tallow's good for many things. At that camp, with that brother who did things wrong, they always kept some on hand.

The Whale, the Sea Scorpion, the Stone, and the Eagle

◇ I G L U L I K   E S K I M O ◇

There were once four young girls who had nearly reached an age to be married. They played together, pretending they had to choose a husband.

One of them saw a whale spouting out at sea, and said, "That will be my husband." And so it came about. Another of the girls caught sight of a sea scorpion lying in shallow water, and said, "That will be my husband." And so it came about. A third found a stone, which she thought very handsome, and she said, "This will be my husband." And so it came about. The fourth saw an eagle hovering high in the air, and said, "That eagle will be my husband." And so it came about.

The girl who wanted to marry the whale was taken and carried off by a whale and brought to an island, and here on this island the whale made a house for the girl of its own bones, and gave her food of its own marrow and its own flesh. The whale was so fond of its wife, and so afraid she might run away, that it would never let her go out, not even to piss. And it kissed her so often, and lay with her so often, that *maktak* skin began to form around her nose and her genitals.

The girl's parents knew quite well that she was out on the island, and went out there themselves now and again, but as they could not get hold of her, they always had to go back home without having accomplished their errand.

The girl knew that her parents were in the habit of coming to the island to try to carry her off home with them, and one day when she was expecting them, she asked her husband to let her go outside to piss. When she said this, the whale answered, "You can urinate in my mouth, and if there is anything more, you can do it in my hand."

But at last one day the whale said she could go out, on condition that she was tethered to a line. She tied the line to a bone, a whale's bone, that lay outside the house, and then said to the bone, "When my husband inside there asks you if I am done urinating and the rest of it, all you have to do is to answer in my voice, 'No, I have not yet finished, I have not finished yet!'"

Then she ran as hard as she could down to her parent's umiak, which lay close up to the beach waiting for her. The girl had not been gone long when the whale began tugging impatiently at the line, and called out, "Have you not yet finished urinating and all the rest of it?"

And the bone to which the line was fastened answered, "No, I have not finished yet."

A little while after, the whale tugged at the line again, and only now did it discover that it was not the girl but a bone at the end of the line. Then it rushed out of the house, gathered up all its bones, so that it became a whale again, and set off in pursuit of the fugitives, who were already far away. But in its haste, it forgot its hipbones.

The whale rapidly overtook the umiak, and those on board, in their fright, threw the wife's outer coat into the sea. The whale came up to the garment and flung itself upon it, and the boat drew a little way ahead while it was busy with that. Then it took up the pursuit again, and now they threw out one of her boots. The kamik again delayed the whale for some little time, and then they threw out the other one, and then her breeches. The breeches, which smelled of her body, kept the whale back so long that the boat got far ahead and reached the shore, running in with such force that it dashed up on land, over two high terraces on the beach. The whale, following close behind, came after it with such speed that it cleared one of the heights, but stopped a little way behind the boat, and the moment it got on shore it died. So the whale lost, because it had forgotten its hipbones.

The girl who married the sea scorpion was carried off and stowed away under a stone, and there she stayed and was never found again.

The girl who married a stone was herself turned into a stone, and as she was becoming a stone, she sang this song:

Men in kayaks,
come to me
and be my husbands;
this stone here
has clung fast to me,
and my feet
are now turning to stone.

        Men in kayaks,
        come to me
        and be my husbands;
        this stone here
        has clung fast to me,
        and my legs
        are now turning to stone.

                Men in kayaks,
                come to me
                and be my husbands;
                this stone here
                has clung fast to me,
                and from the waist down
                I am turning to stone.

                        Men in kayaks,
                        come to me
                        and be my husbands;
                        this stone here
                        has clung fast to me
                        and my entrails
                        are now turning to stone.

                                Men in kayaks,
                                come to me
                                and be my husbands;
                                this stone here
                                has clung fast to me
                                and my lungs
                                are now turning to stone.

   She sang one more verse, but the moment she mentioned her heart, which had now also turned to stone, she died.

The little girl who married an eagle was also carried off, and placed on the top of a high mountain. The eagle was a skillful hunter and often caught small caribou calves, and his wife had plenty of food and plenty of warm skins. The girl found out that her kinsfolk were coming in an umiak to see her, and now she began plaiting a long line of caribou sinews. She lived on a high cliff that fell sheer away down to the sea, and when the line she had plaited was so long that she thought it would reach right down, she made up her mind to try it. One day when the eagle was out hunting, the umiak came to the bird-cliff, and she fastened the line of caribou sinews to the rock and lowered herself down. But the cliff was so high that in lowering herself down she scraped all the skin from the palms of her hands and the inner side of her thighs. But the umiak sailed home with her to her own village.

It was not long before the eagle came flying along, and when it stood above the house, it raised a storm with its wings. It remained hovering above the village, and the men called up to it, "Eagle, let us see what a handsome fellow you are: spread your wings wide!"

The eagle did so, and the girl's kinsmen shot off their arrows; they struck it under the wings, and it fell down dead.

There lay the eagle and rotted away, and it was so big that when its huge head had lost all the flesh and only the skull remained, dogs crept into it to have their litters and brought forth their young inside the skull.

And here ends the story.

PART FIVE

Carried Off by the Moon

Shaman Stories

STORIES ABOUT SHAMANS carry us to the moon and to the Land of the Dead. They show us flying shirts and flying people, spider goddesses, moods as powerful as thunderstorms, miraculous triumphs over the supernatural. From Siberia to Greenland, all across Canada, and on out to the Aleutian Islands, the shaman is the great conjuror and healer, a mysterious figure—man or woman—who deals with wild and threatening circumstances beyond human control. The power to heal the seriously ill, to prophesy, to dream names for children, to resurrect the dead, to control weather, to mesmerize entire villages with violent magic, to bestow luck in hunting: all are the shaman's conspicuous and vital skills.

The term "shaman" is derived from the Siberian Tungus word *shá-man*, and perhaps contains the essence of the Sanskrit word for an aesthete, *šraman*. There are local tribal names for shaman and for the activity of shamanizing; what these share, what each language has absorbed, is the phenomenon of an instinctual, other-than-ordinary, transcendent intelligence. Early accounts of explorers, trappers, and missionaries tended to lump all shamans together as "medicine men," a term far too limited to be of use. While a study of a shaman's life would surely note his or her doctoring skills, it would just as likely include the ability to *cause* an illness in order to demonstrate the power to cure it. Such a study might consider the fact that a shaman could have more than one life; reincarnation may be involved. In addition, a shaman may disappear for a generation or two, having become an ice-ledge or a boulder. A famous Caribou Eskimo shaman was said to have been a polar bear and to have had five or six broods of cubs before becoming human again. Sometimes a shaman may fly over the world for a long time.

In some shaman stories, we see him living off by himself or with an entourage of spirit helpers, or traveling with a lone apprentice. Other times, the shaman has a family. He may sit mending a fishing net, wearing a flannel shirt and trousers, living a life like anyone else's. But then, in broad daylight, he slips through the ice and flies under to visit the Land of the Dead.

"Shamans speak their own language," said Moses Nucaq, a Caribou Eskimo man. Unlike mortals, shamans can readily converse with the spirit world and are used by spirits to convey wishes and whims and instructions to humans. The shaman may be fluent in a number of nonhuman tongues. This sets him apart from mankind in general and is a great source of his power. This type of secret language is unclassifiable—except perhaps to be called "spirit-talking" or "shaman's language"—if only because few ordinary persons have heard enough of it even to mimic its words, let alone hint at its sacred meanings and innermost cadences. Linguists have been privy to only scant bits of shamanic vocabularies, and seldom in the context of a shamanic performance.

Some northern peoples believe that in the beginning there were no shamans. In that distant past there were no animals, so there were no hunting taboos to be broken; people dug up food from the ground. People did fall ill, but there was always somebody who could "breathe or blow away the sickness." And the Great Spirits did not get angry, so did not threaten mankind. But conditions in the world worsened. There came famine, severe and isolating weather, and fatal diseases, and widespread fear and confusion soon followed. This dire predicament gave rise to the need for shamans, people who could confront such overwhelming forces. Iglulik tradition—and several Eskimo tribes are in harmony with this thinking—has it that the first shaman was born when a man suddenly went behind the skins hanging at the back of the sleeping platform and dived down into the earth. He himself did not know what gave him this idea, unless it was the spirits who had contacted him out in the solitude. But he dived down to the Mother of Sea Beasts and brought back game to mankind, thus ending the famine.

In shaman stories, there often exists a state of crisis. When even one person is suffering, empathetically everyone in the village suffers too. An Eskimo hunter, say, breaks a taboo and angers a spirit. Consequently, he may be ambushed or consistently harangued by the offended spirit. He may suffer hallucinations or become depressed, even suicidal. At such desperate moments, a shaman may be hired—

paid for in advance by the family or village—to try and straighten things out, to appease and reason with the spirit. The shaman, then, is a mediator, a liaison between the supernatural—Sea Woman, Moon Man, and others—and humankind.

To heal an illness, to remove the effects of a curse, a shaman needs not only his own consummate skills but, symbiotically, the faith of the people he is helping. Moses Nucaq notes: "We ordinary people deal with things we can see and touch. . . . [Shamans] deal with other things, that only they can see and touch. We believe they can do that, so they can."

Sometimes by merely making a diagnosis, if it is correct, a shaman can put life back in balance. An example of this was recorded by Knud Rasmussen in the early 1920s. The Netsilik shaman Niqunuaq told Rasmussen a story about his own supernatural powers:

> [A man called] Qaqortineq had just come home from Pelly Bay and had told of how so many trout had been caught there that autumn that every night they had been able to hold great feasts on the tasty, frozen fish. A little while after this had become general knowledge, Nuqunuaq came in to Qaqortineq and, in a high, piercing falsetto, told that he had just met one of his most dangerous helping-spirits, who was angry that Qaqortineq had eaten salmon entrails. At our village spring sealing was in full swing and in that season salmon entrails are strictly taboo. The old shaman tumbled about crying and shouting in his pitiable voice that he was mortally afraid of this breach of taboo—it would chase seals away from our hunting camp. Qaqortineq was bound to admit that he actually had eaten salmon entrails and thus broken his taboo; but as soon as the breach had been both confessed and made known, the shaman was able to declare that it would no longer have any fateful influence upon our hunting. The spirit had forgiven the remorseful taboo-breaker. Everyone was impressed at Niqunuaq's ability to discover hidden things.

In the North, there is no single method of becoming a shaman, but recognition of that possibility often comes after a harrowing passage far from home: a man might return from death, experience a vision (often an epiphany) after a lengthy exposure to hunger and cold, or survive a violent encounter with a spirit-being, as in this account from the Iglulik:

Niviatsian, when out hunting, was attacked by a great walrus which came up through the ice, took Niviatsian in his flippers and carried him off. Niviatsian's companions watched helplessly though a hole in the ice as the walrus pierced the man with his tusks. The walrus eventually swam off and when the men finally managed to rescue Niviatsian, he had broken ribs and a deep gash near his collarbone where the tusk had penetrated to his lung, as well as wounds and cuts on his head and different parts of his body. After this experience, Niviatsian was placed in a small snow hut of his own as it was believed that if he had gone to the unclean dwellings of men after the ill-treatment he had received, he would have died. Alone in his little igloo, Niviatsian completely recovered in three days and thus became a great shaman. The walrus, having failed to kill him, became his helping spirit.

Heredity can play a central role in becoming a shaman, though oftentimes a shaman's son or daughter who has inherited this sacred and honored profession must continue to prove himself or herself a worthy successor. In Greenland, a shaman is believed to be born with shamanic proclivities—born *angakkoq* (the Greenlandic word for shaman). Among the Nunivak Eskimo, a person already recognized as having shamanic potential is taken on as an apprentice. The novice may receive an open-ended set of instructions, having then to proceed with his own experiments and investigations. There are great risks involved, as the wellbeing of others is at stake. Things can go badly wrong and the novice, by consensus decision, can lose his important status. But this can happen to an experienced shaman as well. Shamanic skills always need honing.

It is generally perceived that shamans use their powers for the good of mankind, that they are great healers and protectors, even when their methods seem frightening or chaotic. In many stories—consider in this section "Encounter with the Shaman from Padlei"—a shaman turns an insult into a topsy-turvy sequence of frightening predicaments, in order to demonstrate that he is in full control.

Every shaman deals with and behaves in extremes. In that respect, a reader should know about a certain Caribou Eskimo story in which a shaman demonstrates extreme malice. One of a shaman's traditional skills is to locate lost, important objects—ice chisels, rifles, fishing hooks—and traveling parties trapped by a storm or isolated on drift ice. But in this tale, the shaman sees to it that a hunting party drifts out to sea forever. He murders children; he strips huskies of their fur, hurling them into the sky where they defecate down on the village. The evil this shaman causes has no limits. He stomps around, festooned with amulets, bones, and tusks. His hair appears electrified, disgusting snot and saliva blow from his face with gale force. He holds his breath for days, and villagers begin to choke for lack of air. Symbolically, at least, this ear-piercing cacophony of sounds, this horrendously inventive assault, represent some original Chaos. And in the tale, when the village is finally able to defeat this shaman, a profound and jubilant sense of order is restored.

Today in some northern villages, the shaman's drum-dance and his animal-growl chants can still be heard. In shaman tales, the fabric of life is torn and mended: entire landscapes are altered at the whim of a spirit, epic journeys are undertaken, reality can become a mirage, Good and Evil do battle. And at the heart of such events stands the notorious and magical shaman himself.

Carried Off by the Moon

◇NETSILIK ESKIMO◇

Kukiaq was a great shaman who lived not too long ago. Originally, he was from a far place, but after his family died, he moved to Netsilik land, and lived most often around Kingait.

Once he was standing by a breathing-hole, waiting to catch a seal. It was a fine midwinter evening, no wind, and the moon was full. He had his face turned directly toward the moon, and the moon seemed near. He gazed steadily at it and before he knew it, the moon really was coming closer and closer, until it hovered overhead! And then he saw a phantom sledge and a man driving it. There was a team of dogs, and as they approached Kukiaq, he saw that the moon itself was the driver! The dogs were eager to get close to Kukiaq, and the moon had trouble reining them in. At last, the moon stopped and gestured to Kukiaq to come with him. Kukiaq ran over to him. The moon, a big, angry man, stood with his back to Kukiaq near his sledge, which was made of four whale jawbones tied together.

"Close your eyes and sit on my sledge," the moon said. Kukiaq sat down. At once the sledge began to move. Kukiaq could feel the swish and the wind of its speed around him; they were sweeping along. Kukiaq wanted to see where they were going, but could only peek through his eyelids, the wind was so strong. He looked into a tremendous abyss, and almost fell off the sledge. Thoroughly frightened, Kukiaq closed his eyes tightly again. They drove on, and he heard from the resounding noise of the sledge that they were on new ice, bare of snow. In a while the sledge stopped and Kukiaq opened his eyes. He saw before him a large village, many houses, many people: suddenly two of his friends ran up and struck him with their fists! He was in the Land of the Dead, up in the sky!

Now the moon wanted to take Kukiaq to his house, which had bright, beaming windows. They walked to the entrance together. In the passage lay a big dog, so they had to step on it in order to get through. The dog growled, but that was all. The inside of the house was moving in and out, like tent walls flapping in the wind; the walls of the passage moved like a mouth chewing. But they got through safely. The house had two rooms, and in one sat a young, pretty woman holding a child. Her lamp was burning with such a big flame that Kukiaq's neckband became scorched simply by glancing at her. She

was the sun! She waved at Kukiaq and made room for him on her platform, but he was afraid he would forget to go home again, and he hurried away, letting himself slide down from the house of the moon towards the earth again. He fell and fell, and he ended up right back at the very breathing-hole where the moon found him before.

Kukiaq is the last of our shamans who has been up with the sun and the moon.

Story of a Female Shaman
◇ R E I N D E E R   C H U K C H E E ◇

There was a female shaman. She had an only son who fell sick. In the meantime she left her home and went to some other people who lived on the very end of the sea, beyond the margin of the sky. Her husband said, "You are a bad mother. Your only son is suffering, and you leave him and go to the others." "Indeed," said she, "I merit your blame. Still those people beyond the limit of the sky want me so. Their only son is also suffering."

She set off, but while she was on her way the other boy died. She came there. "Oh, he is dead." They had not carried him out into the open because they were waiting for her arrival. She said, "And what payment are you going to give me?"—"Two reindeer teams."—"What kind of reindeer?"—"One grey one, spotted black, and the other a grey one, spotted white."—"All right, I will try."

She struck her drum and restored the boy to life. She spent a year there, and in the meantime her own son died. She went home the next year in the fall. "Where is the boy? Let him come out and look at the reindeer."—"He is asleep."—"Ah, you may awaken him and let him have a look at the reindeer." The father said, "He fell asleep just now. I will not awaken him."

Then she understood and said, "Open him." They opened him. She felt the skin on his arms and it was all rotten, for he had been dead since the summer. Then she said, "I want to have a rest." The husband said, "Why should you have rest? Are you not a shaman? Do something."—"I must have rest," she said.—"You are a shaman. You don't need rest." She struck the drum, but could not find the boy. Then she said, "Rather kill me. I could not find his soul."—"I will not kill you."— "Ah, I could find nothing on the sea. So you must kill me. When I am killed I shall take these reindeer, which were brought from a dead boy in the other world."

So the husband killed her. Then he tied the body on the driving sledge and slew also the grey spotted reindeer team. They went to sleep, and heard a clatter outside. The killed female shaman departed to the sky. She met a raven and the raven said, "I envy you your reindeer team."—"Yes?" said the woman. She drove on and met an eagle. He was chopping wood. He said, "Ah, what a beautiful team."— "Yes, I will give you the other one left at home."—"A female monster carried off your boy. When you come there, you must look well for his clothes. The female monster has taken all his clothes off his body, his coat, cap, and boots. Now you may go away."

She rode away and her bells jingled. She came to the house of the female monster and looked down the vent-hole. The soul of her son was there, tied fast to a pole with arms and legs spread asunder. He asked his mother, "Why do you come here?"—"I come to fetch you home."—"We shall both be killed."—"Did I come to seek life?" She untied the son's soul and carried him off.

The female monster came home and he was not there. "Ah," said she, "I will catch them. Then I will break their bones and swallow both of them." The son's soul told the mother, "Ah, we are pursued." The female shaman called all her assistant spirits to help her, but no one came, all were afraid. The son said, "Leave me alone. Let me fall down."—"I will not. Let her kill us both together." Then she called for the last of her spirits, who was the diver spirit. Two diver spirits came in answer to her call. The female shaman said to one of the diver pair, who also was a female, "And where are your companions? I called for them all and no one came." The female diver said, "Now you must look at the sky. If much blood is spilled and the sky reddens, you may know that the monster has been killed."

The divers flew away. After a while the sky reddened as if the whole world were covered with blood. "Ah," said the female shaman, "so they have killed her." They came home. She called loud, "There, get up." The people awoke. She beat her drum and after a while both creatures she had met on the way, the raven and the eagle, came there and took places by the sides of the corpse. She drummed on. The skin of the body grew fresh and sleek as if on a living body. She snatched the soul and put it into the body. "Wake up. You have slept enough."

Dawn was breaking. The boy awoke. Then only, the mother went to sleep. First she ordered, "Slaughter both the reindeer teams that I brought lately." One team was for the raven and the other for the eagle.

How the False Shaman Was Flung by Walrus

◇ C A R I B O U   E S K I M O ◇

There was a man who arrived in a village and claimed he was a shaman. But there was an old man in the village who didn't believe him. They feuded. It was a horrible argument. Everyone watched it. Both of their faces were contorted as if seen through ice. Both of them displayed ear-knots—out of anger! Both bit lice and spat lice at each other. It went on for some days.

After a few more days it still continued. Ordinary village things began again, hunters came and went. The argument went on in the middle of the village—oh, it was a real skirmish!

"I am a shaman!"

"No, you are not!"

These were the only words they spoke.

Finally, some villagers pulled them apart. Both men were torn up. Both hissed. The elder said, "A shaman can fly—let's see you prove it!"

With that, the visitor paddled out to a floe of walrus. Immediately the walrus flung him amidst their tusks! All day—all day. Then another day. Back and forth the visitor was flung. The floe was bobbing in the sea. Between tusks the visitor was flung. Finally he returned.

"There, you see!" he said. "I am a shaman!"

"No, don't fool yourself. You weren't flying. You don't know how to fly. You were being walrus-flung, is all," the elder said.

The elder looked at his family and said, "Be hospitable to our guest." Then he slipped through the ice. He was gone. He was gone a number of days. He had many sons and nephews, daughters and nieces, and they immediately took over. One after the other they quarreled and skirmished with the visitor. When the visitor went out to piss, there was a son, who said, "What are you doing? You don't know how to piss! What are you doing?" And the visitor was very confused, and held the piss inside him, and grew ill. And things such as that.

Wherever he went, a niece was there. Or a son. Or a daughter. Or a nephew was there. And the elder had been gone many days.

When the elder returned, he went from house to house telling of the Land of the Dead. "I flew under the ice," he said. "I traveled a long way." Everyone heard of his journey. They knew it was true. The elder turned to the visitor and said, "I asked advice. On my journey, I asked advice. And—I received advice."

Then the elder lifted up from the ground. He dangled the visitor by some woven intestine. He flew out over the sea. There, he dropped the visitor among the walrus. The walrus began to fling him. Sometimes a walrus would tumble into the sea, to hunt. But always a few remained, flinging the visitor.

So then ordinary village things started up again, and went on. Once in a while someone would stop and look at the floe. All day—all day. It's true that visitor visited all parts of the walrus floe. But he did not fly on his own.

Things Seen by the Shaman Karawe

◇ C H U K C H E E ◇

I slept and my souls went away.

They set out for way up there to look at—to visit—Sun, Dawn, and Creator.

On the road they said to me, "What's this slow movement of yours? Take our harnesses."

Dawn and Sun spoke in that way. Dawn said, "I'll go with you. It's good for me to go with the drum. When I'm between both of you, keeping up with the drum."

These souls went under the earth and no longer came back, even though I called them back. When they started walking, they were walking on the earth and under the earth, they were seeing everything above the earth and in the high places. They didn't want to return, no matter how much I called them back from there.

But in the summer I was with the herd and fell asleep in front of the herd. Two came on reindeer, the bedding of their sledges worn from traveling so long. The hooves of the deer were ground down from galloping. I looked at them and my mind got confused, my body weakened, and I became like water. I was turned from a strong one into a weak one, fond of sleep, hardly walking in daylight.

To my herd were born such reindeer as in the harness of those people. A wild buck came to the herd, turned tame and quiet, and sired children of the same color. These reindeer of my neighbors— my own.

On the river's steep bank lives a person, a voice there exists and speaks. I saw the master of this voice and spoke with him. He submitted to my power, bent down and sacrificed to me. He arrived yesterday.

Small grey bird with the blue breast, who shamanizes sitting in the hollow of the tree and calls the spirits, arrives and answers my questions. Woodpecker strikes his drum in the tree with his drumming bill. Under the blows of the axe the tree trembles and wails like a drum under the drumstick. It is my helping spirit; it arrives and I hold it in my hands.

My souls are flying like birds in all directions, observing everything there is at once and bringing news to my breast, like food to the nest. It's good for me to fly with my souls in the round canoe.

My friend! Not far away from here I saw that from the river Oloi a great storm is advancing and it hits everything. Between the tents a river was flowing, full of blood. Soon we'll hear news of murder. I heard how Creator was angry that we, the inhabitants of this country, are paying tribute to the Russians—paper of mixed-up colors that we receive in exchange for different skins—are accepting foreign signs, and because of this he makes the pasture of the deer deteriorate and creates limping mothers and young calves with atrophied limbs, so that many of our people have already become poor.

Everything still lives: the lamp walks, walls of the house have their own voice, and even the piss-pot has its own country and tent, wife and children, and serves as a helping spirit. Skins lying in bags as stock for trade are having conversations through the night. Antlers on graves of the dead are walking in procession around the graves, and in the morning they're coming back to their former places, and the dead themselves are getting up and coming to the living.

The Curing-Fox Windigo
◇ SWAMPY CREE ◇

One day a girl in a village had an illness in her chest. When she tried to talk, she coughed. She had troubles in her chest. She had noises in there.

An old curer, whose name was Duck Egg, arrived at the girl's house.

He leaned over the girl's chest to listen. He listened very carefully. Then he said to the others gathered there, "I hear a fox walking over crusty hard snow in there. She is tired. She is weary. She is raspy-breathing hard. She is limping some, too. This fox is panting. She is on a long journey, this fox. The walking is tough. And every few steps she breaks through the snow-crust . . . *that's* the sound I hear in her chest."

With that a hunter said to the sick girl, "We'll bring this fox back to show you." Then, along with some other hunters, he set out. But even with snowshoes the walking was tough, and every so often a hunter broke through the snow-crust. When that happened, back in the village the curer was informing the others still in the village of what was going on.

Out there, the hunters trailed the fox until dark. They had to stop then. They built a fire.

When the hunters stopped and built a fire, the curer, back in the village, leaned over the girl's chest again. He said, "She will have a fever much of the night now."

In the morning the hunters set out. When they saw the fox in the distance, one hunter said, "We are so hungry, we'll have to eat that fox when we catch it! We are so hungry!"

"No!" another said. "We promised to bring it back for the girl."

"We can bring back its fur pelt to show her," the other man said.

"That's not enough."

They set out again. The fox appeared again on the horizon. It was walking along. It was breaking through crusty snow with its steps. "That girl back in the village must surely be coughing a lot now!" one hunter said. They all agreed on that and they were worried about her. Still, they did not catch up with the fox that day.

The hunters had not eaten in days, and they weren't feeling too well. They began coughing. With that, foxes began appearing all around them on the horizon. That was confusing. It made it difficult to know which fox to follow. Then one hunter said, "A windigo is causing all this! A windigo is getting us all sick and weak . . . and now these confusion foxes! It's a windigo's doing!"

The glare off the snow blinded the hunters who were staring so hard at the foxes all around them. They began to wander off in different directions, away from each other! Each hunter stumbled toward a fox.

When the snow blindness left, the hunters saw that one of their group was missing! Then they knew they had to find the windigo and kill it.

Again the hunters set out. Now they saw only one fox. They went after it. This time the hunters caught up with it. They said to the fox, "Are you working for that windigo?"

The fox said, "Why are you following me? Kill me and get it over with. I'm very tired, and I'm sick from not being able to hunt and eat because you've been chasing me! I can't run any more."

One hunter said, "No, we don't want to kill you. We need you to stop a girl's illness, back in our village."

It was then they heard a loud noise behind them. They turned around . . . NOTHING. But when they turned back around, it was there. The windigo was there, where the fox had been.

Back in the village the curer was leaning over the girl's chest. He said, "Her heart is beating very fast. The hunters are afraid."

The curer knew he had to go to the hunters right away to help them. He conjured himself there. When he arrived, he conjured again. This time he conjured up a suckhole of hot tallow. The windigo fell into it. That melted its heart.

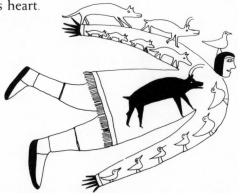

After that, the fox reappeared. The hunters brought it back to the village. The curer, who had also returned, said to the girl, "Sit up and watch the fox walking." This she did. The fox began walking over crusty snow again. The fox was breaking through the surface again, walking away from the village . . . getting farther and farther away. The sound of its walking grew fainter. So did the girl's coughing. The fox was getting its strength back, and it began running. Neither the fox nor the girl was feeling sick any more. That is how they cured each other.

Kinigseq

◇ G R E E N L A N D   E S K I M O ◇

There once was a wizard whose name was Kinigseq. One day when he was about to call upon his helping spirits and make a flight down into the underworld, he gave orders for the floor to be swilled with salt water, to take away the evil smell which might otherwise frighten his helping spirits away.

Then he began calling upon his spirits, and without moving his body, began to pass downwards through the floor.

And down he went. On his way he came to a reef, which was covered with seaweed and therefore so slippery that none could pass that way. But his helping spirit lay down beside him, and placing his foot upon the spirit, he was able to pass.

And on he went, and came to a great slope covered with heather. Far down in the underworld, men say, the land is level and the hills small; there is sun down there, and the sky also is like the one we see from earth.

Suddenly he heard someone crying, "Here comes Kinigseq!"

By the side of a little river he saw some children looking for greyfish.

And before he had reached the houses of men, he met his mother, who had gone out to gather berries. When he came up to her, she tried again and again to kiss him, but his helping spirit thrust her away.

"He is only here on a visit," said the spirit.

Then she offered him some berries, and these he was about to put in his mouth when the spirit said, "If you eat them, you will never return."

A little while later he caught sight of his dead brother, and then his mother said, "Why do you want to go back to earth? Your kin are here. And look down on the shore there: the great masses of dried meat. There are many seal, no snow, and a beautiful open sea!"

The sea lay smooth, without the slightest wind. Two kayaks were rowing towards land. Now and again they threw their bird darts, and one could hear them laughing.

"I will come again when I die," said Kinigseq.

Some kayaks lay drying on a little island. They belonged to men who had just lost their lives while out in their kayaks.

And it is said that the people of the underworld said to Kinigseq, "When you return to earth, send us some ice, for we thirst for cold water down here."

After that Kinigseq went back to earth, but it is said that his son shortly afterwards fell sick and died. And then Kinigseq did not care to live any longer, having seen what it was like in the underworld. So he rowed out in his kayak and caught a guillemot, and a little later he caught a *qartuluk*, and having eaten these one after the other, he died. And then they threw him out into the sea.

It is said that Kinigseq had land at Kigtarajik, a little way to the south of Igdluluarssuit. I have never seen him myself, but my mother has.

How a Bagpipe Drew Hunters from the Outskirts

◇CARIBOU ESKIMO◇

If a shaman gets mad, he might not do anything right away. But he'll look mad. He might say, "I'm angry." Then people know it. And they have to wait. They wait to see what the shaman will do. They might have to wait a long time. But something will happen.

Now, not so long ago a bagpipe washed up. A man from a village found it. He ran in hollering, "A witch is here!" So a number of men went to the bayshore to harpoon the witch. But after they harpooned it, instead of dying it sang! "It's not a witch, then," the harpooner said.

"I agree!" "I agree!" "I agree!" the others said.

Through the harpoon holes, the thing wheezed. Its arms were stiff and waving.

Then the poorest man in the village slung it over his shoulder and carried it home. There he set it on a rack to smoke-dry.

"He can no longer be called the poorest man in our village," his wife announced.

It was true; not with the bagpipe in his possession.

On the rack, in the smoke, it stopped singing. It had sung over the

poor man's shoulder all the way home, with people following behind.
But in the smoke it didn't cough. It just stopped singing. Smoke came
out of holes in its arms.

"It's dead," the wife said.

"No," the man said, "it's just not singing. Burp it like a baby and it
will sing."

So when the bagpipe was dry, the wife laid it over her shoulder.
Villagers were watching. She tapped it on the back, but it didn't sing.

"It's dead," the wife cried.

Just then the shaman from Padlei arrived. "Is my magical instrument
here yet?" he said. "A man I hated used to own it. He made me angry
a long time ago. I waited. He was out in the bay on a boat. Has my
magical instrument washed in yet?"

"No," said the wife. "No—there's no such thing here."

With that, she wrapped up the bagpipe all hidden in a blanket at
her breast.

"Hey—what's *that*?" the shaman said, pointing at the bundle.

"It's my son," she said.

"Let's hear him cry," the shaman said.

With this, the men of the village sprang for their knives.

"I ask to hear a baby cry and you men all spring for your knives,"
the shaman said. "Secrets are being kept from me!"

People were afraid now. They recalled past times when the shaman
was angry. It wasn't good. The shaman held grudges.

In the morning the best hunters went out after seals.

The shaman appeared. "I'm angry," he said. "Here is what I'll do."

The shaman stepped forward, lifted up the blanket, and blew into
the baby's hollow foot. The baby let loose a horrendous wail, a cry, a
howl, a wheeze, then did those things a second time. Then a third.

Soon the first of the great hunters appeared at the village-edge. He
was empty-handed. "I heard our village cry for help," he said, "so I
returned."

In a while all of the hunters had been drawn in from the outskirts,
from seal-haunts far away.

"We're starving," the wife said. "Where's seal to eat?"

"We returned without any," the greatest hunter said. "We were almost
upon some seals when we all heard a cry for help. We returned for
that reason."

"Yes, we feared what was going on here," yet another hunter said.

"What is crying under that blanket?" the shaman demanded to know.

The wife pulled the blanket away and revealed the secret.

"All right, all right," the shaman said. "Give it to me. Now—I have it. Now—all the seals will wait for you. Go out for them."

That night, while people feasted on seals, the shaman played his magical instrument. The music was strange. Everyone listened. But they were happy when it ended and the shaman let people be.

"I'm pleased," the shaman said, leaving.

We say this: what pleases a shaman is unpredictable.

Song of Spider Goddess

◇ A I N U ◇

Doing nothing but needlework, I remained with my eyes focused on a single spot, and this is the way I continued to live on and on until one day from far out at sea a god was heard coming this way with a loud roaring and rumbling. After a while he stopped his chariot over my house.

All around it grew silent. Then after a while the voice of a god came ringing out. This is what he said:

"Greetings, O goddess dwelling in this place. Listen to what I have to say.

"Behind the Cloud Horizon there dwells Big Demon, and he has fallen in love with you and you alone. Because of this, he is now getting ready to come here. I was worried about you and I have come to warn you, in case Big Demon should arrive unexpectedly."

The voice of the god rang out with these words. Nevertheless, I thought to myself, "Am I a deity with weak powers?" Thinking this, I paid no attention. After that, doing nothing but needlework, I remained with my eyes focused on a single spot, and this is the way I continued to live on and on uneventfully until one day a god was heard moving shoreward with an even louder roaring and rumbling. After a while he stopped his chariot over my house. The voice of a god came ringing out:

"It was not a lie that I told you, but you, weighty goddess, seem to have doubted me, for you do nothing about it even while Big Demon is on his way here. This is why I have come again to give you warning."

At these words I turned and looked, and true enough, Big Demon was on his way. Thus, at my sitting-place I set in waiting Thin-Needle Boy. In the middle of the fireplace I set in waiting Chestnut Boy. At the window I set in waiting Hornet Boy. In the water barrel I set in waiting Viper Boy. Above the doorway I set in waiting Pestle Boy. Above the outer doorway I set in waiting Mortar Boy. After that I transformed myself into a reed-stalk and waited.

Just then, outside the house there was the sound of a voice. Without hesitation some sort of being came in, wiggling its way through the narrow doorway. The one who came in was surely the so-called Big Demon, he who dwells behind the Cloud Horizon. He stepped along the right-hand side of the fireplace and sat down at my sitting-place on the right-hand side of the fireplace. He started to dig up the hidden embers in the fireplace, uttering these words while he did so:

"I thought that the goddess dwelling in this place was here just a moment ago, but now she is gone. Where could she have gone?"

Saying these words, he dug up the embers. When he did that, there was a loud snap in the middle of the fireplace. Chestnut Boy popped into one of the eyes of Big Demon. When that happened:

"Hai, my eye!" he cried, and fell over backward.

When he did that, Thin-Needle Boy jabbed him in his rump. When that happened:

"Hai, my eye!

Hai! my rump!" he cried, and stood up and went toward the window.
Then Hornet Boy stung him in his other eye. After that:
"Hai, my eyes!
Hai, my rump!" he cried, and went toward the water barrel.
Then Viper Boy bit Big Demon on one of his hands.
When that happened, Big Demon cried:
"Hai, my eyes!
Hai, my rump!
Hai, my hand!"
Crying this, he went out. Then Pestle Boy tumbled down on top of
the head of Big Demon.
Then Big Demon moaned in pain, crying:
"Hai, my eyes!
Hai, my rump!
Hai, my hand!
Hai, my head!"
Crying this, he went outside. Then when he went out through the
outer doorway, Mortar Boy tumbled down on top of his head. Right
away Big Demon was heard moving off dying with a loud rumbling
and roaring.

When it was all over, everything grew quiet all around.

After that, I came out by the fireside and did nothing but needlework,
remaining with my eyes focused on a single spot, and this is the way
I lived on and on uneventfully.

This tale was told by Spider Goddess.

Desire for Light

◇ MACKENZIE DELTA ESKIMO ◇

There was once a small boy whose father was dead and only his mother
left to look after him. The other people in the place constantly ill-
treated him and made his childhood miserable. Years rolled by, and
he grew older and stronger. One winter the people in the village built
a large dance-house where they used to gather every evening. The boy
spent nearly all his time in the open air; even while the others stayed

in the dance-house, he would often be wandering about outside.

One evening when he was gazing around outside as usual, he saw a bright light some distance away. A great desire filled him to find out about that light, so he started out and walked for a very long time till at last he reached a big dance-house. He was gazing in through the window, but someone inside called out, "What are you standing out there for? Come inside." So inside he went. Men were sitting all around on three sides of the room, and the boy took his place on the fourth side near the door. Time after time the men asked him whether he were not a shaman, and each time he would answer, "No, I am not a shaman."

Finally, a man sitting opposite him on the platform said, "No, you are not a shaman; you are only a poor orphan boy, whom everyone ill-treats. I know all about you and I should like to help you." Then, getting down from the platform, he turned to another man and said, "Bring me my seal spear and my ice-scratcher." The man went out and brought them in. Then the shaman said, "My spirit, help me. Make ice appear in the floor." A moment later a tiny circle of ice appeared in the middle of the floor, and gradually widened until it covered the whole space. A seal-hole opened up in the middle, and a seal emerged and crawled out onto the edge of the ice. The shaman crept up and speared it, cut it up, and distributed it among all the people in the dance-house except the boy. Then the ice disappeared and the floor came back.

The shaman asked the boy if he wished to see more, but the boy was too frightened to answer. "You are a poor boy," the shaman continued, "and I should like to help you. Soon it will be light and then it will be too late. Shall I do some more?" In a voice barely audible the boy managed to whisper, "Yes." The shaman immediately called out, "My spirit, help me." The floor became covered with young ice pierced with a row of holes through which a fishing net was set. The shaman drew it in—it was full of whitefish, which he laid out on the ice to freeze, then divided up among the people on the platforms as before. Once again the ice vanished and the house resumed its usual appearance. Again the shaman called out, "My spirit, help me." This time a moor appeared, and a ring of nooses into which caribou were driven and caught; these too the shaman divided up among the people.

Before daylight the boy was sent back home. A short time afterwards, when all the people of his village were gathered in the dance-house one evening, someone said to him, "You play us something, too." Then the boy thought to himself, "Why did everyone over there ask me if I were a shaman? I am not a shaman, but if they are going to call me a shaman, I may as well act like one." So he sat down in the middle of the floor and called, "My spirit, help me." Everyone remained silent, watching to see what would happen. Presently the floor turned into ice and a seal appeared, which he speared, cut up, and distributed among the people for them to eat. Then he caught whitefish and caribou. Afterwards, all the people of his village were afraid of him. He was a great shaman.

Aksikukuk and Kukrukuk

◇ N A U P A K T O M I U T   E S K I M O ◇

Down at the coast there were people. There were two brothers there. These people always hunted for black whales. Each of those two brothers had a boat, and one time when they were hunting whale the youngest brother's boat caught one. After they caught the whale the eldest brother's boat came along to help. The whale took the boat out into the ocean. When they got far out, they killed the whale.

They tied it to the boats and tried to bring it ashore, but the wind changed and blew strong from the east. The younger brother always had a whale shoulder-blade with a stick in it for his paddle. He always took it when he went out hunting. The other men in the two boats were paddling. They were trying to bring the whale ashore, but it got to be too stormy, so they took the rope off and left the whale to drift. The younger brother started using his whale-paddle; he used it a few times, but the waves were so rough that the stick broke and the shoulder-blade dropped off into the water. Then the men in his boat tried to paddle with the small paddles, but they couldn't make it because it was too rough, so they returned to the whale.

When they got there, they took a large piece of black muktuk off and they started drifting out to sea. They drifted so far they couldn't even see the hills. All summer long they drifted. One day they were drifting in the fog, and after the fog cleared up they thought they saw a black cloud just ahead. They got closer and found out it was land. When they could see the place well, they discovered hills and water. Rounding the point, they landed near a village.

When they got the boat on the beach, they got out. People came, put their hands all over the boat, shook it, and pretty soon it was completely broken up. Then the people took them to the *karigi*. They went in and saw a man with only his pants on, leaning on the bench. He looked pretty tough to them. He had them sit down and said, "When you get to the beach after being on the ocean, you are always thirsty and hungry. So bring them some food."

The women brought some food to the men. After they had eaten, that man said, "When there are strangers in our village, some people like to wrestle to see who is stronger." That man was a man-who-killed-strangers. He was leaning on his side and he straightened up. He talked to them, saying that he never did anything, that he always stayed home and he was getting old and stiff. He finally got up, moving as if he were very stiff. He went to those men, grabbed one, twirled him around, and threw him against a sharp-edged whale shoulder-bone that was on the floor on one side of the *karigi*. He grabbed another man and did the same.

He killed all of them except the captain, the younger brother. The younger brother was kind of heavy and the man couldn't throw him. When the man couldn't kill him, he said, "I can't kill you. You are too tough." So he gave up and put the man by the side of the *karigi* door, saying, "When people come in they will bow to you. If the women come and bring some food, they will bow down to you."

The elder brother was an *anatquq*—shaman—and he started looking with his magic through the villages for his younger brother. He couldn't find him. Finally he went to the village where his younger brother was. He had never noticed that village before. He landed on top of the *karigi* by the window. He saw a man standing by the door with his head down. That man couldn't look up. The elder brother decided he should spit in front of that man to make him look. He spat, and the spittle landed just in front of the man by the door. The man wondered where the spit came from and looked towards the window.

The elder brother recognized his younger brother standing by the door and so he left for home. When he got home he started building a new boat. He finished it all by himself and put the skin on all by himself. When he finished the boat he put it in the water when it was very calm. He wanted to try it out by himself. He drifted out and had the boat stay still, waiting for some ducks to pass. When some ducks came by, the boat started to move all by itself, following those ducks. They were *illiktiuruk*. The ducks started to leave the boat behind. Then the elder brother went back to the shore and said to himself, "This boat is too slow."

So he took the skin off, put another skin on, and went to the ocean again to test it. He put the boat in the water and waited for the ducks to come. The boat moved off by itself, again following those ducks. They were *iinaagiiruk*—ducks who stay in the ocean all winter. He followed for a while and then turned back to the beach. He said, "This boat is fast enough now."

He started getting ready to go to his younger brother. He got some young boys who had no whiskers to go with him. He also got one man with whiskers who was going to pretend to be his father. When they were all ready to go the elder brother became a little boy, smaller than the other young boys, through his *anatquq* magic. He wore a raincoat made of *ugruk* skin that was dyed red and long *ikakliks*—sealskin boots.

When they left, the old man went to the back of the boat and the elder brother got on his lap. The boat moved by itself out into the ocean. The young boys sitting in the boat pretended to paddle, but the boat moved by itself. The old man sat still with the boy in his lap. They went way out into the ocean until they came to a place where two opposing currents passed each other. There were a lot of *uksruks*—seabirds—there. The boat stopped because there were so many birds. The young boys got their paddles and started moving the birds to the side of the boat so that they could make their way through them.

Finally they got through and moved farther on. Soon they saw a dark cloud, just as the first boat had. Coming closer, they saw it was a mountain in the water. They went around the bend and saw the village. When the villagers saw the boat they yelled, "There's a boat, aahee." When they were about to beach the villagers tried to get ahold of the boat, but it backed out from the shore by itself. The little boy said, "When we get to shore, all you boys get out and pretend to lift the boat into the air. It will lift up by itself." When they got to the beach the boys got out and pretended to lift the boat up. The boat went up into the air so high that the people couldn't reach it.

The villagers took them to the *karigi*. The older man in the crew carried the little boy all the way. When they went in, the younger brother was still standing by the door with his head down. He saw the little boy and said, "Aananah, little boy, so cute." He didn't know it was his brother. He said, "These boys have a small boy with them, aananah."

When they went in, the older man and the boy sat down. The older man picked up the small boy and put him in his lap. The man with only his pants on was still leaning on the bench in the *karigi*. He said, "If you've been out on the ocean for a long time and you get to the beach, you are always thirsty and hungry. Bring them some food and water." The women brought it. After they ate it the man that was sort of leaning on the bench said, "Me, I'm always tired. I never do anything." He straightened up and they could hear his bones crack. He stretched and finally tried to get up, saying, "Some people from other villages like to wrestle or try to fight."

He started to walk towards the boys, and at the same time the little boy got up and started to walk towards him. When they got close together the little boy pushed the man in the thigh and said, "You and I, let's fight. All year you have been killing people, so let's try, you and I." The man said, "No, I don't want to fight you. I'd rather raise you."

He wanted to get to the other boys, but the little boy was always in his way and said, "No, you and I, let's fight," and kept pushing him back. Finally, the third time, the boy became a big man.

They started bear-hugging each other. The boy got a good grip and began to press very hard. The man's bones started to break and he began spitting blood. Finally he got weak, and the elder brother put him down because he couldn't stand up any more. After the elder brother put the man on the floor, he went to the young brother, saying, "Now it's your turn if you want to do anything to these people." The younger brother grabbed a stick and began hitting the people in the *karigi*. He killed them all. Then he went outside and killed all the people in the houses. He went back to the *karigi* with his brother.

They all stayed in the *karigi* for a while. Then they started hearing someone in the *kanichu*—storm-shed—of the *karigi*. They waited and waited and finally two old men came in. One had a man's lower arm-bone in his hand; the other had a small bag or pouch over his shoulder. When the little old men got inside they both stood by the door. The one with the bag opened it and pulled out a man's toe-bone and put it in the middle of the floor. He brought out more and set them up in a row until there were as many as there were boys and the older man there. The other little old man took the arm-bone and said he was going to swing it and hit one of the bones, and then the boy opposite that bone was going to die. He hit the bone and a boy died. He kept hitting those bones until all the boys died and only the elder and younger brother were left. Then those two old men left. When they ran out, the *anatquq* started working on the dead boys, and they came alive again. They became themselves again.

Soon they started hearing someone in the shed again. They waited and waited, and two old women came in and stood by the door. They looked really fat. Their parkas were all puffed up and they had ropes tied around their middles. They let the ropes loose and a whole lot of feathers flew out. There were so many feathers that the whole *karigi* was smoky. The younger boys started dying because they couldn't breathe. The feathers got in their noses and mouths. Only the two brothers lived. The two old women ran out. When the feathers had settled down, the *anatquq* worked on the young boys again and soon they were alive.

They waited for a while and nothing further happened. They left the *karigi* and went to the boat. It was still up in the air. They pretended to put it down, and it came down by itself. They put it in the water and headed for home. They had to go through the *uksruks* again, and they used their paddles to put them aside. Thus they made their way, got through, and reached home. The eldest brother was named Aksikukuk and the younger brother Kukrukuk. The end.

I heard this story from Kakan, Grace Bailey's grandfather.

Encounter with the Shaman from Padlei
◇ C A R I B O U   E S K I M O ◇

At that time the shaman wore a shirt and held a shirt. He lived for a while near Baker Lake, too. He lived here and there, but then he would disappear for years. Nobody saw him. Then someone might say, "Oh, I saw him at Eskimo Point," "He was seen over by the Churchill River," "Over by Padlei." How did those people know it was him? Because of the smelly shirt he always carried. He was a powerful shaman. One time he walked into a meeting of hunters and pointed at them, saying, "If you hunt out there today, you will all die." The hunters stayed home.

"This shirt"—he would hold it out in front of himself—"has been traveling all over. Flying all over. It tells me what goes on in all the villages." It was just a rag, a torn-up shirt!

But sometimes people angered him. What I want to tell about was a time when he was angry. He had called a meeting. He said, "The weather in the easterly direction is treacherous. You'll all die if you go hunting in that direction."

The hunters in that village laughed.

The shaman was angered. He said, "No place will be familiar." Then he began thumping. Wretched thumping. It was as though seal bladders were bursting just under the ground.

"He's angry!"

He was angry. Someone had laughed at his power, and the thumping continued. Then the people called a meeting. "I found that shirt of his in my house!" someone said. "All around it was wretched thumping."

"Yes, that shirt has been all over the village," said someone else.

He was angry. He entered the meeting. He said, "From now on, nothing will be familiar." The first thing that happened was that some hunters set out, and they traveled to a place they knew very well from former visits. There they stopped. They were tired, so they made camp and slept. When they awoke, they said, "Where is this place?" It was not recognizable. "If we don't know where this place is," they said, "how can we find our way home?" "Well, we are here now, so let's hunt," a man said. It was geese they were after. They went out to find some. Some geese landed. The men shot them. When they walked up to the geese, they saw that they were made of stone. "It will be a shameful thing to bring home stone geese," a man said.

"Let's go back."

"How? In which direction?"

Just then, a very long, folded-up tent-cover rolled by. The men were thrown down by its wind and drawn forcefully to it. They clung to it. It rolled them back to their home village. But they were badly bruised and broken-boned. When they arrived home, the thumping shaman— who had now ceased thumping—was waiting. He called a meeting. He displayed the broken-boned hunters. One hunter couldn't move. He was dead. He lay on his back. His mouth was slack. The shaman said, "I'll return him." He used his magic, and the man came back to life.

He was still angry. The shirt flew by overhead. He said, "I'll leave the others with broken bones for a while." He did that. In a few days he cured them as well.

He was still angry. He demanded an ear-pulling contest. The pull-strings were handed out. One by one, men pulled against the shaman.

He wouldn't even have to move or blink, and they'd be flung a great distance. Then the most powerful ear-puller went up against the shaman. He was flung the farthest. He stumbled back, saying, "This is not familiar."

After he proved his powers, the shaman said, "Things will be familiar again." They were.

PART SIX

Thrashing Spirits
and
Ten-Legged Polar Bears

Stories of
Strange and Menacing Neighbors

THE STORIES in this part show how all manner of strange, violent, truly wild spirits have entered the imagination of northern peoples. "Up here," said Wayne Nucaq, a Caribou Eskimo man, referring to the Hudson Bay region, "a lot of neighbors are spirits." Stories about spirits, in which people do battle with dwarves, giants, ten-legged polar bears, ghosts, or monster fish, are called upon to explain what is extraordinary and tragic, or at least to describe in detail events beyond human comprehension. Some spirits aid human beings; their presence lends calm, happiness, and security to life. However, many others wreak havoc and cause death. They are great tacticians of fear. "When I was a girl," said Sarah Greys, a Cree elder, "a *thing* visited our home. It walked right in. 'Gimmee food,' it said. We were frightened. My mother set out soup. It ate loudly like a moose—slurp slurp, like that. Later, after it left, we heard that it murdered some people. But then my mother wept: 'Oh, I gave it strength to kill those poor folks.' It was a terrible thing. It ate like a moose."

Manlike spirits such as Susquatch or brushmen may barge in on two feet. Weather spirits may ambush from the sky. Spirits of the dead may crash up through the sea ice. In Greenland, a giant worm may appear on a distant horizon; the villagers' panic grows as the worm makes its way from the outskirts of their mythic reality toward its center. There are spirits of snowdrifts, valleys, ice hummocks, rapids, forests; they have jurisdiction over those locales, and many northern places are named for spirits. Yet others may lurk in the nooks and crannies of a village, occasionally interacting with human beings in the most intimate ways, as in the Naskapi tale "Ayaje's Wives with Forearms Like Awls," in which a man is actually married to gruesome spirit-folk, in this case two cannibals.

In the early 1920s, Aua, an Iglulik man, offered the ethnographer Knud Rasmussen this remarkable litany of fears: "We fear the weather spirits of earth, that we must fight against to wrest our food from land

and sea. We fear Sila. We fear Takanakpsaluk, the great woman down at the bottom of the sea, that rules over all the beasts of the sea. We fear evil spirits of life, those of the air, the sea, and of the earth, that can help wicked shamans harm their fellow man." Such mortal fears have been through centuries routed into taboos, those formal and sacred instructions as to the hows and whys of going about one's life in order not to offend the presiding spirits. Cautionary tales featuring breaches of taboo are very popular in the North, often touching on events believed to have occurred as part of humankind's earliest associations with spirits.

The Eskimo of the Canadian arctic host a remarkable gallery of minor spirits, each with its power and reputation. Yet there is a common belief in three major deities. Tarquip, or Moon Spirit, is generally well-intentioned toward mankind, though capable of dread punishments. Tarquip can make barren women fertile, can lead starving hunters to seals and caribou, can even comfort those on the verge of suicide, lulling them with an invitation: "Come on, come to me, it is not painful to die. It is only a brief dizziness."

Then there is Sila, god of the air, who detests humankind. Sila lives "up in the air," between sea and sky. Fickle as the weather she personifies, Sila is easily offended. She may lash down murderous hailstones, cause fog to settle thickly enough to blind a traveler, or lock an entire hunting party in a blizzard.

Even with these powers, both Tarquip and Sila have less control over the destinies of human beings than the most feared of Eskimo spirits, Nuliajuk (or Takanakpsaluk). Sometimes referred to as "the Mother of Sea Beasts," Nuliajuk persistently monitors human behavior for the slightest breach of taboo—"she knows everything." When offended, she swiftly retaliates in the most devastating way: by hiding all the game animals. She shuts up all the seals in a drip-basin beneath her lamp, in her house at the bottom of the sea. To make things worse, Nuliajuk maintains a frightful entourage of sycophants, menacing spirit guardians who encourage her eternal grudge against mankind. The Netsilik tale "The Mother of Sea Beasts" in this section is but one of many versions of Nuliajuk's origins, though they all interweave common themes of betrayal, abandonment, and cruelty.

"We sometimes are troubled by hermits gone crazy," said Albert Johnson Teases-Crows, a Slavey Indian. The "wild man" of the wilderness (Bigfoot is one popular example), a solitary, often hairy being who lives at the edge of civilization, is one of the oldest and most persistent of folk beliefs. Among the Athapaskan, we find brushmen, who are sometimes believed to be "crazy white men," feared as kidnappers, murderers, even sorcerers. In the Vanta-Kutchin tale "Brushmen," we see a milder portrait, that of a basically mysterious, fleeting, in fact philanthropic presence—"Brushmen were always good to poor people."

In a number of subarctic communities, there is knowledge of Big Man, another manlike spirit who is neither Susquatch nor brushman. He may dwell for centuries inside a boulder, or "travel off the earth" entirely. One belief is that a sighting of Big Man is a harbinger of terrible times ahead for Indian people. His presence is a warning that mankind is tampering with sacred trusts, destroying rivers and lakes; even if outsiders are essentially responsible, Indian peoples will suffer.

The malevolent antagonist Windigo is also mightily feared. Windigo is most commonly associated with the Cree, though neighboring Chippewa groups have a group of windigo tales. Generally, Windigo is considered a horrible personification of starvation. Some accounts have Windigo as a giant cannibal, with a rattling ice skeleton and a heart made of ice. These are capable of flying overhead with feet on fire, howling in weird tonalities like a thousand ghostly wolves. Another view is that Windigo is no giant at all but rather a man "possessed," demented by the stress of failing to provide food for his family. This person, often exiled, is called "He-Who-Lives-Alone." Whatever form they take, windigos have populated the forests and icy swamplands of the Cree for centuries.

The North is a world of natural perils and extreme conditions that often quicken the extremes of imagination. Out of all of this, we are offered these magnificent tales about spirits, which bring us face to face with luck, disaster, and death.

The Birth of Tchakapesh

◇ N A S K A P I   I N D I A N ◇

Once a man and his wife were chopping down some trees for firewood. They were making so much noise that they woke up Mammoth. "What creature is disturbing my sleep?" Mammoth said. He found the man and crushed him into the ground. The woman was pregnant, and he ripped open her womb and with his tusk flung away a little boy-child. Then he crushed the woman into the ground, too.

Now this man and wife had a daughter who'd been left behind to tend their camp. She wondered why her parents were so late in getting back, so she put on her snowshoes and walked off in search of them. Near a clearing she found the little boy-child sitting quietly on a rock.

"Who are you?" she asked.

"I am Tchakapesh, your brother," came the reply.

The girl picked up the little boy and placed him in a kettle to keep him warm. She fed him rich suet for three days, and in those three days he grew to manhood. Stepping from the kettle, he said, "I am going to kill Mammoth because he killed our parents."

"Our parents are dead?"

"Yes, I'm afraid so, and Mammoth must die for it."

Tchakapesh chopped down a spruce tree, which he carved into a bow. He took a smaller spruce tree and this became his arrow. Then he stood inside one of Mammoth's footprints in the snow and called out for his brother Wolf. He said, "Tell Mammoth I am going to kill him."

Wolf's message made Mammoth very angry. He could imagine being killed by Bear or maybe even Wolf himself, but not by an ugly little human being. So he searched around until he found Tchakapesh standing in the footprint. "I must punish you, Mammoth, for killing my parents," Tchakapesh said. Whereupon Mammoth made a lunge at him with his tusks. Tchakapesh was quicker, however, and he pulled back on his spruce bow and shot his arrow directly into Mammoth's heart.

"You have killed me, Tchakapesh," Mammoth said. "You may eat any part of my body, but just remember this: don't let grease from my head fall on a woman's hands."

Now Tchakapesh cut off Mammoth's ears and head. He took the head to eat and the ears as a pair of warm blankets. Then he cut out Mammoth's heart and stomach. The heart he took to eat and the stomach as a quiver for his spruce-tree arrows. The tail he used to tie down his tent.

After he did these things, he curled up in the snow and went to sleep. His sister came along and she happened to touch Mammoth's head. The instant grease fell on her hands, the head came alive again. It began hopping as best it could toward Tchakapesh, its eyes red with anger. Tchakapesh woke up and shot it with another arrow, and then it died again.

"Now we will always be safe from Mammoth," Tchakapesh said.

But he was never safe from Mammoth. As long as he lived (and that would be forever), Tchakapesh heard the hopping of Mammoth's head in the night, coming after him, and each time he had to take up his bow and kill it. Each time he killed it, he was only bringing it back to life again, for grease from Mammoth's head had fallen on his sister's hands.

The Thrashing Spirit with a Bearded Seal for a Whip
◇ IGLULIK ESKIMO ◇

There was once a great village where the people loved to get together for a festival in the dance-house. When the adults gathered, the children all went into a big house and often played on a big drying-frame made of sealskin thongs. Often, one or another of them got hurt, for they were only children and had no one to look after them. When they got tired of playing inside the house, they would scream and shout outside, or play at being shamans, pretending to call up spirits.

One day, when the adults were dancing, the children let the lamps burn wrong, and they began to smoke thickly into the air. The children shouted, they called up spirits, too—things got crazy. Finally, they ran outside. What they saw then was the great, horrible Thrashing Spirit coming toward them! The children were terrified, but managed to get back into the house. Inside, they were running every which way, looking for hiding-places. One boy said, "Lift me up," and some others hoisted him up onto the drying-frame, where he crouched in back. Children crawled under the bench, they crammed together in corners, they crept into cupboards where skins and furs were kept. The last child had just hidden when the Thrashing Spirit hissed in through the passage. In front crawled its whip, a live bearded seal. Once it got inside, the Thrashing Spirit picked up the bearded seal by its hind flippers, swung it like a whip, and thrashed—thrash! thrash! thrash!— all the children to death. The Thrashing Spirit did its work. Only the boy who'd been hoisted up on the drying-rack was left alive. The Thrashing Spirit didn't see him. Then the Thrashing Spirit hissed out of the house and disappeared.

All this time, the grownups were singing in the dance-house. When they returned at last, they found that all their children had been killed! The men wanted vengeance. They got ready.

Next day, they held a song festival in the dance-house, just as if nothing had happened. But this time, some of the men hid in the house where the children had been murdered. Now and again, one of them peeked out to see if any spirits were on their way.

At last, the Thrashing Spirit approached. One of the men clambered up onto the drying-frame, taking with him a lamp and some oil that had been heated up. The oil was scalding hot. The Thrashing Spirit hissed into the house. In front of it crawled its whip, the live bearded seal. When the seal got into the house, it got scalding oil poured on it. There was a fizzing sound—and then a bunch of men sprang out and stabbed it! The bearded seal died right away, but the Thrashing Spirit escaped, and even though a lot of men ran after it, none could catch it.

But after that, the Thrashing Spirit never visited people who were singing in their feasting-house, now that it had lost its whip.

The Mother of Sea Beasts

◇NETSILIK ESKIMO◇

Once, in times long past, people left the settlement at Qingmertoq in Sherman Inlet, to find new hunting places. They were going to cross the water and had made rafts of kayaks tied together. There were a lot of them, there was not much room on the rafts, and they were also in a great hurry.

At the village was a little orphan girl whose name was Nuliajuk. She jumped out onto the raft together with the other boys and girls, but no one cared about her, so they seized her and threw her into the water. In vain she tried to get hold of the edge of the raft; they cut her fingers off, and as she sank to the bottom the stumps of her fingers became alive in the water and bobbed up around the raft like seals. That was the origin of seals. But Nuliajuk herself sank to the bottom of the sea. There she became a spirit, the sea spirit, and she became the mother of the sea beasts, because seals had been born of her fingers. She became mistress of everything else alive; the land beasts, too, which mankind had to hunt.

So she had great power over mankind, who had despised her and thrown her into the sea. She became the most feared of all spirits, the most powerful, and she controlled the destiny of men. Many taboos are directed toward Nuliajuk, though only in the dark period when the sun is low and it is cold and windy on earth—then life is most dangerous to live.

Nuliajuk lives in a house on the bed of the sea. At the bottom of the sea there are lands just as on the earth, and she lives in a house that is built like a human house.

Nuliajuk lives like a hermit, quick to anger, terrible in the ways she punishes mankind. She notices every little breach of taboo, she knows everything. Whenever people break a taboo toward her, she hides all the animals; for one thing, she shuts up all the seals in a drip-basin she keeps under her lamp. Then mankind begins to starve. People then have to call on shamans to help. Now, some shamans let their helping spirits do all the work, and the shamans themselves remain in their houses, summoning and conjuring in a trance. Some shamans rush at Nuliajuk to fight her. And there are some who draw Nuliajuk herself

up to the surface of the land. They do it this way: they make a hook
fast to the end of a long sealskin thong and throw it out of the entrance
passage of a special house; the helping spirit sets the hook deep in
Nuliajuk, and the shaman hauls her up into the passage. There everybody can hear her speaking. But the entrance from the passage into
the living-room must be closed with a block of snow, and Nuliajuk
will keep trying to break it into pieces, in order to get into the house
and frighten everybody to death. And there is great fear in the house.
But the shaman watches the block of snow so that Nuliajuk doesn't
get in. Only when she has promised the shaman to release all the seals
into the sea again does the shaman take her off the hook and let her
go free.

In that way a shaman, who is only a human being, can subdue
Nuliajuk and save people from hunger and misery.

In her house, Nuliajuk is surrounded by a lot of frightful beings.
Just inside her house passage sits *kataum inua*, the ruler of the passage,
who keeps an exact record of all the breaches of taboo committed by
mankind. Everything he hears and sees he reports to Nuliajuk, and he
also tries to scare away any shamans.

Farther into the passage there's a big black dog, and only the greatest
of shamans can get past him.

Nuliajuk herself lives with Isarrataitsoq—"The-One-with-No-
Wings, the-One-with-No-Arms"—a woman, but nobody knows who
she is. She has the same husband as Nuliajuk, a little sea scorpion.

A child, too, lives with Nuliajuk. The child's name is Ungaq, "The-One-Who-Screams." She was once stolen from a sleeping mother when her husband was out hunting at the breathing-holes.

This is all we know of Nuliajuk, the sea spirit. She gave us seals, but she'd like to get rid of us, too.

Brushmen

◇ V A N T A - K U T C H I N   I N D I A N ◇

Once there were two old women who sat drying fish at the traps while the rest of the people were up in the mountains. All through the summer they were troubled by three brushmen, one of them a little boy. One day, while one of the old women was dozing over her fish-cleaning, a brushman crept up and stole a little knife out of her heedless fingers. On another occasion, one of the brushmen crawled along, mostly under water, till he reached the fish-traps to steal some of the fish in them, but one of the women saw him and hit him on the head with a piece of iron.

Later in the year, when the people had come back from the hills, they decided to leave that camp. One of the younger men sat down to rest on top of a rounded knoll. All was quiet, and suddenly he heard the sound of laughter. He looked about him, expecting to see some of his own people, but nobody was in sight. He kept very quiet, and soon he heard people laughing again and somebody saying, "Do you remember when I slid the knife out of the old woman's hand?" Very quietly the young man went away and rejoined his people. They were living in opposed pairs of caribou-skin tents. In those days, when a man or woman had seen something unusual, they would say nothing until their silence was so evident that people would ask what was the reason for it.

This evening the young man neither spoke nor ate, and the people in both tents noticed it. That night he shook his father to wake him up and told him what he had seen. Next morning when the people were ready to go on, the old man announced that his family was going to stay behind for a little while to snare rabbits.

As soon as everybody had gone on and all was quiet, the old man went and sat on the little knoll; for a long time nothing happened, and then he too heard laughter and talking. Suddenly he called out aloud, "Help! Please help me! I and my family are starving!"

At once the sounds of talk and laughter stopped. For a long time both the old man and the invisible people kept silence. Then he heard them laughing and talking again of the old woman's knife, and called again for help, adding that nobody was there but his wife and son and himself.

Soon he heard the sound of wood on wood, and a small section of brush in the side of the little knoll moved aside and three brushmen appeared. They gave the old man and his wife and son food, and they all stayed together until the snow started to disappear in the spring. Then the man and his family went on and rejoined their own people.

Brushmen were always good to poor people.

One winter a brushman made a young girl's needlecase disappear by his medicine. These people happened to camp close to this brushman's cave on the edge of a lake with a hill behind it. He made the girl drop the case, and she didn't miss it until they had reached the next camp. When she missed it, she went back to the old camp to get it. When she was in the middle of the lake, he made a bad storm come up. She couldn't see because of the thick snow. Suddenly she heard a noise beside her: it was the brushman. He grabbed her and took her to his cave. Her people knew there was something wrong, because she was so long in returning. When they went back to look for her, there was nobody in sight. They cried and called, and she could hear them; the brushmen told the girl that she should go back to them, as he felt sorry for them. But she didn't want to, because he had three rooms in his cave all full of good meat, berries, bone marrow, grease, dried food, and so on.

She wanted to stay with him; so he let her stay, and her relatives gave up the search. A year later the brushman made some big hunting snowshoes, as large as six feet long, and by this time the girl was ready to lace them with babiche. Just above the cave was an open place covered with snow. There was snow under the snowshoes, too, so she could see to work. The brushman had to stay hidden. Suddenly she saw a shadow pass over the snowshoes, and then it was repeated. She said, "Look at this, it's as though somebody was passing the cave."

The same people who had lost her the year before had returned and were starving. They were on the same trail again, and were walking with sticks because they were so feeble.

The brushman said, "They don't have any food. I can tell by the way they are walking." In these days there were lots of people, two or three hundred. She finished the snowshoes at once, and he put them on. He told her to get food for them so that he could go out to feed them. He took a whole caribou skin full of pemmican for them. He put this on his back and followed along their trail. He got to where they had made a camp, just a little place, because they were so weak. The brushman stopped on the edge of the camp and cried out, "Folks, is my father-in-law here? If you have a lost girl here, it was I who stole her. If her parents are here, let me know." As soon as they heard this, the people all ran up to him, and there among them was her father, who called out thanks for news of his daughter's safety. Three men were unable to carry all the food the brushman had brought. Each one got a piece about four inches square. They drank a soup of dried caribou tripe first. He told them to go back to the lake the next day and he would give meat to each family. He told the girl that her parents were among the people, and the next day they all came to his cave, and he gave everybody enough meat to last until spring, and even then he had plenty left of all kinds.

Then he joined his father-in-law and lived with him, but he was so used to being alone with plenty of food that he could not stay. One morning he was gone, back to his cave perhaps. That is the end of that story.

Ayaje's Wives with Forearms Like Awls
◇ N A S K A P I   I N D I A N ◇

Ayaje decided to get married. He looked for a wife. What he found were two prospects, sisters who had forearms shaped like awls. "Hey," they said, "marry us, we'll prick and stab you when we sleep together. We roll around in our sleep."

Ayaje thought about it. He said, "Let's get married. Let's go to sleep."

"The last husband we had we rolled over on, and our forearms poked him and his blood ran out."

"Did he die?"

"Yes."

"No matter, it won't happen to me. Let's get married and go to sleep."

"First let's meet your family."

"Okay."

They had a family gathering. The two women with forearms like awls stabbed a lot of people. They couldn't help this. They stepped up close. Then someone would yell, "Awgh! I'm stabbed by a forearm!"

"It doesn't matter," said Ayaje. "Let's get married and sleep."

That is what happened. They got married. But right away they took a journey to the ancestral home of the two women. They didn't sleep at all along the way. Part of the way they walked, part of the way they traveled by canoe. It was a long journey. Finally they arrived, and Ayaje saw a lot of people with forearms like awls. Also, there were the skulls of other people—not awl-arm people, though—hanging from poles. "Who are they?" Ayaje said.

"Those were people a storm washed up to us," one of the wives said. "My people stabbed them."

They sat down for a meal. Big slabs of meat were set out, and the awl-armed people stabbed at the meat, then gobbled it. After supper they sharpened their arms, and Ayaje saw sparks. Then everyone went to sleep.

"I think I'll stay awake and walk around the village awhile," Ayaje said.

"Suit yourself," one of his wives said.

In the night, Ayaje took the skulls down from the poles and fled the village of the awl-arms.

He fled fast.

When he got quite a ways away, he was tired. He set down the skulls all around him on the ground and fell asleep. He woke up. There was a moon out. By the light of the moon, he gathered up the skulls again and fled.

He ran and ran, dropping and picking up skulls, until finally he reached his home village. It was now morning. The people there were up and about. "Hey, here's Ayaje with a bunch of skulls!" someone said.

"I killed these people," Ayaje said. "It was a horrendous battle. Each of them had forearms like awls, and I was stabbed often. But finally I defeated them."

"Have some food," someone said. Ayaje ate. He was an important man with skulls all around him. He ate and fell asleep.

In the morning, he woke up and found that all of his people were quiet. "There's no morning noises in camp," he said. He went outside to look. No one was around. Then he saw a number of skulls on poles, all around the camp.

Then he heard, "There's just you left, Ayaje." It was one of his wives speaking.

He was surprised to see her.

"Where's my other wife?" he said.

"She's gone back to our village," she said.

"You get out, you have killed my people. You get out and leave and don't come back."

"You wanted to marry us," she said.

"It was a mistake."

She left the village and didn't come back. Now here was Ayaje, with the old skulls on the ground and new ones on poles in the air. The wives with forearms like awls appeared on the edge of the village. It grew dark. They sparked their arms together and made a fire. They sat there all night. But in the morning Ayaje wouldn't go with them. He stayed behind. And he lived there a long time. His mistake had cost the lives of his people. He lived with the skulls for many years, and he died in that village, too.

Three Sisters and the Demon

◇ A I N U ◇

Long ago, there were three sisters living by themselves in a settlement. Because their parents and brothers were dead, they alone hunted and fished for their food.

One day the eldest sister said to the other two, "Since it's so hard for us to live by ourselves, I'm going to find myself a man to marry." She put on her best clothes and adorned herself with earrings and a necklace. Setting out, she hung a disk from her necklace on the wall. "As long as I'm alive," she said, "this disk will stay on the wall. If I should die, the disk will swing, then fall to the floor."

Far from home now, the eldest sister climbed a mountain. As the sun was setting, she saw a grass hut with smoke coming out of the skylight. She went to the hut and coughed, which was the traditional way of announcing she had arrived. Then she heard an elderly woman reply, "Who in the world has come to my door at this late hour and coughed? I am too tired to get up and show you in. Come in."

When she went inside, she saw an old woman weaving threads for shoes. When the old woman saw the eldest sister, she wept tears of joy. "There's a terrible demon in our settlement," the old woman said. She then served her supper. After eating, the eldest sister said that she wanted to continue on her journey, even though it was dark outside. The old woman reminded her of the dreadful demon lurking about. "Don't go out at this time of night," the old woman said. "The demon lives in a two-story house just down the road."

Despite the warning, the eldest sister left the hut and walked up the road. She soon came to a golden house. At the entrance to the house, she coughed. A young girl appeared and said, "Come on inside. I have three brothers. The eldest is a dreadful demon. You can eat quickly, and you can hide before they return from hunting."

Soon the eldest sister hid, and the three brothers returned and made a lot of noise. The eldest brother said, "There's a human smell. I can smell human flesh." They found the girl and dragged her out. They tossed her in a nearby swamp with hundreds of sharp bamboo spears sticking up from the bottom. Swooning with pain from their points, she fell motionless to the ground.

At that moment, back in her house, the disk swung rapidly and fell to the floor. The two remaining sisters cried and cried and said, "We told her to stay at home!" They put the disk back on the wall. Meanwhile the old woman in the grass hut, who was a deity, became very worried.

The eldest sister lay in the swamp unconscious. When she came to, she found herself lying in a pool of blood. This pool had been created by the blood of all the people who had been thrown there by the demon-brother. Finally, she managed to escape from the swamp and went back to the old woman in the grass hut. As she coughed at the back entrance, the woman appeared and said, "I warned you, but you insisted on going. See what happened to you!" The old woman treated her wounds and healed the eldest sister.

Meanwhile, in the settlement of the three sisters, the middle sister said to the youngest, "I am going to follow the trail of our elder sister." She hung her own disk on the wall and set out. She followed her elder sister's footprints, which led her directly to the demon's house. "Go away quickly," the young girl there said. But it was too late, because the demon caught the middle sister and flung her in the bamboo-pointed swamp. This sister passed out, and when she woke up she was in the pool of blood. Finally, she escaped. She made her way to the grass hut, cleared her throat, and was shown in. There she found her elder sister, who had completely recovered. The deity cared for the middle sister the same way.

Back in the settlement, the youngest sister was all alone. When the disk swung and fell to the floor, she decided to follow her other sisters. Soon she saw smoke from the grass hut, and there she found her two sisters. The deity said, "Your sisters narrowly escaped death."

The middle sister said, "It's our eldest sister's fault, let's throw some snot at her!" "No—it's the middle sister's fault," the eldest sister claimed. "Let's throw snot at her!" Then they all threw snot at each other. Later, the deity got them safely home.

The Giant Rat

◇EYAK INDIAN◇

A man and woman and their child were boating along, looking for berries, when they came upon the cliff where the monster reputedly had its hole.

"I wish we might see it," said the woman.

The man said, "Shhh! Don't ask for trouble!" And just as he spoke the rat emerged behind them, capsizing their canoe. The woman was lost. The man grabbed the child and jumped onto the back of the big rat.

It took them into its hole, where they jumped off. The man held the child. She was afraid of the monster. Nevertheless, they lived a long time with this giant monster rat.

When it got dark the rat would go out hunting. It would bring home seals and ducks for the man and his child. Then it would lie down on top of them to cook them. When the food was cooked, the rat gave it to the man and his child and they ate it. They were living this way for some time. The man would try climbing the spruce-roots which hung from above, while the rat was gone. He got out. But he knew the rat would look for them as soon as it came back, so he hurried back in. When the rat returned, they were sitting there. It laid in under itself what it had killed and gave it to the man and his child to eat.

His child was a little girl.

When it was pitch-dark the rat would leave, returning as it began to get light out. One day just before it got light the man put the girl on his back and climbed out of the rathole. He was going along, and had not yet gotten very far, when the rat returned. It immediately missed them and started banging its tail around, knocking everything down.

The man and his daughter returned to their people safely. He told them, "Go get some young ravens. Snare them. Snare lots of them." They did as he asked.

When the moon was full, they went there. (The rat would stay in and never go out when the moon was full.)

They sharpened their knives and axes, packed the young ravens on their backs, and headed for the rathole. "Now dump the ravens down into the rathole to see if they'll be quiet." (If the birds remained quiet, that would mean the hole was empty.) Immediately they clamored. The rat jerked his tail partway down but the people chopped it off, thus killing the monster.

The rat moved forward as it died, but only about halfway out. They were going to tow it down to shore but it was too big. They had to leave it there, until a big tide came and carried it down to the shore.

The monster rat was more massive than a very big whale and had enormously long upper teeth. Its hair was longer than a black bear's fur.

The corpse of the giant rat floated out and as it washed around, they towed it ashore. They butchered it to get the skin. When they cut it open, they found all sorts of things in its stomach. People who had been disappearing mysteriously, they now found, had been killed and eaten by this big rat. They found people's skulls in its stomach. The people butchered it for its skin. The hair was already going in some places, but where it was good they dried it.

After this, they called a potlatch and exhibited before the people's eyes what had been killing their relatives. Now, not just anyone could use that ratskin; only a chief could sit on the monster ratskin. At the potlatch the people kept saying, "No cheapskate will sit on it. Only chiefs. Too many people have fallen victim to this rat. Those poor wretches, all killed. That's why only chiefs will sit on it."

Word spread of the giant ratskin and a tribe from some distant land wanted it for themselves. These people from another land came and made war over it. Many people died, but the ratskin was not wrested from them. The chief who used to sit on it was the first to be killed in the war for that ratskin. Therefore it could not be abandoned. It was of no concern to them how many would perish on its account, or how many would die in the pursuit of that skin. They fought to a finish.

When the battle ended, they took the chief's corpse from among the other dead people and put it inside the rat's tail. Then they wrapped it in the ratskin and burned it.

(In the old days people didn't bury one another. Whoever died was cremated and his charred remains were gathered in a box.)

Thus they did to their chief's bones. But then the other tribe found out about the box and stole it and packed it up the mountain and threw it in the water.

Then there was another battle, between that other tribe and those whose chief's bones had been thrown into the water. They were all wiped out, except for old men and women and children. They killed all the young men. That's what happened to those whose chief's bones were thrown in the water.

Their children grew up and wanted revenge, but never got revenge. They got wiped out, those whose chief's bones were thrown in the water.

These people were just like each other, though living in a different land. There are people from Sitka living here at Yakutat just like we do. Though they are foreigners, they live harmoniously with us. But these people waged war over that ratskin, people just like each other. What good is a ratskin? They did that, though, and nothing more could happen to them, no more wars with anyone. They were wiped out completely.

That's all.

The Ghost

◇ M A C K E N Z I E   D E L T A   E S K I M O ◇

Long ago at a place a little south of Nome there were three houses standing together. A man died in one of them, and the other inhabitants left the settlement and went to live some distance away. With them was an orphan boy named Oyupkataliq. One day he was gruffly told to go off and get some food for himself, as he could not expect other people to provide for him all the time. He said, "All right, I will go tomorrow." He borrowed some dogs, a sled, and a pair of mittens from the man with whom he was living, and set out the next day for the deserted settlement. There he unharnessed the dogs and took them with him into the dead man's house, leaving the sled beside the rack. Inside he found a lamp, and soon he had everything arranged for passing the night.

All was quiet for the first hour or two, then suddenly he heard a voice calling him: "*Oyupkataliq, Oyupkataliq, anu tapanmik tunyum piciaktun, taycoqpaum uqyoa timakli-i*—Oyupkataliq, go out quickly, the spirit is going to seize you, the sea-salmon. Let the spirit devour its oil." At first the chant was sung slowly in a low voice, and the boy took no notice, but after a little while it was repeated louder and faster. The boy was rather frightened and hid behind the lamp. A third time the chant was sung outside, louder and faster than ever, then came a crash on the roof, and a moment afterwards the door was pushed violently open and the spirit entered. It searched all round the room without finding the boy and went out again.

All was quiet for a while, and the boy began to think that the spirit had gone away altogether when he heard the song again, and a moment later it burst into the house a second time, made another futile search, and went out. The boy, now thoroughly alarmed, fled outside and hid on top of the rack among a pile of king salmon. Then he noticed a light, rather like a lamp, on the dead man's grave. Presently he saw the spirit emerge from it and enter the house, then come out again quickly and follow his tracks to the rack. Hurriedly he pulled some salmon out of a sealskin poke and threw them down. The spirit stopped, picked them up, carried them on its back to the grave, and vanished.

Soon it reappeared and came towards the rack again. This time the boy threw down a few pieces of the poke itself, which the spirit carried off similarly. Then the boy jumped down, harnessed up his dogs as quickly as he could, and raced off. He saw a ball of fire pursuing him. The terrified dogs traveled their fastest, but gradually it overtook them and drew near. The boy took off one of his mittens and said to it, "Help me, my pup," and threw it back at the fire. There was a short fight; then the fire ate up the mitten and continued the pursuit. Far in the distance the boy saw his home, but the fire was close behind again. He hastily drew off the other mitten and addressing it in the same way, threw it back; again the fire swallowed it up. But now the house was near at hand, and with one last effort the boy gained the entrance and rushed inside. Dark matter oozed from his nostrils and he fell on the floor exhausted. "What's this?" said a shaman who was present. He looked out and saw the fire, but by the power of his magic he killed it and saved the boy's life.

The Giants

◇ P O I N T   H O P E   E S K I M O ◇

There once lived at Point Hope an Eskimo who was very short but very strong. He heard that somewhere there were three giants, two women and a man, so he set out eastward to find them.

One day he saw a giant down below him on the sea ice; he was spearing white whales from the top of an ice-keg. The Eskimo climbed onto a higher keg above him, broke off a lump of ice, and threw it down on his head, but the giant merely said, "It's beginning to snow." The Eskimo broke off a larger piece and let it drop. Now the giant looked up and saw him. "Hello, my nephew," he said. "Where do you come from?"—"From Point Hope," he replied. "I want to see you." So the giant gathered up in one hand two whales that he had speared, and took his guest home with him.

There were two houses, both very large, but one was larger than the other. The giant led him inside the smaller house and began to cook one of the white whales, broiling it over the fire. He gave a small piece to the Eskimo and ate all the rest himself. Then he said to his guest, "You saw the second house over there. Two women live there, giants like myself. They have one son who has only one tooth. Those two women are always trying to kill me. Tomorrow you must take a copper adze and stand outside the door and sing:

> There are two women with one son,
> and he has only one old tooth.

The Eskimo said, "Very well." So the giant broke a small fragment from his great copper adze and made of it a smaller adze that the Eskimo could handle more easily. Then they lay down to sleep.

Next morning the Eskimo went outside and, standing near the door, sang out:

> There are two women with one son,
> and he has only one old tooth.

Immediately two giantesses with breasts full of milk rushed out of the other house. They did not wait to put on their coats, but ran into the giant's house and shouted, "Where is that son of yours?"—"I have no son," he replied.—"But someone called out just now, 'There are two women with one son, and he has only one old tooth.'"—"It may be so," he said. "I don't know. I heard a noise too, but you see there is no one here." The women went out again, but as soon as the first one emerged the Eskimo struck her on the heel with the copper adze and slew her. He killed the second one in the same way. The floor was flooded with water and dirt, which put out the fire.

The giant and the Eskimo then went to the giantesses' house and the giant tore out the window. Entering, they found an old man with one tooth lying on the sleeping platform. The giant dipped up water from a great pot and poured it down the old man's throat until his stomach was distended like a huge bag. Then the giant squeezed him till he burst and so died.

When they had all been slain, the giant turned to the Eskimo and said, "Thank you, my nephew." But the Eskimo went outside, and when the giant followed, he struck him also on the heel with the copper adze and slew him.

The Woman Who Ate Men

◇ EAST GREENLAND ESKIMO ◇

The usual thing: kayaks went out eastward and never returned. At last only one of the hunters was left: he also rowed out to the east to look for his fellows. As he rounded a point, someone called out to him.

"Come up."

"No, I will not come up."

"Come up, do."

And as she persisted, he did so.

"Bring up your kayak."

"No, I will not bring it up."

And as she persisted, he did so.

"Take out the things in it."

"No, I will not take them out."

"Take them out, do."

And as she persisted, at last he did.
"Turn the kayak upside down."
"No, I will not turn it upside down."
"Turn it upside down, do."
And as she persisted, he did so.
"Place the stone on the kayak."
"No!"
"Place the stone on it, do."
And so he did.
"Now, go in."
"No!"
"Go in, do."
And so he did.
"Take off your furs."
"No!"
"Take them off, do."
And so he did.
And she hung them up to dry.
"But what are we going to give him to eat?"
And then she set about cleaning a great round wooden tray and
went out to fetch food.

When he looked about him, he saw that she had taken his former
fellow villagers and used them as pictures for her house, sticking the
skin of their faces on the walls.

In came the woman, carrying a bag of berries. The man began to
eat, but when he thrust his hand down into the bag, he caught hold
of a boiled human hand, and when he saw it, he said he couldn't eat
such a thing.

When evening came they went to rest.

The man pretended to sleep, and when he snored a little, he could
see that she took up her knife, but as soon as he pretended to wake,
there came a clank of iron as she threw the weapon down.

At last the woman fell asleep. The man caught up his clothes and
put on his kamiks, and taking his kayak under his arm, ran down to
the shore. He got down into the kayak and the woman, who had set
off after him, just managed to touch him, though she could not catch
hold of him.

When he came home, he told them this:

"Don't be surprised when those who go eastward never return. There's a man-eating woman there who lives on them!"

When the next day dawned he rowed back to her, and when he was outside her house, she cried out.

"Come up."

"It was you who nearly killed me yesterday," he answered.

"Never mind, come up. It wasn't me but the other one up there."

"Yes, but the child in the pouch has such dreadful nails," said the kayak man.

Suddenly afraid, she turned around and cast the child into the sea, and when it hit the water it fell to pieces, which sank to the bottom. The eyebrows became blue mussels, the guts seaweed, and the hair sea plants.

And now the old woman was angry.

"If only I could stab him," she burst out.

At this his kayak nearly upset.

"If only one could send a harpoon through her," he cried in answer.

At this the woman nearly fell down.

"If only one could stab him," she cried again.

And again he nearly upset.

"If only one could send a harpoon right through her, and that with full force," he cried back.

At this she fell on her knees and cast away her knife.

"If only one could reach him," she cried.

The man's kayak was almost under water, so near was he to upsetting. But he managed to row away from her and reached home.

And here we may end this story.

The Wrong-Chill Windigo

◇ S W A M P Y   C R E E ◇

In a village lived a man named Teal Duck. There was much illness from hunger in his village at that time. Many fevers, in children and others. Teal Duck went out hunting to try to find food to eat. He went out alone. It was when the first ice was breaking up on streams and lakes. "Maybe some ducks will arrive soon," Teal Duck said. It had been a hard winter, with little food.

Some days before, Teal Duck had found a wide stream that was mostly clear of ice. He set out for that stream. It wasn't too far from his village. But when he arrived, the stream was frozen over again! Just then he saw an owl fly down. "Why did you freeze this stream back up?" Teal Duck called to the owl.

"Get out on the ice and shiver, then I'll thaw this stream open again!" answered the owl.

With that, Teal Duck walked out on the stream. He sat down on the ice. He held himself tightly with his arms. Then he began shivering.

But the owl said, "No! That's the wrong kind of shivering! You've got the wrong chill in you! That's a chill from a childhood fever!" Then the owl flew away.

Teal Duck stood up. That's when he heard in the distance another ice breakup! He said out loud, "Maybe *that's* where the ducks are!" Teal Duck walked toward that sound. When he arrived at the distant stream, he saw that it too had frozen over! Again he saw the owl. The owl was sitting in a tree. Teal Duck shouted, "Why are you doing this to me?"

Again the owl said, "Get out on that ice!"

Teal Duck, farther away from his village now and starving, walked out on the ice. He sat down. He shivered.

But the owl said, "No, that's not it! That's the shivering from a nightmare dream, when you sit up in fear . . . awake! That's the wrong chill. That's the wrong shivering." Then the owl flew away.

So Teal Duck had shivered up the memory of a childhood fever and he had shivered up that other thing—a nightmare. "That's enough for one day!" he called out to the flying owl. But just then ice was cracking in the distance, farther yet from his village.

Again Teal Duck walked in hunger toward cracking ice. Again he arrived at a frozen stream! Again, the owl was there!

The owl said, "The right chill will thaw this ice for ducks to arrive. Then you can get food. Then you won't starve."

So Teal Duck went out on the ice to shiver. He sat down. With his fever he sat. With his nightmare he sat. He shivered. He shivered past those two things, past those days. He was very hungry.

Then a windigo arrived.

Teal Duck knew where the chill came from. The windigo sent the chill into him. The windigo did that.

Teal Duck called at the owl, "You've been working for this windigo, now you'll do so for me!" With that, Teal Duck conjured all the fevers from his village into that owl! The owl began burning up! Then Teal Duck shouted, "Strike your talons into it!" The owl did so. The owl struck its talons into the windigo's chest. That melted its heart. The windigo was dying. It howled loud in a tremendously fearful way. Then it died.

That howl brought the others all the way from Teal Duck's village. They arrived. Teal Duck said to them, "As the owl is now working for me, I'll make it thaw more ice!"

Teal Duck said, "Owl, get to work!"

With that, the owl thawed open more ice. It had such powers, it cracked open the ice on many lakes and streams. Teal Duck and the others could hear the owl in the distance on the ice, thawing it. The owl, full of those fevers that Teal Duck had conjured into it, was hissing in the water.

So that is what happened.

After that, there were ducks to eat.

Ipiup Inua, the Spirit of the Precipice

◇IGLULIK ESKIMO◇

It happened that people were disappearing, and no one knew how. It happened that children running about outside at play were suddenly lost, or that caribou hunters up inland did not return. And then it is said that three children of the same parents were out one day playing together. The oldest carried the youngest. One of them found a little bird carved out of walrus tusk, and at that they all fell to searching eagerly about in the hope of finding more, and so intent were they on their search that suddenly, without knowing how, they found themselves in a house. The moment they got in, a woman came and placed herself in their way, so that they could not get out again.

The oldest girl understood that they had come to the house of a spirit which ate human beings, and so she said, "Before we begin eating this tender calf I am carrying, just turn around and eat a little of the earth by the door opening. Then close your eyes and cover them with your hands, and howl at the top of your voice."

The girl had the jaw of a seal in her hand, and as the Spirit of the Precipice began eating away at the passage, she herself fell to digging in the ground with the jawbone. The girl had just managed to dig a hole through the ground when the Spirit of the Precipice was about to open her eyes, so she said, "Do not open your eyes. Eat a little more of the earth by the doorway, then you shall soon have the tender little calf to eat."

The Spirit of the Precipice closed her eyes again and fell to howling with all her might, and at the same moment the girl sent out her two little sisters, making them go first through the hole she had dug. Then as she herself was about to follow them, the spirit tried to grasp her, but only managed to get hold of a piece of her clothing, which she tore off and kept in her hand. Thus the girl got away.

The Spirit of the Precipice called after her, "Did you see all the heads lying about in here, all these human heads? When I have nothing to eat, I suck the snot from their noses."

The girl took her little sisters by the hand and they fled homewards as hard as they could. They had got a good way when the spirit came out of her house and cried after them, "I had not thought you could be so artful!"

When they got home, the children told what had happened, and thus the fate of all the children and all the caribou hunters that had disappeared became known. It was the Spirit of the Precipice that had taken them. None of the men were at home, so the women of that village all set about to take their vengeance. One of the women took down a new sealskin thong, one that had never been used, and then they tried to do exactly as the children had done. They began looking about on the ground for small figures of birds carved out of walrus tusk. One of the women found such a figure, and before she knew where she was, she had been drawn into the house, and at once she spoke to the spirit and said, "The whalers cannot kill the whales they catch, so I've come to cut your claws."

At these words, the spirit stretched out her hands, and said, "You are right. My nails have got so long."

"Let me see your feet as well," said the woman. But as soon as the spirit had stretched out hands and feet, the woman bound them with the sealskin thong and cried out to the others outside the house to pull. The spirit tried to resist with her feet, but the women outside pulled so violently that one of the spirit's hips was broken, and at last they pulled her out of the house. Then they dragged her away, hauling her along over the ground. They tried to pick out the most uneven parts, so it was no wonder the spirit was soon at the point of death. Then suddenly she spoke:

"Wait a little before you kill me, wait a little. Let me tell you a little story first. My entrails are made of beads. Wait a little, wait a little before you kill me. My liver is made of copper. Wait a little, wait a little before you kill me. My lungs are made of a hard white stone, but I do not know what my heart is made of."

Hardly had the spirit spoken of her heart when she breathed her last and died.

Then they cut up the dead body to see if what she had said was true, and sure enough: hardly had they slit up the belly when they saw that it was full of beads, and they took out the beads and made bracelets and necklaces of them. But there were many more than they could use, and they took the rest home.

They lay down to sleep, decked out in all their fine beads, but when they awoke next morning, all the beads had turned into ordinary human entrails.

Inugpasugssuk the Giant
◇ N E T S I L I K   E S K I M O ◇

There was once a giant named Inugpasugssuk. He was so big that his lice were as large as lemmings. He used to fish for salmon at Kitingijait, a wide and enormous ravine in the Netsilik land. Through the ravine runs a river so deep that no one can see the bottom. There Inugpasugssuk used to catch salmon, standing astride the ravine. He took the salmon with his hands as they lay under the stones, and although they were very big fish he called them salmon fry.

Sometimes he caught seals. He waded out into the sea with a stick in his hand and killed the seals when they bobbed up out of the water, striking them with his stick.

He was always very careful with humans and always afraid of doing them harm, and therefore he used to move those that lived on the low, flat shores up onto the higher islands in the bay. Once he waded out at Arviligjuaq as usual to hunt seals. He had to swim a stroke in order to get at a seal, and it made a wave so enormous that it washed people out into the fjord. That wave went far in over all the land in the vicinity and washed quantities of fish up on the shore. It is those we now find as fossils and use as wick-trimmers for our lamps. There are all types of small fish, small sea scorpions, small cod with large eyes, sticklebacks, salmon fry, cod, and many other kinds.

Another time Inugpasugssuk raised a wave that flooded the whole district of Arviligjuaq. As usual he was out sealing when he accidentally struck his own penis; it had shot up out of the water but was so far away that he thought it was a seal putting its head up. The pain made him tumble over backward so that he sat down, and that movement raised a sea that went right in over the land.

Inugpasugssuk was very fond of humans and often camped close to where they were. He once fell in love with an Inuk woman and exchanged wives with her husband. The arrangement turned out so badly, however, that Inugpasugssuk never tried it again. The Inuk man who was lying with Inugpasugssuk's wife fell into her genitals and never came up again. He dissolved inside her and his bones came out with her urine. But the Inuk woman with whom Inugpasugssuk was lying was split right across and died.

Inugpasugssuk was sorry he had killed a human. To console himself he adopted a human son and reared him in such a manner that he grew and grew and became much bigger than humans usually grow. The foster son helped the giant with all kinds of work. When evening came and the giant lay down to sleep, he loved to be loused; but his foster son, who was afraid to take the big lice out with his naked hands, always wore mittens when he loused him.

One evening, it is said, the giant gave his foster son two stones, a small one and a big one, and said to him, "Tonight I expect that big game will come to our house. If a bear should appear in the ravine you must awaken me, and you must do it by first knocking on my head with the little stone. If I don't wake up, take the big stone and thump my head with it."

Then the giant lay down to sleep and the foster son kept a lookout through the window.

It was not long before a big bear appeared away up the ravine, and at once the son knocked his foster father on the head with the small stone. The giant woke up, saw the bear, and laughed heartily, saying, "Yes, but that's only a fox."

Nevertheless he went out and killed it, and lay down to sleep again. The boy kept watch again, and it was not long before another animal appeared, and this time it was so big that it turned quite dark in the ravine. Once more the foster son took the small stone and hit the giant's head with it. But by this time the giant had become sleepy, and as he did not wake up quickly enough, the boy seized the big stone and began to hammer away at his temples with it. Only then did he awake. As he looked up towards the ravine, a slight shiver passed through his great body; it was hunting ardor, and he said, "Yes, this time it's a real bear," and placing his foster son in the strap around his kamik, he ran out and killed the bear.

Once Inugpasugssuk's foster son wanted to visit his family, but as they lived far away and he did not know the way, the giant gave him his magic wand, saying, "Every evening, when you lie down to sleep, you must stick this wand into the ground. When you wake up, it will always have fallen over and will be pointing in the direction you have to go."

And it happened as the giant had said, and the foster son safely reached his old village. But it is told that he had now grown so tall that he could no longer get into the houses of humans. So he soon went back to the giant, and since then nothing has been heard of them.

The Four Cannibals

◇ S H U S W A P   I N D I A N ◇

A man lived with his young wife, who was very wise and gifted with magic. She said, "Danger threatens you; therefore I will make for you four arrows, which you must always carry in your quiver and never use for shooting deer or other animals." He cut wood for her, and she made the arrows and tied them together. When the man went hunting, he carried these arrows but never used them, not even when his quiver was empty of other arrows and game was in sight.

One day he was hunting below Big Bar on the west side of the Fraser River. The ground was good, but here and there broken by bluffs of rock. Looking over one of these, he saw below him a large band of mountain sheep. It was impossible to approach within arrow-shot without being seen. He said to himself, "If somebody would only shoot the sheep for me!" Then again, he thought, "If someone would only drive them for me." Just then he heard a man's voice behind the sheep, calling "Xwoo'o!" as some Indians do when driving game. The sheep all looked around. Then a voice sounded from below and another from above, and the sheep all started to run one way. A fourth voice then sounded from above, "Run to Gap-in-Stone, sit down there, and shoot them." Thinking that the voices were those of Indians hunting, and seeing the sheep heading towards that place, the man ran there and arrived just in time to see the first sheep emerge from between the rocks. As they came out, one after another he shot them, until all his arrows were discharged. Just then four large rams with enormous horns came along. He said to himself, "Why does my wife forbid me to shoot her arrows? I have been carrying them a long time, now I will use them." He untied the four arrows and shot the rams with them. The dead sheep lay close together, and he skinned them and cut them up. He put all the rib-pieces in one pile, the forelegs in another, the heads in another, and so on, thus making eight piles. He took a large tripe and filled it with blood to take home. When he had finished, he lit a fire and roasted four pieces of meat.

While he was eating the meat, four men appeared carrying spears to the handles of which were attached strings of human nails and teeth, which made a jingling noise as they walked. He was afraid when he

saw their fierce appearance, and offered them some of the roasted meat
to eat. One of the men swallowed the meat at a single gulp, so he gave
them more. They looked threatening, so he threw the raw legs to them,
one after another. They finished these in a few gulps, and thus he gave
them one pile of meat after another, and at last the skins. When all
was gone, they attacked him, shaking their spears and crying, "Nem,
nem, nem!" Then he picked up the tripe, intending to give it to them,
and the blood inside made a noise. When the cannibals heard this,
they drew back in fear. When they returned after a little while, he
shook the tripe at them again, and they ran away some distance. The
fourth time they returned, he threw the tripe up in the air; it fell to
the ground and burst with a loud report, and the blood came running
out. The cannibals were very much afraid and ran off a long ways.

Then the man seized his empty quiver and ran for home as fast as
he could. The cannibals chased him, but when they came near, he tore
up the earth with his fingers and threw it back between his legs. This
made them run away, but they always returned. Four times he did this,
but they still continued their pursuit. By this time the man was very
tired. While running along, he heard the sound of chopping, and came
upon two women who were felling trees with chisels. He asked for
their assistance, and they transformed him into a baby, saying, "You
must cry hard." Then they changed one of the chips into a cradle and
put him into it, and one of them took him on her back and resumed
her work. Just then the cannibals arrived and asked the women if they
had seen a deer (meaning the man) pass that way. They answered,
"No." The cannibals said, "His tracks lead right to this spot," but the
women said nothing had passed them. The cannibals searched in vain
for the man, and at last gave up the pursuit and disappeared.

Then the women changed the man back into his natural form and
shortened the distance that separated them from his home, so that it
became quite near. They said, "Go straight over that hill and you will
see your camp." He would not believe them, and said, "You must be
mistaken. I know where my camp is, and it is a long way from here."
Finally he went, and was much surprised to see his camp just on the
other side of the hill.

When he reached home, his wife asked him what had happened,
and he told her the whole story. She laughed and said, "Now you see

the result of disobeying me. I made those four arrows for the four cannibals who torment the country. If you had kept them, you would have killed them when they attacked you. By not listening to my advice, you have nearly lost your life."

Kivioq, Whose Kayak Was Full of Ghosts
◇WEST GREENLAND ESKIMO◇

Kivioq's beloved wife died. He buried her under a pile of stones and then lay down to sleep away her death. But he was unable to rid himself of her. He woke up even sadder than before. So he decided to leave the place where he lived and travel far away from his memories.

All at once his little son, whom he planned to leave behind, burst through the door. The boy had a big smile on his face and he said, "I've just seen mother. She's outside with another man."

"Your mother is dead," Kivioq said. But he went outside to look for himself anyway. And sure enough, there was his wife rubbing stomachs with a man he did not know. Neither paid any attention to him.

Kivioq was furious. He struck down both his wife and the other man and buried them in a second grave. "Now," he said to his wife, "perhaps you'll stay dead." And then he made good his resolve to flee from that place. While his little boy slept, he packed his goods into his kayak and hastened away. He was already quite a distance across the fjord when he thought he heard the boy calling for him to come back. But he paddled on.

Now Kivioq was attacked by sea-lice. They ate up half the skin from his kayak. Then he was nearly sucked into a whirlpool. As he paddled out of the whirlpool, a claw-troll scratched at his eyes. Then he came upon two icebergs. He was unable to paddle around them. "Well," he thought, "I'll just paddle between them." And as he went between them, suddenly the icebergs closed on him and he was almost crushed to death. It was with relief that he turned his kayak toward land.

But his troubles were only beginning. Once he pulled onto the shore, he met a woman who gestured for him to enter her house. He followed her inside. There he saw another woman—a wrinkled old creature whose dugs reached almost to her toes—lying on some tattered sleeping-skins. This old woman offered him berries mixed with fat, which he ate with great gusto. "These taste very fine," he said as he chewed.

"Small wonder," replied the old woman, "for the fat is from a very young man."

Now Kivioq feigned sleep. And he heard the two women talking away.

"Let's kill him now," the old one said. "I'm hungry."

"No," said the young one. "Let's wait. I want the chance to make love with him first."

"Well, let me have the first taste of his head, then. It's been a long time since I tasted head."

"All right, but I want his genitals. Especially if he turns out to be a good lover . . ."

Whereupon Kivioq jumped up and dashed out the door. After a while he came to another house inside which lived only a baby. This baby had an enormous, bloated stomach. All around were various frozen parts of bodies. The baby took one look at Kivioq and said, "How nice of mother and grandmother to send me over some fresh food . . ."

If the sea is dangerous, Kivioq thought, then the land is twice as bad. He ran back to his kayak. He had hardly set out when an eagle swept down and tried to carry him off. He escaped only by smashing the eagle's head with his paddle. Then the ghosts of drowned people rose up from the water and sat on his kayak, for they hoped to drown him as they themselves had been drowned. Yet Kivioq paddled on, despite so much extra weight.

Now he was joined by the ghosts of his wife and her lover. The drowned people complained that there wasn't enough room for all of them on the kayak, but the wife and her lover found a place anyway.

"It was very unkind of you to kill me," she said to Kivioq.

"But you were already dead . . ."

"To kill a person who is already dead," she said, "that is the unkindest thing of all."

Years seemed to pass with all these ghosts on the back of his kayak. He seemed to paddle everywhere, up and down every fjord, everywhere in the entire country. Each year the kayak got heavier and heavier, but he paddled on. At last he came upon a number of other kayaks and they were dragging along a huge whale. On the back of this whale stood a very robust young man. Kivioq recognized this young man as his own son. He hailed him: "I am your father, dear boy. I am old Kivioq."

But his son did not recognize him. "Oh, that could not be true. My father died years ago. He was sucked down into a whirlpool. You're just a crazy old man in a kayak full of ghosts." Then the son was pulled away by the others.

And old Kivioq buried his head in his arms and wept.

The Ten-Legged Polar Bear

◇ B A R R O W   E S K I M O ◇

There were some people living between Icy Cape and Wainwright. They had two houses. In one house were a man and his wife and their many children. In the other lived quite a few related people. Now it happened that one winter the people in the second house got a walrus. They kept all the meat for themselves and gave none to the family with the many children. The father of the family with the many children, a man named Kucirak, was very unhappy. Food was scarce and he didn't know how he was going to provide for his children.

The next day he decided to go out sealing. He went out on the ice. In among the pressure ridges, he noticed a huge glacier, bigger at the top than at the bottom. Walking by it, he saw a big hole. In the hole there were seal lungs floating about. And he knew at once what he had stumbled into—the lair of the *kukuweaq*, the ten-legged polar bear. He was very frightened, but he decided that his family needed food too badly. So he sat down by the hole and waited. Soon the huge head of the *kukuweaq* came out of the water. Taking his seal spears, Kucirak blinded the monster, stabbing out first one eye and then the other. The bear came up out of the water roaring. It followed the man by the smell of his footprints. As the man ran, he saw the ten-legged bear gaining on him. He began to circle around but still the bear followed him, coming closer and closer. Soon he doubled back to the inverted glacier. He circled again, noticing that there was a narrow passage in between the ridges. He ran in between them and the monster, following him, was caught tight. The man crawled around behind it and stabbed it to death.

Then he cut off one of its ten legs and brought it home as food for his family. As soon as the people in the other house heard of his catch, they came over with plenty of walrus meat. Next day, he and his wife went out and began butchering the carcass. It was just as though they were cutting up a whale. And they gave freely of their food to those people in the other house.

The Monster Fish in the Lake

◇ G W I C H ' I N   I N D I A N ◇

Long ago, on the shore of a big lake called Vank'eedii, there lived one man, his wife, and his only child, so they say. Living far away from any neighbor, the man went out hunting alone. With big-game snares he snared moose, mountain sheep, and caribou. He also fished with a net and with hooks. There was a lot of small game, and in the fall there were berries of all kinds. With all this, they had a good life.

Now, this lake on whose shore they lived was a very big lake. In fall, when the days are short, it took one whole day to cross it. At its edge, big rugged mountains rose to the sky. The mountains extended far down it, and only at the outlet were there no mountains. When the clouds were thick, the lake was so big that the sky and earth appeared to meet in a flat line. Whenever the wind blew, its surface became terrifying with great waves.

On the shore of this lake at the upper end, on the bank up in the woods, this man had set up a skin lodge facing the lake, so they say.

One spring when things were starting to grow again and everything seemed fine, he was eating at midday with his son and his wife; the sun was shining and the wind was not blowing. They were eating boiled meat, and just as they were finishing, they sighted something. A caribou had apparently gone into the water to escape the mosquitoes. In excitement they leapt up. The son grabbed his arrows, jumped into his birchbark canoe, and pushed out into the water. With all his might he paddled after the caribou. However fast the caribou swam, he matched it, for he was a young man. He paddled quickly up to it and shot it under the foreleg. After it kicked a few times, it started floating, and he glided up to it. Before he had time to think, a whirlpool formed and he disappeared, sucked down by the current. The canoe and the killed game too disappeared. The water closed over them and became entirely calm again.

The man and his wife had been so proud of their son, and before they knew what was happening he had disappeared. Helplessly, the man and his wife burst out weeping, and he burned his hair. How could it be that his son had come to die? It was said that a giant fish had lived in this lake since ancient times. "It must be this fish that has swallowed him," it suddenly occurred to him. In his sorrow, he did not know what great work he would do. But he said, "Before I die, this fish will perish for sure."

Several winters passed while the old man set about his work. He chopped a lot of wood, and what he chopped he piled on the frozen lake. After several years had passed, the entire surface of the lake was covered with firewood. Upon this wood he piled rocks. Around on the woodpile he also poured oil. One spring, on a warm day, he set the lake on fire. Since the wind was blowing quite a bit when he did this, the lake soon blazed up like grass. For four days it burned, but nothing happened. After about six days, they say the water became lukewarm. All kinds of little fish and little water creatures started coming up to the surface. After eight days had passed, the water began to boil. Not knowing what was going to happen, the man and his wife climbed to the top of a high mountain. From there they watched the lake closely. It was like a big boiling pot, because the hot rocks had dropped into it. After ten days, they began to feel that something was about to happen. As evening fell, the earth seemed to shake. There was a sound like thunder. When it was almost night, far down toward the outlet, what looked like a hill thrust itself up. With a crashing noise it flapped about, and then it became still. The old man who had said "I will kill the fish" had done so.

The news spread among the people in all directions and they gathered together near the big fish. They lived on it for an entire winter. They found antlers in its stomach. Other than that, there was nothing they could recognize. Even to this very day, the bones of the fish are there, so people say. And the trees against which the fish beat its tail are still to be seen.

The Attainable Border of the Birds

◇ C H U K C H E E ◇

On the other side of the sea there is, on that far shore, a large forest without end. In that forest live "the invisible ones." When they come to trade, one can see only the fox and beaver skins that they carry in their hands, for they themselves are imperceptible shadows. It seems as if the furs themselves are moving in air. They come to meet the traders on the borders of the forest, and shout, "Let us trade!" Then the merchants throw a bundle of tobacco, as if into the farthest depths of the forest. "Oh, oh, tobacco, tobacco!" rings through the forest. At the border sounds begin, arguments. But whoever is creating this noise cannot be seen. After a while beaver skins or a bag of fox skins come flying from the forest. For one bundle of tobacco they are prepared to give a full bag of fox skins.

Farther on there is a lake. On its shores, beneath the trees, sit the "half-people"—split right down the middle—who, when they hear any-one's footsteps, put their halves together and throw themselves into the water. They also desire tobacco, paying for it with large fish and otters.

Still deeper in the woods is a land of burrows, and in these burrows live people as small as hares. They also desire tobacco, and buy it with the skins of lynx and muskrat.

Then again there are others, great ones, taller than standing trees. They live in volcanoes, in the mountain caves, and when they cook their food, fire comes out of the top of the volcano. They also desire tobacco.

And there are shaggy people with the bodies of polar bears and the faces of men. These pay best of all, since for a small piece of the black deposit from a pipestem, not larger than half a finger, they are ready to pay a red fox.

For all the people of that shore covet only tobacco throughout their lives.

Now, in the open ocean, in the deepest waters, stands a tall tree. In the tree is a large hollow. In the hollow lives a spirit. The branches of this tree are numerous beyond counting; on each branch there are twenty times twenty twigs, on each twig a crooked thorn. The tree lies on its side, submerged in the depths; when it arises, the whole ocean is white with fish. On each thorn is a white fish—all of these fish fall into the hollow and serve as food for the spirit. If a Chukchee boat comes too close, the tree falls on it and, catching them with its branches, pulls all the people into the food of the spirit.

Beyond this sea is a continent, but beyond this continent is another sea, and beyond that sea is the attainable border of the birds. Here the solid sky falls down, striking against the earth, rebounding, a gate that never ceases its opening and closing.

Beyond this gate is the country of the birds, to which the birds fly in the winter. But the sky comes down so quickly that many do not succeed in flying through, and they are caught in the gate's closing as in a trap. Before this gate the ground is covered with a thick layer of crushed birds, greater than the height of a man, and their feathers are continually floating about there, drifting in the wind.

PART SEVEN

The Day Auks Netted Hid-Well

Hunting Stories

"THE DREAM THAT CAME BACK," the Cree Indian tale that begins this part, goes right to the center of the northern hunting experience, as it deals with the providing of food and the emotional odyssey of the hunt. In this story, a man has an unsettling dream about an old woman and her two children before setting out to track a bear and her two cubs. As he deciphers sets of tracks in the snow, he discovers a startling fact: the polar bear is in fact tracking his own son, Albert, who is out setting fox snares. The man follows. Finally face to face with the she-bear, and still haunted by his dream, the hunter is struck by an intense, familial empathy. Nonetheless, he kills her for food.

Hunting stories take us out of the village, sometimes on long, arduous journeys on which hunters take nothing for granted, and from which they sometimes do not return. A story may take place in strange, distant lands, as in the Iglulik tale "Agdlumaloqaq, Who Hunted at the Blowholes in a Far, Foreign Land." But arctic oral literature can also telescope aspects of a hunter's life, as in this Polar Eskimo song:

> The third day now
> I stand
> bent over
> a hole in the world,
> back-bent
> all day
> over an ice-hole.

Harpoon at the ready, a hunter may make such a song part of his vigil, as he bobs a seal-lure under the ice, watching for a telltale snow-bubble to signal a seal's presence. After hours of waiting silence, there may be a sudden crescendo of activity—the seal is struck!—and given the reverberating acoustics of sea ice, news of a kill travels fast to scattered hunters and their families: "A seal!" Children come running. The hunter melts a little snow in his hand, then dribbles it into the seal's mouth.

"I know you gave yourself up for a drink of fresh water," he says. Now dogs growl and snap the air, intoxicated by the powerful smell as the hunter takes up his knife and spills open the seal's innards. Pieces of blubber are doled out. For the hunter there is much exhausted joy in the moment, deep gratitude and satisfaction; his family and village respect and honor his skills. But the waiting came first. Implicit in all northern hunting tales is the lesson of patience; nature works in its own good time, and human beings cannot hurry it.

In the most basic sense, then, hunting tales are about making a living. And so certain stories manifest a rather matter-of-fact tone. The Gwich'in story "The Moose Among the Chandalar River People" is like a zoologically based meditation on the moose and moose hunting, complete with the refrain "it is very pleasant." And a reader will notice that while the Polar Eskimo story "The Day Auks Netted Hid-Well" features the logistics of the hunt, as well as a number of wild episodes, it still ends with people sitting down to supper.

Though it is not often clearly spelled out, all hunting stories are informed by a profound moral code, which has been brought down from a time when animals and people spoke with each other. Some Algonquian peoples refer to it as "the old agreement," implying an ancient pact offered by animals to mankind for their mutual benefit. Richard Nelson writes of this among the Koyukon Indians: "Human existence depends on a morally based relationship with the overarching powers of nature. Humanity acts at the behest of the environment. The Koyukon move *with* their surroundings, not attempting to control, master or fundamentally alter them. They do not confront nature, they yield to it. At most they are able to placate and coerce nature through its spiritual dimension."

The "old agreement" is a constant and pervasive moral exchange. The give-and-take between animals and humankind is the hunter's most sacred trust. Hunting taboos must be observed, praise-songs sung, and praise-poems spoken. Animals must be flattered, and as an equally vital part of life in a hunting village, a food-animal must be prepared properly, its bones hung outside the village or pieces of its fat placed in the fire so that through smoke or on the wind the animal's spirit may be returned to the world.

The "old agreement," then, is the spiritual foundation of a hunter's existence and not merely a rhetorical salute. John Rains, a Cree Man, addressed this directly: "Animals expect us to act properly. We can't cause them any suffering. That's why we have to teach our sons to shoot well, so that animals don't suffer. If we behave badly toward animals, they leave. We have to let our territories rest—sometimes for two or three years. That way, the animals can replenish themselves. If we insult them—if an insult is put on the land—we have to stay away from it for a long time. If we take more animals than we need, if we are greedy, then we are punished for it."

Since hunting had to be one of the earliest of human enterprises, it is no wonder that certain hunting tales seem to materialize out of the mists of time itself. The Kobuk River story "The Mammoth Hunters," for instance, is unique in evoking ancient shamans. In the story, a man named Ataogoraachuak is out hunting marmots when he notices "some great big animal walking along, as though it was floating, barely touching the ground," followed by three men with spears, who also walk in the air. The scene is like an animated cave painting—shamans stalking an ivory-tusked mammoth. In this respect, in a chilling, almost hallucinatory moment, Ataogoraachuak encounters his own ancestors. And as it turns out, it is a fortuitous meeting, because the shamans have chosen him, despite his protestations, to be a shaman. Finally, he is given the power to "know where bears hole up in the wintertime," certainly a bear hunter's dream.

Patience, traditional skills, and intuition are critical, of course, in any hunting endeavor. Yet also necessary for a successful hunt, whether for marmot or whale, is *luck*. Luck is a mysterious power. In tales one person may say of another, "He is a great hunter. He is respected by everyone. He has great luck in hunting." This statement indicates that the hunter in question is under the good graces of the presiding spirits who give luck, and in a larger sense it means that the hunter's world is itself in balance. Luck, to many northern peoples, is a finite entity, certainly tangible enough to have entered the language. It is an omnipresent force, with its idiosyncratic jurisdictions and personality. Certain objects may be infused with luck—rifles, fishing hooks, bullets, harpoons; in turn, any person who steals a tool may also have stolen its luck. Luck may be bestowed on young or old; likewise, it may stay with a person or a family for generations, then suddenly vanish. Luck may be the reward for astute and respectful behavior toward animals: "Animals give us luck," said Tommy Black, a Chipewyan hunter. Whatever its sources and manifestations, without luck there can be only terrible fate in all its infinite variety—illness, starvation, depression, loss of pride, death. And yet in times of feast or famine, a hunter, his family, and his village know that luck, like life itself, is to a great degree unpredictable. The "old agreement" has its difficult dramas. Let us end with an account of a walrus hunt by a group of Polar Eskimos in Greenland:

> Those of us in the boat were watching intently. This type of hunting is extremely dangerous. The Eskimo must strike the animal near the head with his harpoon. If he misses, the enraged walrus will go on the offensive. He will charge straight on. With his red eye, the walrus quickly takes the measure of the battlefield, and the hunter must absolutely not let the animal drag him toward the *querencia*, the territory where the animal and the rest of the herd like to stay. A kayak is very likely to be overturned in this area and stove in by the maddened beast. This happened recently to Kaalipaluk. He described to me how the summer before, his kayak had been dragged toward the main herd and had been literally crushed by one of these formidable sea elephants as he was getting ready to harpoon it. He couldn't get clear of the wreckage in the icy water. Had he been alone, he would have been lost. His companions were hard put to create the necessary diversions by shouting and striking the water with their paddles.

The Dream That Came Back

◇MISTASSINI CREE◇

I have heard of many people having dreams which actually happened. I have had many dreams myself. I will tell you one of the dreams I had. I had this dream early in January, before my wife's death. I was married to this woman for a long time.

We were out along the coast. I had just returned to the wigwam after a hunt. That night, I dreamt about a woman, I dreamt of a woman. When I went out hunting, sometimes I used to wander off the trails which led to my traps, as I tried hunting for partridges. I used to do this often. In my dream, I was doing this. I dreamt I was wandering off among the trees. I dreamt I was wandering off and finally I reached a woman. I imagined the woman was sitting inside a wigwam, although my dream was not clear if she was in the wigwam. The woman looked very old. She had two children. As I looked at her, I did not feel very comfortable. I had a sad feeling towards her. I dreamt I was unable to speak to her. Then, I dreamt about one of my children who passed away. I dreamt she was here with her mother. Finally, I woke up from my dream.

When I woke up, I did not tell my wife about this dream. I was thinking about my dream and I thought, "Maybe I was dreaming about a big kill." I did not tell this dream to my wife or anyone else.

There was no marten near the area; we were only trapping mink. I had set traps for the mink. There were plenty of rabbits, too. My oldest son Albert was a fully grown man then. He used to accompany me when I was setting traps far away. My second-oldest son was able to hunt, too. I only have two sons and one daughter living, of all the children my wife had.

Albert and I were checking fox snares. My other son was out checking rabbit snares with his mother. We were going to take him with us but he was out with his mother. It was February fifth when we were checking the fox snares. It was very far from camp where the snares were. I was carrying my gun. I had my gun loaded as I thought I would shoot at partridges if we saw any. The gun was able to hold six shells. As we were walking, I shot at a partridge and that left five shells. I checked the next fox snare.

Then we stopped and made a fire. It was a very clear day with a slight wind. While we were eating, I had a very strange feeling. I had a feeling which wanted me to continue walking. I was very anxious to continue. Quickly, I packed my things and set out, without my son, on the journey. I came to a lake, which I crossed. The night before, it was snowing very heavily. As I came to the middle of the lake, I saw a person's tracks. I wondered who the person could be, I wondered who it was. I did not worry about it. Then I remembered it was snowing heavily just the night before. When I realized it was a person's tracks, my wife came to mind, first. As I came close to the tracks, I recognized that they were not human tracks. I followed the tracks and then I saw another set of tracks. Then I realized it was a polar bear's tracks. I decided to follow them. The tracks led up a river towards the coast. My son had gone to check fox snares along the coast, very close to where the bear was heading. I thought the bear would reach my son before I could catch up to it. I thought if the bear was walking in the woods, I probably could kill it. I kept following it and soon I saw my son Albert's tracks. His tracks were heading back inland. Then I saw the bear's tracks going in the same direction my son was going.

The bear had followed him. I knew my son had not built a fire because he was going very fast. As I came close to one of the fox snares, I could see the polar bear at the trap. Then the bear started to walk towards another lake. It was going across the lake. There were two cubs, following the mother. Sometimes the bear would look back at me. Just before the bear went across, I saw my son Albert's tracks again. The bear started to run towards the woods. I continued to follow it and readied my gun. It was going to where some trees had fallen. I followed it. I did not want it to go any farther into the bush. I had very light loads—ammunition—with me. I did not want to let go of my axe, in case the bear attacked me. I shot it. I hit one of her eyes, thinking she would not be able to wander very far. Then I could shoot her elsewhere. People believed that if you talk to a bear, it will understand you. I started talking to the bear, saying, "What are you trying to do?"

Then, the bear started to walk away and moved back a bit. I moved to an area where there were many fallen trees. The bear started to walk away with her cubs. I looked at them. The mother was not moving. I could not see the cubs. I had only one bullet in my gun, as I shot her again. The bear was not very far when I shot her. I left my packbag, still carrying my axe. She started to move. Then I followed her across a very clear area. When my son was young he was very short. I used to encourage him when we were out hunting. The bear was hopping along in the clear area (like my short son's movements). I said to the bear, "Albert, why are you leaving me behind?" The bear sat down. When I reached her, she was looking at me. I was very close to her and she was hardly moving. All of a sudden, I felt sorry for her. I was wondering what I was going to do with her. I did not have a strong rope with me. I had some string, but it was weak and I figured it would break if I dragged her by it. I decided to use my gun and shot her right under the arm.

I went up to her; she was about the size of a large husky dog. I buried her in the snow and covered her with boughs. When I returned to my son he was making a fire. He said, "Did you kill a lot of meat?" After I finished eating I made a trail leading to the bear. I built another fire. Then I followed this trail back and followed another trail leading to the snares. When I finally reached home, I told everyone I had killed a bear. I gave the mother bear to my father and the young cubs to my son. This is when I finally told about my dream, the dream that I had. I told them, "There was a woman with two children. I dreamt that I was walking among the trees when I reached her and her children. She had two children. She acted very strange. I felt very uneasy with her. Then I started to dream about my wife. Then I woke up."

My father said to me, "Your dream meant that you were going to kill the bear and her cubs." I was really convinced about this dream.

Then, that same month, my wife died. When she died my dream came back to me.

The Hunter and the Goats
◇THOMPSON INDIAN◇

A party was out hunting goats in the mountains of the Utamqt country. They consisted of a father and several sons. The father was known for his wisdom. They hunted many days, but could not find any game. The father knew what was going to happen.

One night when they were in camp, a goat came within sight. Now, the youngest son had been training for the hunt, practicing his running and shooting. He was very swift, so his father told him to run out and shoot the goat. The boy killed the goat in one shot. While he skinned and cut up the meat, he prayed and treated the remains very respectfully. He spread fir boughs on the ground, and laid the pieces of meat very carefully on them. Then he tied the meat together with packing line and wrapped fir twigs around everything.

He had finished, and was just about to leave for camp, when he saw a woman approaching. She was good-looking and had a white complexion. He wondered who she could be. He knew nothing about her. She came up to him and asked him to accompany her home. He said, "No, I can't go with any woman. I'm in training, and it would ruin hunting for me. I must keep myself pure." She praised him for his skill in hunting, for being so careful with the meat, and for showing so much respect for the goat. Then she told him that if he went home with her, he would gain the knowledge to become an even greater hunter. He said he'd go with her. Leaving his pack of goat meat, he set out. She carried his bows and arrows.

Finally, they arrived at a high cliff and entered it through a crack, which immediately closed behind them. Everything seemed very strange; suddenly the young man passed out. When he woke up, he saw that he was in a large cavern, and there were goat men and goat women talking to each other. They all welcomed him. Then the woman he'd traveled with said, "For now, I'm your wife. This is the cavern of the goats. You hunters can't find us here. I'm a goat too. This is rutting season."

Now all the other goats left. The woman took a very large skin belonging to an old male goat and put it around the young man. "Let's go and join our friends," she said. She opened the cliff, which shut again once they'd passed through. Bounding off to a grassy slope surrounded by cliffs, she said to him, "Jump on the rocks!" He did that. Then she said, "Are you now a goat?"

"I am," he said.

"Then," she said, "go to the female goats and rut with them."

The other goats were all on the grassy slopes above, and he went up there, but the younger he-goats attacked him and gored him badly. He went back to the cavern and told the woman how he'd fared. He said, "I am too heavy." Feeling sick, he lay down. She changed his skin, replacing it with a younger goat's, then sent him out to rut again; but the male goats ripped him up. He returned to the cavern. Then the woman changed his skin to that of a middle-aged goat and sent him back; but the he-goats drove him away.

Now it was nearly morning, so she changed his skin for that of a young, strong goat in his prime; then she went to the band of goats herself and mingled with them. The hunter felt much lighter now. When he reached the band of goats, he drove all the he-goats off. Then he rutted with all the female goats, old and young, including his wife and mother-in-law. He finished just at daylight. Then all the goats went home and slept.

When he woke, he saw an attractive she-goat and tried to rut with her. She refused him. "You have to wait till night," she said, "and rut with me and all the others, too."

He rutted for four nights in a row. Three times each night the he-goats drove him off, but the fourth time he won out. He had all the she-goats to himself. He slept all day long.

After four nights and days, his wife took his bows and arrows and said, "Follow me." He went with her, and all the goats followed too. They came to a very high precipice of slanting rock. She said, "You must slide down with us to the bottom." She slid down first, and he followed her. The other goats all slid down. Reaching the bottom in safety, the goats all said good-bye to the hunter.

His wife said, "Here's your bows and arrows. Now you'll be a great hunter and will be able to follow the goats on the precipices where they walk. When you kill goats, treat their bodies respectfully, for they are people, too. Don't shoot she-goats, for they were your wives and they'll bear your children. Don't kill kids, for they may be your offspring. Only shoot your brothers-in-law, the male goats. And don't be sorry when you kill them, for they don't really die, but return home. The flesh and skin you keep, but their real selves go back home." Then she lifted up his pack of goat meat and fitted it to his back. "If you keep my counsel," she said, "even when you carry an entire goat on your back, it will seem so light that you will hardly know you are carrying anything."

They parted, and she went home and the hunter returned to his father's camp. When he arrived, he roasted the meat for his father, and after they had eaten it all, he gathered all the bones together and wrapped them up carefully. He put them in a pool of water, and bathed in the pool. The next morning, when he washed himself, he couldn't find the nose-bone of the goat. When he went to the camp, he wouldn't talk or eat, because he knew that his father had taken the nose-bone. He discovered the bone in his headband. He was angry with his father and said to him, "Why do you insult the goats?" His father said, "I only wanted to find out if you had learned anything during your stay with the goats. I did it to test you." The young man then took the bone to the pool and tossed it in.

Now, his brothers had left before he'd gotten back from the goats, and had gone to another part of the mountains to try and find game. So he went searching for them. He found them in camp. They were starving. They'd had no luck and had become so weak they couldn't walk. Immediately he went hunting and killed some goats. He fed his brothers, and soon they were strong enough to walk.

They all set out for their father's camp. On the way they saw a she-goat and kid on a hillside. The young man told his brothers that he'd kill the goat, and said for them to travel on home. He got close to the goats and was about to shoot them when the she-goat cried out, "I am your wife. Beware of shooting your wife and child!" He felt ashamed. "I'm sorry," he called out. "I was too hasty, and forgot your advice." The she-goat went up and embraced him. "Be sure to follow my advice," she said. "If you don't, it will be worse for you. You nearly shot your child just now. Never again think of shooting a kid. Don't you know they are all your children? And never think of shooting a she-goat. They are your wives."

Now the she-goat and kid went away and soon were out of sight. A he-goat appeared in sight within easy range. It came near the hunter and stood still. He shot it, and carried the meat to his brothers, who he soon caught up with. His brothers said, "That's not a she-goat." He said, "No, she ran away too fast."

"You don't have to lie to us," they said. "We already know all about your living with the goats, and that the she-goats are your wives and the kids your children."

Soon they arrived at their father's camp, and on the following four days the young man hunted and killed many male goats. They had all the meat they could carry; so they went to their home on the river, all carrying heavy loads of meat.

Agdlumaloqaq, Who Hunted at the Blowholes in a Far, Foreign Land

◇ I G L U L I K   E S K I M O ◇

Agdlumaloqaq told his fellow villagers that the places where he went hunting every day at blowholes were so far away from their customary hunting grounds that it was like hunting in a far, foreign land. But nobody believed him. And since nobody would believe him, he invited one of the neighbors to go with him on his hunt. They set off very early in the morning, but it was dark before they got to the hunting ground. During the night they passed two small cracks in the ice. It was now well on in the night, and they still kept on. Then they came to a piece of land, crossed over that, and went on over the ice on the farther side. Here at last they came to a blowhole, and Agdlumaloqaq made ready his implements and prepared to wait until a seal came up to breathe. Towards morning, Agdlumaloqaq got a seal, and they now prepared to set off home with it. Agdlumaloqaq proposed that they should go home together, but his companion wanted to stay and try to get a seal for himself.

Agdlumaloqaq then hurried off home alone, and arrived on the same day he had caught the seal. Now that he was alone, he made good time. But the whole day passed, and his companion did not return. At last several days had passed, and still he had not returned.

It happened in this way with the companion: he had caught a seal and had set off toward home with that seal, and had gone on day after day and in the end had eaten up the whole seal, and was now nearly dying of hunger. Finally, he found his way back to his village, half dead. And now at last the unbelieving neighbors understood that Agdlumaloqaq had been telling the truth when he said he went to hunt in a far, foreign land.

The Moose Among the Chandalar River People
◇ G W I C H ' I N   I N D I A N ◇

We hunt moose year round, but hunting is especially good in the fall. In fall during the rutting season, moose have a lot of fat on them and are not hard to kill. When we hunt moose in winter, it is too cold and there's a lot of snow and it's difficult. In early spring there is a lot of water and mosquitoes, so it is not good to hunt moose then. Also, in early spring, there are young moose, and the adults aren't fat. For all these reasons, fall, when the leaves are getting red—early September— is the only good time to hunt moose.

It is difficult to hunt moose. Even when one is sleeping far away, it hears noises. It has good eyes. It can smell things far in the distance. As soon as a moose sees something, or smells something, or hears something, it flees. Because moose are this way, they are not often killed. We only go hunting for moose when we think there is a good place for one to feed. Moose stay around little streams where there's lots of willows. When we go after one, we search for its fresh tracks. We look to see if it has eaten recently and defecated. In fall one hunts it more than at other times, and it is very pleasant.

To call a moose, one rubs two sticks together or scrapes on a tree with a shoulder-blade, and the bull moose, thinking another moose is there, comes to the hunter. When it comes to us, we shoot it. As soon as it sees we are humans, it flees from us. If it should prove to be another moose, they would begin to fight for the cow moose. Sometimes they lock their antlers, and unable to free them they die right on the spot. When the bull moose is in rut, it does not eat for a space of two weeks. It smells the cow's urine, and wherever there is a smell of urine it tears up the ground. While they are in rut this way, they are very fat, so it is not hard to deceive them; furthermore, it is not cold, and so this is a good time to hunt moose, we say.

When we kill a moose in the fall, we just cut it up and leave it there. We lay its skin over it, and above that we put something on a stick which will blow in the wind and frighten away animals. During winter, we pile snow over it. On this too we sometimes put something on a stick. Since the moose is big, it is hard to carry it home. Sometimes its two hind legs make a heavy load for one toboggan. Sometimes where we have to carry it is steep or there is a lot of brush, and then it is very hard work for us. In winter we travel with dogs, and that is hard, but in summer it is even harder to get it; among the tussocks the mosquitoes are many, the sweat pours out on us, and we stagger around here and there—it's really fun! While the mosquitoes are swarming, our packs get caught on things, and we have to free them—it's all a lot of work. Sometimes it is so hard to bring the moose back that we just move to the moose.

There is also a lot of work involved in handling moose. In fall when it is still warm, when we kill one we cut it up and dry it. We build a drying-house for it and keep a fire burning under it and dry it; we take care of its marrow, its fat, and all that very well. After the moose is dried, we bundle it up and put it in an underground cache. Sometimes we put it up on a platform cache. When we have prepared it well for winter and cached it away from the animals, we move from there and kill moose farther on and do the same thing. In winter we do not dry it, since it is always cold, but in spring, summer, and fall when it is warm, we dry moose meat in this manner.

The moose is good for many things. Dried meat with fat is tasty and its marrow is very good, and we eat pounded meat—"Indian ice cream"—made from it, and we make many things from it. There are many kinds of clothing made from it: boots, mittens, and parkas are made from its hide. The women work very hard on it, scraping the skin, smoke-tanning it, and making big boots that are quite good for going hunting. The skin of a young moose is very desirable for making babiche, rawhide thongs, for lacing snowshoes. When we make snares, we make them only from the cut-up skin of a moose. People in the old days also made bowstrings out of moose hide. Since we use it in these many different ways, the moose is truly an important animal.

When we kill a moose, we give some away. If two men are hunting, the one who does not kill a moose always gets some. If a fair number of men are hunting, the one who is the leader decides how to dispose of the kill. The food is always distributed properly. We distribute food to everyone equally, to sick people, old people, and people who are well. Young men do not eat young moose. Children and young men do not eat the marrow of a calf moose. This is because it would make it hard for them to run, so they say. Whoever we give the moose to always cooks it. He boils the head, the hump, and the breastbone all together, and after we eat, we all tell stories and sometimes we dance. The children do not drink the broth made from the head. Such it is here in the Chandalar country; enough has been said about how we handle moose. It is always a lot of work for us, but when we are young men, hunting is very pleasant.

The Woman Who Put a Bucket over a Caribou's Head

◇ POINT BARROW ESKIMO ◇

There was a married couple living close by some other people in a village. After a while, they left to go hunting by themselves far away. Now, the man was a skilled hunter. He came to the place where there were many caribou and he killed a lot of them. Other times, he'd hunt seals; he was a great hunter on land or sea. And his wife never wasted any meat. She always went after his catch and brought it back and treated it right. She always gave water to animals from the sea, to thank them for letting her husband kill them.

When the couple went to the far place and the man hunted, killing many caribou, the wife stored the meat, dried it, and put the skins up on the rack. When he'd killed caribou, the man took the sinew and the skins and sent his wife after the meat. He did his hunting in the summertime, and usually got enough meat for the year. Usually, he took just enough. This year, the couple moved far away from the village and settled among some old houses. People hadn't lived in these houses for generations. He hunted, and he and his wife kept busy.

Pretty soon, the woman got tired of the hard work she had. She was tired of the nasty mosquitoes. She stopped looking forward to summer. She started to hope that her husband came home empty-handed. Then one day she saw an empty bucket that was thrown away by someone. She found the bucket on a day when her husband had killed a caribou nearby. She knew that her husband had not yet cut off the caribou's head. She thought, "I'll put the bucket over the caribou's head." She did that.

And it seemed that putting the bucket over the caribou's head brought the husband bad luck. The next day, he had to travel a great distance before he found a caribou. And the next day he had to travel even farther away. And then one day he came home empty-handed. "The caribou," he said, "were just too far away." It was nearly winter and he was having no luck in hunting. He said to his wife, "If this keeps up, we'll starve in the winter." He tried hunting once again, but killed nothing.

Toward spring, their food was low. The woman ate with her husband when he returned from hunting, but otherwise she ate nothing all day. At last, their food was gone. Then they ate sinew and the sealskins they'd been storing. They both became very weak.

The hunter wondered why there was no game. In his weakness, he could scarcely walk, although he tried to hunt every day. Soon he had to use a staff to support him, but he still had no luck.

One day, as he staggered along trying to find game, he saw something black moving, stumbling over the tundra. He started toward it but it was hard to catch up. And when finally he came near, he heard a sound, "Haw!" It was dark now and he thought it might be another person. He thought, "This person must be suffering from hunger, too!"

When he got nearer he thought he saw a caribou, and when he was up close, he saw it was a caribou with a bucket over its head. The caribou was talking to itself: "Haw! Haw! Who will take this bucket off my head? Aaaaawh haw!"

The man walked up and put his hand on the bucket. He took the bucket off and the caribou saw him. "Even though your own wife did this to me," the caribou said, "I'll see to it that luck comes your way. Tomorrow, all sorts of game will appear."

As soon as it was light out the man came upon a caribou herd. Because he was so weak, he was able to take only one caribou. He took the back fat and haunch and started back to camp. He walked home past a lot of caribou. When he got home, his wife immediately took the meat from him and cooked it. Soon they had a feast.

After the meal, the hunter said, "Did you do anything to that caribou I killed a while back, the one that disappeared?"

"I put a bucket over its head," she said. "I'll never do that again."

For a few days after that, the man killed a lot of caribou. The wife would go out and fetch the meat, and both of them kept walking past

the caribou that had had its head in the bucket. It would always be feeding nearby, but it paid no attention to them.

The next summer the man and his wife moved down the river a ways, and were hunting seals at the seashore. The caribou that had had the bucket over its head followed them and hung around their camp for a while. In the autumn, he went away. The couple worked hard. She'd learned to be afraid of hunger. After that, they always had enough food.

The Day Auks Netted Hid-Well

◇POLAR ESKIMO◇

His name was Hid-Well. This was the way he hunted auks: He'd travel out to the rocks on a hillside and stare hard out over the water. When he sighted an auk, he'd hide well among the rocks. He'd duck down. He'd crouch down.

He'd crouch, and his legs would cramp. But he'd stay put. His back would cramp, his arms would cramp, his eyes, too, from staring hard. He'd wait for auks.

His auk net on its long pole would be upright. He'd hold it tightly if there was wind. He knew the weight and balance of his auk net so well, it was like one of his arms.

Now, an auk is a small bird, but a flock of them make a wide net in the sky. They make a net, each auk is a knot in the net, and hovering overhead the knots are moving every which way.

Hid-Well loved the auks, he loved to net them, he loved hunting auks and did so whenever he could.

One day he woke up and said to his wife, "I'm going out to net auks."

He said to his son, "You can't go this time. This time, I'm going on my own. Next time you can go."

He said to his daughter, "Your brother will want to go but he can't. If he tries to follow me, throw a sinew-rope around his legs, trip him up, then put all your weight on him and hold him down until I am out of sight. Also, cram some dirt and pebbles into his mouth, so it will muffle his voice. I don't want to hear him cry out."

He said to his wife, "If our son tries to follow, our daughter will take care of him. This will leave you free for other things."

He had breakfast with his wife, son, and daughter. Then he set out for his auk-netting place. It was a secret place. Only he knew where it was. Not even his own son knew. Whenever he'd taken his son there, he'd kept him blindfolded until they arrived. All the way his son would protest, making high-pitched noises such as auks make. Finally, he'd take off the blindfold, and they'd be at the netting place. They'd be at the rocky hillside. They'd both stare hard, looking for auks.

Well, so, as Hid-Well set out, of course his son began to protest. His auk-noises started up. Just a few steps from camp, Hid-Well grew angry and spun around and netted his own son. He said, "You can't come this time. I told you. This time is different, I can't say why. You can't come along." Then he lifted his son high into the air, as high as the auk net would go. His son was up in the air, crying out. He lowered his son to the ground. "Okay—now, go ahead," he said to his daughter. "Do as I ordered." With that, the daughter leapt on her brother. She was the older. She sat on him, then tied his legs up with sinew-rope. Then she muffled his cries with dirt and pebbles.

The great auk hunter now felt free to travel to the auk-netting place. The secret place.

He traveled through some weather that was just overhead, then ran into some weather that was down on his level, close to the ground. He saw a different weather out to sea, roiling up. He traveled through it all, and finally he came to the secret auk-netting hill. There it was, covered with big rocks. He looked around. He glanced about. He looked hard out to sea. Then he made his way halfway up the hillside. There were a few small avalanches. He clung to the hillside, he held on to his auk net.

When he reached his favorite hiding-place, he was panting. He was tired. He rested there in the sun. Then he cleared away a few rocks. He crouched there, hidden well. His auk-net was sticking up. There was little wind. He wedged rocks against it, and it held fast. He crouched and crouched. He got cramped up. He rubbed his legs.

He dozed off, but the sound of auks woke him. He saw auks in a flock. They were flying toward him. "Get ready," he said to himself. He got ready. He held his auk net tightly.

First a single auk hovered overhead, and it flew near his net, but he let it go. He was waiting for the flock. He knew this auk would go back and tell the others, "Come on, come on." He held his net still. There was no wind.

Soon the flock appeared. So many auks. So many.

They formed a net in the sky, the knots going every which way.

The auks hung in the air, right over the great auk hunter. He marveled at them. Then he stood up, and waving his net back and forth he let out a skillful cry, "Aaaaiiiii!"

Now, in the past, he would have netted a few auks. He would have been successful. He'd lower his net and take out the auks and break their necks. He'd put them in a sack.

But this time was different. This time when he lowered his net and looked in it, there were no auks to be found. The entire flock had eluded him.

He was puzzled. He said, "Bad luck." That was all he said. He rubbed a few cramps out. Then he crouched again. He held on to his net.

In a while, the flock returned. They hung overhead. There was a loud racket in the air.

He lifted himself up, he rose to his full height and waved his net, and suddenly his net flew from his hand!

"What?" he cried. "What has happened?"

And then he was lifted up, he was lifted up by auks. The auks had scooped him up and he was high in the air with them. He was in the auk net! He struggled, but it was no use. He didn't want to fall, nor did he want to stay up there. He didn't like either choice.

Now that the auks had netted him, he cried out a long ways across the land to his camp. He cried for his son. His son heard him and set out to find him. But since in the past he'd always been blindfolded, he couldn't find the secret auk-netting hill. His son wandered around, but finally gave up and went sadly home. He listened, but his father no longer called for him. He thought it might have been a daydream.

The auks decided to hover him here and there. They took him out to sea and hovered him over the water awhile. Then they took him over jagged rocks, and later they took him over deep, dangerous crevices.

Finally, the auks dropped him near the hillside. Just like that, they decided to let him go. He broke a few bones. He hobbled back to his camp. As he drew close, his wife saw him and ran out. "What happened?" she cried. "Auks netted me," he said. His wife was greatly puzzled, but said nothing. She helped him to camp.

The next day his wife's family came to visit. They expected a feast of auks. "Let's sit down and eat," said his father-in-law. "We've come a long way, and we're hungry."

"There are no auks," the wife said.

"Why not?" the great auk hunter's father-in-law asked.

"Look inside the tent," she said.

Everyone looked inside the tent. There they saw Hid-Well, who was mending under a blanket. He looked very weak, and besides that, he seemed ashamed.

"What happened to your husband?" the father-in-law asked.

"He went out to net auks," the wife said. "But auks netted him! They hovered him. Then they dropped him and broke a few of his bones. Now he's in the tent."

"It is a hard thing to believe," the father-in-law said. Then he passed around some plaits of sinew and some rancid walrus meat. "This will be our supper," he said. Everyone ate that. Without auks to eat, they were all disappointed. Some cousins groaned and complained. Inside the tent the great auk hunter heard this, and he felt ashamed. He wept.

The next day, when everyone woke up, the great auk hunter said, "I'm hobbled and I have a few broken bones, that is true. But I'm going auk-netting. I'll be gone awhile. Wait here."

Of course, the great auk hunter's son protested. He said, "I'm going too!" And this time his father said, "Yes, all right. I have a plan for you."

Still, he blindfolded the son. They traveled to the hill. There he took the blindfold off.

"Now," said the father, "I am too weak to climb up to my usual place. You go up there. When you get there, hide well among the rocks. Then make your auk-call."

The son climbed up and hid. Soon he made his auk-call, which echoed out to sea.

The father stood with his auk net, waiting.

"Cram rocks into your pockets," he called to his son. "If the auks try to net you, you'll be too heavy." The son put rocks into his pockets and he held fast onto a big rock. All the while, the son made auk-calls.

The auks flew in. The flock hovered, and the father netted a few. The auks flew out to sea, and when they returned the father netted a dozen. The son had killed some with rocks, too.

They put the auks in a sack.

On their way back to camp, the son said, "Did you fall down on the rocks?"

Angrily his father said, "Auks netted me! That is what happened."

They walked to camp.

At night, a campfire was built. People feasted on auks. Everyone asked how the day went. The father and son told of netting auks. The son said he made auk-calls. The father said the son made auk-calls and he netted auks. The son said that his father netted auks and that he, the son, killed some with rocks.

"And the auks lifted you into the air today?" the father-in-law said.

"No," said the auk hunter. "Today they didn't."

"No," said the son. "Not today."

Lake-Dwarves

◇EYAK INDIAN◇

A man was out hunting on foot. He came upon some lake-dwarves. He stood there and watched. Before him, boating around, were two little canoes filled with these lake-dwarves.

Just then a mouse came out. To their eyes it was a brown bear, that mouse. The dwarves got into a scurry over the mouse. Many dwarves shot at it with their bows and arrows, until at last they killed it. Then, lo, they saw a second mouse, and they were going to kill this one too.

The man was watching that. "Wha—? What is that?" he pondered.

After the dwarves had killed the second mouse, they landed their canoes and proceeded to tow the two mice to shore. These wee people began butchering the mice the way brown bears are butchered. They took off the skin. Then they cut up the carcass. It was quite a struggle to load that mouse meat into their boats. It took two dwarves to carry the hind quarters, the mouse thighs. They worked very hard until all the meat from the two mice was loaded into their boats—the ribs, the spine. They took the mouse spine too. That lesser little mouse, for them, was a black bear.

While they were bustling about over their work, preoccupied with the mice, the man reached down and plucked up one of the wee people. He took him and tucked him under his belt.

The dwarf pleaded with the man. "Please, these things I hunt with, I'll give them to you if you release me. They are yours if you let me go. You will become a great hunter if you free me." The little fellow was begging the man quite pitifully. "I will show you my weapon." He handed it to the man. It was the size of the man's thumb, like a strawberry leaf. Then the dwarf said, "Put this inside your rifle whenever you are going to shoot anything." The man set him free.

The other lake-dwarves were at their boats and ready to leave, waiting for their comrade who was missing, who had disappeared from their midst. The hunter had freed him and he was running back to his people. When he arrived they asked him, "Where are your weapons?"

"I gave them away. That's how I managed to get back here. A huge man, big as a tree he was, grabbed me! I got him to release me by giving him all my things."

"Maybe it was a tree-man," they said to him.

"No, no. He was a person. He was the size of a tree, though. A huge person. He was enormous. He had clothes on and he stuck me under his belt. I offered him everything to pay him off. I finally gave him my lucky hunting-leaf and for that he let me go."

"Quick! Hurry up! He'll come upon us again."

The dwarves put out their boats, paddled across the lake, and got home.

My, how their women came running down to meet them! Their little husbands had killed a brown bear and a black bear and had come boating home to them. The little people brought the meat ashore. Although it was already evening, the women hung the meat in the curing-house right away, just as it was. The next day they would cut it into strips. Some went to bed, but it was expected that at any time the man would come.

They had boated clear across the lake. There was no way for the man to walk across, because it was such a deep lake.

He too went home. After all, he was out hunting for black bear when he came across these lake-dwarves.

The Mammoth Hunters

◇KOBUK RIVER ESKIMO◇

Now and then, mammoths come around. One time, near the Salmon River, a man was out hunting. His name was Ataogoraachuak. He was hunting marmots in the mountains. He wasn't wearing any boots, he never wore them while hunting on the rocks—he was barefoot. That time of year the marmots were fat. In a while Ataogoraachuak had caught two marmots, and he ate them both. But while he was up on the mountain the weather got foggy. He stayed on the mountain trail, and when he looked down the creek he saw some great big animal walking along, as though it was floating, barely touching the ground. He could see its breath.

Ataogoraachuak trailed this animal, which was floating just above the ground. And then he saw that three men were following the animal, tracking it. The men had spears and they too were walking along without touching the ground. And soon, two of the men walked right up to Ataogoraachuak while the third man went on following the big animal. The two fellows said to Ataogoraachuak, "Our companion will catch up with that mammoth just up ahead."

"I don't want to go see it," Ataogoraachuak said.

The two men thought Ataogoraachuak was lazy and offered to pay him to go down and see the mammoth. "If you go down there to the mammoth," they said, "you'll become a great shaman. You'll always know where bears hole up in the wintertime. You'll be a great seer."

But Ataogoraachuak didn't want to go down. He said, "If you will fix it so I can cut jade and drill it with my little finger, I'll go."

To Ataogoraachuak's great surprise, the men said, "Sure, okay, it's done. From now on, you'll be able to drill jade with your little finger."

So, they all walked down the path and soon they got to the mammoth. It was lying dead by a lake. This was a great, huge animal with long curved ivory tusks growing out of its head.

The three men, who walked without touching the ground, went to work divvying up the mammoth.

Now the three hunters said to Ataogoraachuak, "Go and fetch some wood and build a fire so we can cook mammoth meat."

Ataogoraachuak got the wood, all nice and dry, and piled it up, but when he tried to light it, it acted like green wood and wouldn't burn. And when the wood wouldn't burn, one of those hunters took off his clothes and walked to the lake. Then he went under the water and fetched some wood! And when he got back with wood from the lake, right away he built a fire with it and it burned like it had kerosene on it. Then the three hunters started to eat, and when they'd eaten some, they put some meat in their packsacks. Before they set out, they told Ataogoraachuak, "Go on home, and when you've walked a ways, turn around and try to look at us."

So Ataogoraachuak started home, and in a while he looked back at the three fellows, and they were up in the air! They were walking with their packsacks up in the air!

Now, when Ataogoraachuak got home, he took out some jade and found he could cut it and drill it with his little finger. Everyone in his village knew then he was a great shaman.

Those fellows that hunt the big animal with ivories live up in the air, halfway to the sky above us. They too are oldtime shamans. From the past. When the weather is bad around here, those fellows go hunting. When the weather is fine, and clear, they stay home. Only shamans can see them. The name of the big animal with ivories is *kilyigvuk*.

Why Woolly Mammoths Decided
to Flee Underground
◇ CARIBOU ESKIMO ◇

I heard about Noah in church, and I found out later for myself what really happened. This story is about Noah. Noah and his family were starving. By the time they got north, they had eaten all the animals. Finally, the wife and children died. It was just Noah left. So he was out looking for more animals. He had eaten every animal on the boat. A long travel. Very long. Finally, after all this travel he found some animals around ice floes. This was far north of here, where walrus live. Bible says two, two of each got on that boat, but that's not it. Around the ice floes, a lot of animals got on the Ark. Walrus got on. Seals got on. Gulls—other birds.

All the people drowned where Noah came from. But up there, Eskimos were around. They saw the Ark out there. They were curious, and came around. Well, the thing was that Noah didn't know what to do. He didn't know how to hunt. So some people showed him some things. He was not good at calling in animals, but still some got on his boat.

Well, one day some people were out hunting woolly elephants. These had big curved tusks. People were hunting one and closing in on it. The elephant was chased out near the sea, so it swam out and got on the Ark. But the tusks tore into the sides. Some people went out in kayaks and repaired it. The ones who were after the elephant repaired it. They said, "Now, in exchange for our help, let us have that elephant." But this Noah said, "No, I need it. I'll kill it and eat it." With this, the people got in their kayaks and left for home. They did not allow the Ark to stop at their village.

Now, Noah managed to get more walrus on the Ark. So he had plenty to eat, awhile. But in the winter, the ice locked the Ark in. People saw an elephant walk right out away over the ice. The boat was locked out there, and Noah ran out of food. He'd eaten all the walrus. He didn't know how to hunt seals through breathing-holes. He didn't know about ice-fishing. He walked to the village and begged for food. But the people there stuck him with spears. They didn't poke them into him—only pushed him away. He went back.

Now, some people were out hunting another elephant. It was bad weather. Again, they were chasing it. They were almost close enough to kill it, but then it ran onto the Ark and its tusks went in and it got itself up onto the boat. The people said, "It's ours. We need it." But Noah said, "No, it's mine. I'll kill it." But as he didn't know how to use a spear properly, when he threw he missed the elephant. With this, the elephant left the Ark and fled underground, so as not to be killed improperly by this person. After that, elephants lived underground. During the thaw, the Ark sank.

Sometimes a Seal Hunt Goes Like This

◇ S O N G I S H   I N D I A N ◇

The wife was a troublemaker. The husband was not lazy. He simply had poor luck in hunting. He hardly ever brought any food home. The wife's two brothers—now, *they* were great hunters. They'd built a sleek canoe. They'd go out, and they'd lug home seals, porpoises, and fish.

Well, one day the husband walks home and says, "Whew, I'm tired! Whew, I've been gone four days hunting."

He says, "Is there any supper?"

"No," says his wife.

I told you the wife was a troublemaker. Because the truth was, her brothers had brought home lots of food. They'd fed the whole village! But the wife made her two children sprinkle ashes on their wooden platters and glue ashes to their lips to cover any food-grease. "No, my brothers gave us no food."

"Did they bring any home?" asked the husband.

"Yes," said his wife. "They lugged in some seals, porpoises, and fish. They sat over there. They ate. They feasted. We could hear them all day and night. 'Hey, toss us some fishbones at least!' No, no, no, they said. They said no between gulps and bites. Me and the children watched."

"I see you've fed our children ashes," the husband said.

"Now I know you want to kill my brothers," said the wife, "but I'd rather you just put a spell on them. My grandfather taught me one. You turn a seal into a magic seal. I'll tell you how." And she taught her husband the spell.

The next day, the husband hollers, "Look! Out on that rock in the harbor! Isn't that a big seal out there, where you usually hunt? Look, it's arching its back."

The brothers-in-law looked and grew eager. They said, "Hey, thanks." They got their canoe. It was light. It was sleek. It was their great hunting canoe.

"You'll make short work out of that seal," the husband said.

The hunters paddled out, and got near the seal-rock. The seal arched its back, it showed off its fat and meat. The seal-hunting brothers were eager, they harpooned the seal.

The seal slid into the water, and when it surfaced it let out a roar. "It's roaring a whirlpool!" one brother yelled. It was true—a treacherous whirlpool had spun into view. It caught up with the canoe and spun it, spun it around, and one hunter cried, "Let go of the harpoon rope!"

"I can't!" the other shouted. "I'm stuck to it!"

"This isn't natural!"

The seal's whirlpool spun the brothers to a mysterious place. "Where are we?" "I don't know."

Instantly, the world was covered with fog. The seal pulled the sleek canoe along, the seal dove and surfaced, dove and surfaced. Each time they came up for air, it was a new day. The canoe was pulled along for many days and nights.

Finally they came to an island. "I think we're under a bad spell," one brother said.

"Has to be," the other said.

"Where's that seal now?"

"Pull in the harpoon rope."

One brother hauled in the harpoon rope, and pulled up a gnarled tree. It was mostly a stump—it was horrible-looking.

"Take a look at that," one hunter said. "That horrible thing pulled us all this way. It's part of the spell."

"Where's the seal, then?"

"Long gone."

"That's the most hideous-looking stump I've ever seen!"

"It's part of the spell, all right."

"I think we've crossed the ocean."

"Let's haul the canoe ashore and lie down and hide."

They hid a long time, and then suddenly a child came into view. The child was paddling a canoe big enough to hold an entire family. He looked like a human boy—looked like it, but the truth was, it was a hideous dwarf disguised as a boy. That's what it really was. It was part of the spell.

Suddenly the boy dove from his canoe into the water, and when he surfaced he held two big halibut in his mouth!

He flipped them into the boat, and there were two other halibut already in there. He was a great halibut hunter, this boy.

"Did you see that dive?" one seal-hunting brother said.

"He went deep for halibut," the other said. "He was down a long time. He has good lungs."

Now the child dove again. He was down a long time. When he surfaced, he had four halibut in his mouth.

In hiding, the seal hunters whispered, "It sure makes us hungry, watching the boy catch halibut."

"Hey," one said, "next time he's down, let's grab some halibut from his canoe. He's got a lot. Let's grab some and eat them. My mouth's watering."

The other brother said, "All right." He agreed. His mouth was watering, too.

They quickly got their canoe down to the edge and paddled out and grabbed some halibut. They got back on land, down behind some driftwood. They got there with the stolen halibut. But pretty soon the boy surfaced with a loud gasp. "He's up," one brother said.

The boy looked around. He counted his halibut and saw that some were missing. He stood up, and this is what he did: he started pointing, he moved his hand along in the air. He was pointing toward shore and suddenly he stopped, and his hand pointed *right* where the seal hunters hid. His hand pointed at them.

"What's he doing?" one brother said.

Suddenly—this happened very fast—the boy leapt to land, wrestled down the two seal hunters, and put them in his canoe. He then fastened their canoe to his, and towed it along. He'd kidnapped the seal hunters!

He took them a long ways until they landed on an island. It was a strange place. There were some red houses! There were a few striped houses! And lots of people lived there.

Everyone was a dwarf, tiny little people, lots of hideous sorts. When the seal hunters next looked, the one who'd kidnapped them was pretty awful-looking, too. In fact, now he was crunching some shellfish in his mouth.

Lots of mollusk shells were piled around. These dwarves were great divers and shell hunters. "Did these dwarves put a spell on us?" one brother said.

"I think it was somebody back home."

Now, it turned out that the dwarves treated them pretty well. They were fed soup—soup at first, because their stomachs were empty. Later, they ate king, silver, and dog salmon.

"These people are great divers, shell seekers, and salmon hunters," one brother said.

"They are hideous-looking, but they can truly dive," the other brother said.

"I think they know some things, too," one seal hunter said. "I think they can tell us by their magic who put a spell on us!"

"Listen," one brother said to the dwarves, "gather all your people together. We have a story."

The seal-hunting brothers carefully explained what had happened— no, no, they *began* to tell. Suddenly the oldest dwarf said, "We know already what happened." The dwarves knew about the seal hunters' misfortunes. They knew about the whirlpooling seal, about the long journey, and about the horrible stump. They knew about the fog.

"You are wise," the brothers said. "So, who put a spell on us?"

"Your sister," the older dwarf said.

"No!" the brothers cried. "No, it couldn't be!"

"Well," said the dwarf, "it was your brother-in-law, but he learned it from her!"

"We'll have to kill her," the brothers said, mournfully.

"The halibut hunter will escort you back," the dwarf said.

That proved to be true. The halibut-hunting dwarf, whose halibut they'd stolen, escorted them home. It took many days. When they got home, they went to their sister's house, intending to prick her with duck quills for a whole night. They had decided they couldn't kill their own sister. They were going to stab her a lot of times with duck quills, though.

But when they got to her house, they found that their sister, her husband, and their children were gone. There were ashes on the wooden platters. "Of course they're gone," one seal-hunting brother exclaimed.

"Of course," the other said. "They'd have starved here alone without us." They cleaned off the platters, and put fresh halibut they'd caught on them.

Now the story's done. A lot happened to the seal hunters.

Don't forget, I told you that wife was a troublemaker.

And anyway, sometimes a seal hunt goes like this.

PART EIGHT

Wolf's Bride,
Star Husbands

Stories About
All Sorts of Marriages

LOOKING BACK ON THREE MARRIAGES of his own (he was widowed each time), Thomas Iliuq, a Caribou Eskimo, said, "Marriage . . . it was the funniest thing that ever happened to me. And the most dangerous." Covering as wide a spectrum of human emotions are the stories about love, courtship, and marriage in this part. Here we find jealousy, sibling rivalry, lust, abiding love, adultery. These tales present marriage not only as part of tribal tradition but as a fitting complement to the fundamental strangeness of life in the North, in which little is stable, absolute, or predictable.

Take, for instance, the Eyak tale "The Woman and the Octopus." While out doing the everyday chore of picking blueberries, a woman is abducted by an octopus. Once they remove to the octopus's lair, where he "turns into a man with her," the woman experiences a kind of enchanted delusion and sees what must surely be a cave under a rock as a big house: in her mind, then, she has connected the domestic worlds of land and sea. Later, we hear a touching acknowledgment: "The woman had gotten to know him. In fact, she had gotten quite used to the octopus." The interspecies couple move from familiarity to intimacy: "She had octopus babies, two of them."

But then again, in mythic times all sorts of marriages took place, part of the commonplace social intercourse between animals, spirits, and mankind. Such marriages quite often strengthened these bonds, but they could also create permanent hostilities. "In Indian stories," said Michael Elk, a Blood Indian, "anyone took up with anyone else. Otters you saw every day could marry off their son to a girl in a people's town. Sometimes it worked out, other times no." In this section alone we have a raven, a jay (whiskey jack), a whale, an octopus, a wolf, and a grizzly bear, each in his own fashion and for various periods of time wed to a human being. Men or women marrying bears is an especially popular motif across the entire arctic and subarctic.

Full of heightened emotion, whimsical complications, long journeys, hope, and abandonment, these tales tell us that much of love is in the waiting. And if the wait for a mate is a long one, it often reveals the infinite capacity for longing and expectation we all share. This is touched upon poignantly in the Athapaskan tale "The Star Husbands." In this story, twin sisters lie awake at night considering the possibility of marrying attractive stars. Suddenly, as though their very musings were wishes come true: "My goodness! Someone was sleeping with them!" The star husbands take them to the sky. Yet in the end, the twins' longing is not well met by reality. Their marriage to the stars cannot sustain them and they return to earth. "Well," as one twin explains to the stars, "we were lonesome. You think we'd stay where we can't see our daddy, our mama? We don't see our sister or brother?" The human family is reunited.

Clearly, even when love arrives, fate may intervene. In the Snowdrift Chipewyan story "Go Away" we witness an unrequited love that, in its tenacious grip on a man named Crazy River, has something of an epic tragedy about it. Crazy River loves One-Who-Squints, who does not return his love. Eventually she marries another and has children. One night, even as Crazy River sleeps elsewhere in her village, she whispers emphatically to him, "Go away." Finally, Crazy River becomes a great hunter and uses that reputation to woo One-Who-Squints. Alas, she remains faithful, even though her own husband is a poor hunter. Given his desperate love for One-Who-Squints, it would perhaps not be far-fetched to say that Crazy River was inspired to *become* a great hunter as part of his ill-fated courtship. In many northern cultures, a man's prowess as a hunter, a provider, meant he would therefore make a good husband. "In old days especially," said Mary Kiladvuak, a Copper Eskimo, "a good hunter, you'd say: He's a good catch."

Of course, marriage was an emotional partnership. Yet it might be said that, historically, the tradition of marriage in the North was predicated most importantly on economic necessity. In her oral memoir, Quajukasuaq, a Polar Eskimo, says, "Families kept each other—took care of each other. The men brought in animals, women fished, too, but there was much work to do at home. It was good to be married, to be part of a family, and have it work well." The family and extended family, then, constituted the economic unit sustained by the community's central enterprise: hunting. As a rule, in Polar Eskimo villages a young man had to prove his abilities as a good hunter before marrying. He had to show that he could support a household. As many accounts bear out, life wasn't easy for widows, widowers, and single persons in the North—a man without a wife or daughter, for example, found it hard to keep up his household. And many northern tales deal with barren women, some of whom had husbands who abandoned them. Indeed, sometimes a marriage was not really recognized unless there were children. By and large barrenness was considered a harsh fate. Such women were pitied, even ridiculed, and in rare instances shunned and feared as bewitched. In certain arctic tales, unmarried women, too, are depicted as suffering great stress, often resulting in wild, irrational, even murderous behavior.

Courtship and marriage rituals varied tremendously across the North. In Inland Tlingit villages, for instance, where the entire social system stressed relative seniority, women often married much older men. Arranged by elders of the tribe, marriages strengthened ancient lines of kinship and power. A considerable bride-price was often paid, and a son-in-law might be required to provide for his wife's parents until their deaths. Yet in certain Eskimo groups, the attitude toward marriage seemed at best lackadaisical; we hear of couples "falling into" or "happening into" marriage. They simply begin living together and—even into old age—may move freely in and out of each other's lives. According to the St. Lawrence Island Eskimo tradition, families might arrange an infant betrothal; when the children grew up, they would be married. At some point in adolescence, a sequence of events that were recognized as a "marriage" took place. A groom would begin his "groom-work," which lasted for about a year. He had many duties, including hunting with his future father-in-law. During that year, he lived with his wife-to-be's family, but finally the couple moved in with the young man's parents. When this happened, a group of the bride's immediate kin would arrive with a sled loaded with walrus-hide rope, tools, food, and other useful items. With this event, the marriage contract was complete.

When the ice-hearted giant threatens the tradition of marriage in the Cree Indian tale "The Windigo Almost Prevents a Marriage," it is living up to its reputation of violating some of the most vital elements of the human life-cycle: birth, lovemaking, marriage, even funerals.

And while in this tale the entire community rallies to fight the horrific windigo, it is the groom himself, One-Who-Is-Quiet (a good hunter), who is the most powerfully resourceful; he actually turns into a weasel, the one animal that can kill a windigo. As a weasel, One-Who-Is-Quiet climbs down the windigo's throat and chews its heart. The storyteller, John Rains, told this tale a number of times; when he told it in July 1970, he ended with a humorous aside: "Whew, that man musta really wanted to get married, eh?"

Raven Didn't Stick Around

◇TLINGIT INDIAN◇

Pretty far north of here, up up there, lived a beautiful woman who didn't want to get married. She had a lot of suitors, but she turned them all down.

But one day a handsome young dude shows up. He was dressed in the best. He had on a ground-squirrel parka, long wolverine trim, and these fancy mukluks. He was dressed!

She fell right in love with him, in hardly no time. It happened fast. Snap your fingers—like that fast.

"Hey, hello," he said. "Hello," she said. "You in love with me yet?" he said. "Yes," she said. Like that.

She brings him home and says to her father, "We're married."

The father says, "Can you hunt caribou?"

The dude just scratches at the ground with those fine mukluks.

"Okay," the father says. He gives his son-in-law some arrows.

Off he goes to hunt. But he comes back, all the arrows are busted up. He's got blood all over him. He's got nothing to show for it, either, no game.

The dude just stands there, and the father-in-law starts to sniff. Sniff, sniff, sniff. In the air, like that. He says, "I smell a raven's asshole," he says. Everyone started searching for the raven, including the handsome dude. They search all night, using lamps. Sniff, sniff, sniff, but they don't find it.

One day, after the dude goes off hunting, the father-in-law tells a young man, "Go follow him. Come back and tell me what you see."

When the dude gets a ways from the village, he stops by a big rock. He takes off a mukluk and scrapes it, and then he scrapes the other one. He tears up the boots. He pecks at them, tears them up. Then he shoots arrows at the rock, busting them. Then he punches his own nose. He punches it and it's bleeding all over the place. Then he goes home.

But the man who'd followed him got back first.

The beautiful woman's father gets everyone together, and he says, "I've found out that somebody here has three toes!"

He goes around. "Everybody take off a mukluk," he says to the men. When he gets close to the son-in-law, the dude cries out, "What's wrong with three toes? Why's five toes so great?" He takes off a mukluk, and everybody sees he's Raven.

"Daughter," the old man says, "now you see you've married Raven. Raven's busted up his own nose a lot of times. He's torn up his mukluks. He can't hunt caribou."

"No, no, no!" she cries. And she takes off with the dude Raven. "Let's go to your parents' house."

Raven takes her to his village. They walk into his house. All there is to eat is caribou stomachs. "It all smells like ravens' assholes in here!" she cries.

"Hey, here's a meal," Raven says. "Stop complaining."

"I'm going back!" she cries.

Raven says, "Okay." He flies off. He didn't stick around. He didn't stay married long.

This story comes from up Eskimo way.

Kivioq, Who Left His Home Because His Wife Was Unfaithful

◇ E A S T   G R E E N L A N D   E S K I M O ◇

There was once a man named Kivioq, and he had a wife. But a young man came seeking her favor. When the husband came home after he had been out in his kayak, he would always find the young man sitting inside passing the time with his wife. And if he had brought home any catch, his wife's mother would go down and haul it up, while his wife herself and the young man would look on holding each other by the hand.

Kivioq, displeased, made up his mind to go away on a long journey. And now whenever he came home with a saddleback he would say, "Here is skin for mittens." He would require a great store of these on a long journey.

And at last he had many, for each time he came home he said he had lost one of his mittens.

One day someone asked his wife's mother to beg a little blubber of him.

"This is for your winter store," he said.

"Where is he thinking of going now, I wonder?" said his wife's mother.

And then one day when he was out in his kayak, he rowed right out to the open sea. And when he turned around to look at the land, it was almost out of sight.

He rowed on again, and when he next looked around, he could no longer see the land. On his way he came to a place which was full of sea-lice. (When we see a piece of driftwood which is full of holes, then we know that the sea-lice made them). He flung his bird arrow out at them, and they ate it up in a moment. And then, seeing that he risked losing his paddle if he tried to row through them, he took a piece of the skin which covered his seat, and cutting it into thongs, bound it about the paddles. In this way he rowed safely through the swarm, for sea-lice do not eat thongs.

And thus passing on his way, he came later to a place where the snouts of many spotted seal were to be seen sticking up above the water. And these he simply passed by.

And still passing on his way, he came to a place where the guts of bearded seal were to be seen, all bulging out as if they had been filled with water.

"Who can have filled them out thus?" he thought, and rowed on.

But at the same time he heard a voice out of the air, which said:

"This place is the Middle of the World!"

Then he rowed on and came to a place where the sea went bubbling around in a whirlpool.

"What can this be?" he thought.

"This is the Navel of the Sea," said the voice in the air.

And after a time he sighted land, and went up to look for a house. And he found one, and likewise a number of kayaks placed on trestles.

Then he went into the house.

"I left my village because I was jealous," he said as he entered. And then he stayed there.

In this house there were two women; they had no husbands, but used the frame-post of the house.

Now he lay down on the bench, and there he lay, looking at the frame-post, which had many projecting knots in the wood, and it was these which the women used.

He was so angry at this that he sprang up and cut them all off with an axe.

When it grew light in the morning, the women said to him, "Tell us when it is low water."

And he went out, and came back a moment after and told them that it was now low water.

And then they went out and looked at the land and at the sea and said, "No; you must not call it low tide until the sea has passed out of sight."

And when the sea had passed out of sight, the two women went out hunting, and the man would have gone with them.

"No," they said. "You must not go with us until you have grown accustomed to it."

Nevertheless he went with them a little way, but when he saw a great number of strange creatures lying about in places which at other times were covered with water, he was seized with fear and went back again.

Later in the evening the women came home with bladder-nosed seal on their backs.

On the next day they went out again, and this time he went with them. And after they had traversed all that land which at other times was the bottom of the sea, and at last reached the water, there lay the seal, crowding together like crawling maggots.

Now the women sought out their game, took a couple of fjord seal that had recently shed their old coats, and went home with these seal on their backs.

"When you hear a rushing noise, make all haste in to land," said the women.

And then they heard a roaring far out at sea, and the women set off at a run towards land, but the man could not keep up with them.

At the moment when he was about to spring up onto the land, a wave closed over him. But they caught hold of him and hauled him ashore.

When the next day dawned, they went up inland to a lake to catch eider duck. And in the evening they came home with as many as they could carry.

On the next day the man went up, taking an axe with him, to look at that lake. He took off his clothes and went into the water. When he got out into the lake, a great penis rose up out of the water, and as soon as it appeared, he hacked at it with his axe, cutting it through, and red blood spread out over the lake.

And now he saw that it was for this the women had gone to the lake, and that all the eider duck they had brought home were its gifts.

When he got back, he sat down on the platform as if nothing had happened, and when they spoke to him, he answered carelessly.

Next morning while it was yet early, the women went off as usual to the lake, and sat down on the shore to wait. But as nothing appeared they went home again.

And now they began to suspect the man, and turned from him in anger.

On the next day the man went down to his kayak, feeling now ill-disposed towards the two women. And he rowed home.

He came rowing along, and was nearing land, and his wife had gone up into the hills as usual, but a falcon, which had seen him, flew over the woman's head and cried:

"There was once a time when there lived a man named Kivioq!"

But the wife went down and told her mother what the falcon had said. Her mother grew sorrowful at this and bowed her head.

Then the wife went out again, and saw a kayak come rowing in towards land. The man was wearied, for he dipped his elbows in the water.

"That looks as if it really might be Kivioq," said the wife. "Thus he was wont to row when he came home wearied with much rowing."

And she went down to the shore, holding the young man's hand as usual. And when Kivioq saw them thus, he turned his kayak outwards again and cried, "Now I am filled with longing for those stranger women once more."

But he was then so close in to land that an old woman was able to grasp the bow of his kayak and hold him back. And she persuaded him with words, until he stepped ashore and went up to his house.

And there he sat, in the guest's place, his wife and the young man in the place of the host. But now he turned to the young man and said, "Let us pull arms, and the stronger take the woman."

And wearied as he was, Kivioq seated himself on the floor and began wrestling with that young man.

And the young man could not match his strength.

Thus this matter was brought to an end, and Kivioq went up into the host's place beside his wife, while the young man crept shame-facedly to the side platform.

And here ends the story of Kivioq.

The Windigo Almost Prevents a Marriage

◇ S W A M P Y   C R E E ◇

In a village lived a man who did most things very quietly. You could hardly even hear him eating soup. "He's quiet," everyone said. "Yes, he's quiet."

"That's him over there, whittling on some wood. He never talks louder than the sound of whittling." That too was said about him.

This man was going to be married soon.

So he lived there, in the village. Of course, he was a good hunter, too. Quiet is good to take hunting with you. Quiet helps in catching many things.

One day he said, "I have a trick. I am going to hide somewhere in the village. You try and find me." He hid then. Others tried to find him, but they couldn't. They looked everywhere in the village, but they couldn't find him.

Then someone shouted, "Look, over there, what's that noise?" Every-one looked over to a kettle. From inside the kettle came a loud noise. "Something's in there!"

"It's One-Who-Is-Quiet."

"Yes, he's in there!"

"No, it's too loud to be him!" another man said.

"Calling out from inside a kettle can make anyone loud!" still another said.

They went over to the kettle. They looked inside it. There they saw some snow had gathered. On this snow were some weasel tracks.

"He's turned into a weasel!" a man said.

"I'm not going to get married in that kettle," said the woman who was going to be the wife.

Then she said, "Don't use that kettle for cooking. That would cook my future husband!"

Then she said, "Come out of there, out of that kettle!"

Just then another kettle, across the village, began making noise. Everyone went over to it. When they looked inside, there too was snow. Again there were weasel tracks on it! "He's tunneling through the village, from kettle to kettle!" someone said. Everyone agreed.

With that they gathered the rest of the kettles together in the middle of the village. There they waited for One-Who-Is-Quiet, who was a weasel now, to arrive in a kettle. They waited by the kettles for him, for the kettle-weasel.

"Let's eat some food!" someone said.

"No," another said, "we can't use any kettles yet!"

"But we're starving," a man said.

That went on for several days. It was getting difficult not to use a kettle, and someone said, "We'll have to take our chances in cooking that weasel up!"

"No, it's a windigo causing all this!" an elder said. "We have to find it and kill it."

Some hunters set out. They walked all day. That night, they made a camp. They made a fire with a kettle over it. They had brought one kettle with them.

Soon the windigo arrived at the hunters' camp. When it arrived, one of the older hunters shouted into their kettle, "We know you're in

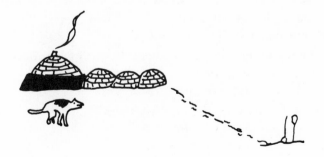

there! Help us now!" And with that the weasel ran out of the kettle snow and down the windigo's throat. It bit the windigo's heart, which killed it. So the hunters returned to their village. There they found the man who was about to be married. He was in his house. He said, "I've been here, waiting." Later, the wedding took place.

That is the story.

The Star Husbands

◇ A T H A P A S K A N ◇

There were twin girls, and their mother and daddy are still alive. But these girls haven't gotten married yet. They're full-grown women. So one night they get ready for marriage.

Nighttime, and they're asleep. Then one sister says, "Look, sister, if we want to marry those two stars in the sky, do you think they'll marry us? I like that one star, there, the one that's a little grey."

The other sister says, "I like that one, the one without any grey, the one that just shines bright. I want that one for a husband."

They talked about it and talked about it. They don't know if they're good-at-hunting husbands. In those days, people married lynx, wolverine, everything. Or a wolf or a marten.

The twins slept then.

My goodness! Someone was sleeping with them! One sister wakes up. The man sleeping with her has grey hair. He looks good. She looks for her sister. Somebody's sleeping with her. She calls, "Wake up!"

"Yes," the sister says, "I'm awake."

"Where did we get these men from? Where are we?"

"Well," the men say, "last night you talked about us. You wanted to marry us. That's why we got you."

"Where's our daddy?" the twins said.

"Well," the men said, "he's down there on earth. Your daddy, your mama, they can't come up here."

The twins have nothing to say.

"Well, what do you eat?" the men ask them.

"Well, we eat meat, fish, like that."

"All right, we're going to get that for breakfast." The star husbands go off to get a gopher.

The one girl didn't like her husband. He was a little bit old, you know. Her sister had a nice young fellow.

Quickly the husbands came back, bringing ten gophers. The one girl knew how to cook gophers. She singed them, skinned them, cooked them up.

Well, on earth their mama was looking around. Everything was the same, except that her daughters were gone. Her daughters were just gone!

The sister married to the older man told him to bring home lots of game, lots of caribou, lots of marten.

"You want a blanket?" one husband said to his wife.

"Yes," she said, "a marten blanket."

He brought her marten skins, and she made a blanket from them.

"What do you want for a blanket?" the other husband asked.

"Lynx," the other sister said.

He got her a lynx, and she made a lynx-fur blanket.

Then the husbands say, "You know the village we found you in? Your daddy and mama miss you there."

The oldest husband says, "We're going down there. Going to kill game for them. Going to leave it. What does your mama like to eat?"

"Well, she likes caribou and sheep to eat, and she likes marten and lynx fur."

The mama and daddy were asleep. They don't know that the star husbands have arrived. The daddy gets up early to hunt. The sun's not up yet. My goodness, right in a pile, marten, lynx. The meat's already cut up. Fat. Everything. He wakes up his wife.

"Get up," he says. "It's our daughters who sent this meat to us. Oh, just fat, meat, fur, everywhere."

Next, up in the sky, the girls say, "We like fish. Bring mama and daddy fish."

The daddy fixes up his camp. He doesn't want to leave camp now. He wants to stay for good. He fixes an Indian stick-house. They make a big place.

Now the sisters talk together. "You think we can go down to earth?" one says. "My husband says it looks far but really it's not. It's just our eyes that make it seem far away." Then the twins make skins into a saddle, put a string down the middle, and sit on it and say, "Let's slide down."

"Well, I'm going to take my marten skin," one says.

"I'm going to take my blanket," the other says.

Their husbands say, "We're going hunting for two nights. Two nights we'll camp and then we'll come home."

Those girls get ready. Who's going to slide down first? "Me!" one says.

"All right."

They put on their clothes. It's hard work going down. They aren't far apart, the sisters. They go down, they go down, they go down . . . When two of their mittens get friction holes, they put on new ones.

Oh my! They land.

Their daddy fixed up a camp about a mile up the creek. They walk around and find it.

They run to their mama. "Mama, we got husbands!" they cry out. "We married stars. That's where we've been. But we came down on a string."

Gee, she's surprised, that mama.

Up in the sky the husbands miss their wives. They know where they've gone. At night they make their wives dream-call for them. They wake them up. But they can't take them back any more.

"Why did you run away?" the husbands ask.

"Well, we were lonesome. You think we'd stay where we can't see our daddy, our mama? We don't see our sister or brother? It's pretty hard. You people up there just stay in one place."

"Yes, you're right," the star husbands say. "Well, we're going to feed you. We're going to give you what we've got. Anything you want, you tell us when you go to sleep. Call our names." Gone.

Some people tell this story a different way, but this way is honest, you know. Some people say they landed in a tree and they can't come down. Then a man comes and says, "I'm going to marry you."

After that, the girls married Indians.

The Girl Who Married the Bear

◇ T L I N G I T   I N D I A N ◇

Some people had been staying one day at the mouth of the river, and they were putting up dry fish—salmon. Well, they finished. They dried the salmon and stored it, and they were ready to go off to get berries. The women, just about ten of them together, went out to get berries. One young girl goes with them. There are ten women, and she is young.

She fills up a basket that big [gesture]. She fills up two baskets. Fifty pounds she has. And she puts the baskets together, one on top of the other.

When they were coming down to the camp, it was all dark. The young woman was tired of packing so much, and after a while she slipped on something. She slipped down, and she spilled all the berries from the top basket. Then she wanted to know what it was she slipped on. That's where the bear goes out [i.e., defecates]. And the girl wants to know what was on her foot. It was where the bear goes out. You know, like down on the salt water where they [bears] eat berries and go [defecate]. It's big, that big [gesture]. That's what she slipped on.

She got mad at the bear. "Where this dirty bear went out, I fell on it myself!" And she called that bear bad names because of it. And maybe the bear heard it.

So she takes the berries again that she had spilled from her basket, and some of the other ladies helped her put them back in the basket. When they had finished, she packed [carried] the baskets again.

She goes along packing the baskets one on top of the other, and after a while the packstrap across her shoulders broke, and both baskets fell onto the ground, and the berries spilled out.

That was because the bear wished it.

But the ladies came in to help her put the berries back again. One was just about half empty, and the other is full again. And she was about half crying. She put the berries back again, and all the ladies went again. It's dark. It's in the fall time. Everybody goes again.

They had gone only a little ways, and then the strap broke again on both sides. And then all the other older ladies were kind of cold. And it's raining—raining hard. And the old ladies are getting cold. So one old woman said,

"I'm going to go home now." And pretty soon all the other ladies wanted to go, and they left her alone to stay and pick up those berries all by herself. She had a husband at home, and when the last woman left her, she told her to tell her husband to come and meet her.

When the young woman started for home, she had just gone a short little way when she saw somebody coming. He had a little bearskin on his back. It was a man. She thought it was her husband. He used to wear a bearskin on his back when it was raining. And she kept crying. And when he was coming, he said,

"What's this crying for? I'm here." He wiped her eyes. "Quit crying. Let's go now!"

The husband was packing the berries. And they kept on going and going. That is a bear taking her away now.

They go and they go, and after a while he tells that young woman to walk quick. "It's getting dark on us!"

And after a while she sees a big windfall about five feet high. You know, down on the coast there are big trees. He goes under it. That's really a mountain. The lady thinks it's a windfall, but that bear knows it's a mountain, and he goes under. And then they go and go, and after a while they go under again. She thought it was another windfall. And they go under again.

And after a while they go on the side of a mountain, and they camp there.

"We're lost," he says. "We go the wrong way," he tells the lady.

Next morning she wakes up. She sleeps all right, but in the morning early, just before the man wakes up, she wakes up, and she knows it [i.e., what has happened]. She is sleeping on the ground, but in the evening she had thought she was in a house, her own house. But in the morning when she wakes up and opens her eyes, she knows it's a camp around her. And that morning she sees bear claws on her neck.

Then after a while the bear wakes up, and that lady shuts her eyes. She doesn't want to move. When the bear gets up, she looks at him, and it looks like her husband walking around. And he makes a fire and cooks. And when he finishes cooking, she gets up and eats. She doesn't see it. Lunch too. But all the same, the man cooks. She doesn't see where he does it.

In the morning after they have their breakfast, the man says, "I am going to hunt for groundhog. You stay home and make fire," he tells her. He goes.

In the evening time he comes back home. He packs a big sack full of groundhogs and gophers. He cooks it, and when they are going to leave, he packs it.

When he comes back in the evening, they go to bed again. And in the night the lady wakes up again and wants to know for good what's wrong here. Then she knows it's a grizzly bear that sleeps with her. And then she is quiet again and goes to sleep.

Next morning she wakes up again. In the evening time he had packed home what he had gotten—groundhogs—but there is nothing left. They are all gone. And she doesn't say anything. She doesn't see anything around, but all the same the man is cooking something. And when he puts it down, it is groundhog that is cooked already. And she takes it and eats it again.

When they are through eating in the morning, he tells her to stay home again and get lots of wood. "I'm going to kill groundhogs." And when he came back in the evening he had a big pack again full of groundhogs and gophers and things like that. And he did the cooking in the same way.

And they stayed there about a month and did things that way. And they didn't save anything at all. In the fall, late in the fall, the man says,

"We are going to be late in having a winter camp, a winter home. Let's go look now for where we are going to stay in the wintertime to make a home."

And then they go, and they have a big pack with dry groundhogs. She never sees it when they stop, and she never sees him drying them at all, but when they walk off from the camp, her husband has a big pack of dried groundhog just the same.

They camp in four camps in four days. They were on a high mountain. It's near a big river on the Alaska side at Chilkat. It's called *tsu.m.* It's the highest one.

You see where the mud comes down from the mountain, that's the place the bear found on the mountain, where all the rocks wash down and spread out in the valley below. That's where the bear dug a hole. As soon as he finished digging the hole, he told his wife to get boughs.

"Don't get them where the wind blows the boughs and the brush," he told her. "Get them down low."

So the girl goes out to get the brush, and she breaks the trees up high. She breaks the boughs off way up high . . . She brings the brush back and throws it down by her husband. The bear comes out and smells that brush and tells his wife.

"Why did you break the brush up high? Somebody is going to find us!" he said. She breaks off the brush too high, so they are going to see it. Bears break their brush over and under their arms. People break brush by turning it down.

Then he is mad. The man gets mad and slaps his wife. And he goes himself to get the brush . . . And he gets the brush and something just like roots for putting on the ground. He brings the brush and everything together for the ground. The ground is icy, and he throws roots and brush into the hole and breaks it up. That way he finishes the hole.

When he comes in the evening time, he wants to eat. He cooks something. It's groundhog meat and gopher, but the woman never sees the groundhog. All the same, the man cooks some.

Then they camp three nights. It seems as though it is three nights, but really it is three months. The man told her, "Feel outside how soft the snow is!"

The woman is going to put up on the door-place, because she is getting used to staying with the bear. The woman has begun to carry a baby. It seemed like it was only three months, but the baby seemed like six months. She feels the baby already. That's because the bear has babies quicker than people. She has a big body showing she is having a baby.

After a while, when she is going to feel the snow outside, first she feels her husband all around his body like she is loving him. She hugged her husband and stroked his hair all over.

Then she moved outdoors and felt the snow. Then it's soft. She makes a big snowball with her hands, and she knows the snowball will slide down. She knows that the den is high above a snowslide. She throws the ball down to the bottom of the hill to the creek.

The girl has four brothers staying at the mouth of the river.

After a while, in April when the fourth month comes, the girl feels sick because she is going to have a baby. In the middle of the night which was really half a month, two little baby boys are born to her. In three and a half months she has babies. When they are born, the palms of their hands are like a person's [indicates smooth], but the backs are all hairy. It is all hairy on their backs too, but their stomachs are like humans'. Their feet were the same way.

In April when there first began to be a crust on the snow is the time that the brothers would want to go hunting bear with their dogs. The oldest brother has two dogs, bear dogs—big dogs—good hunting dogs.

For a long time her brothers and all the townspeople had known that the girl was really taken by the bear when she was out berrying. The four brothers went out together. The youngest one was only a kid. The other three have wives.

The oldest brother tries first, but he never gets any bear. Next time the second oldest one tries to get the bear. He comes back home in the evening, and he has got nothing. The next day, the third one tries it. He doesn't get anything.

The youngest kid is always sleeping. When the oldest brother comes back and his kid brother is sleeping yet, he says,

"You're no good! Do you think you are going to get your sister?"

Well, he just wished to himself that he would try it; he knows he is going to get his sister.

So the third one tries. And the next day that youngest boy never sleeps. After a while he puts his moccasins on. And he goes, and keeps on straight to the high mountain. He keeps on to where they used to go in the summer, and he has those two dogs with him.

After a while, he sees that snowball. And the dogs get into the place and smell the bear. And he follows them to where the snowball came down. And the two dogs run up the mountain. And after a while he hears the dogs barking up there. And he walks up and up. And after a while he sees there is a bear. He sees the hole, and the dogs are in it. He sees the two dog tails in it. They are barking and barking.

He has no way to hit the bear. He has a bow and arrow, but he has no way to shoot it, because the dogs are in the way. He tries to pull them out. And after a while he hears somebody talking inside that hole. The voice was talking to the dogs. One dog's name was *calsaᵘa*

[?]. The other's name was *kusadago ic* [*kucda^{kw}ic*, little otter, father, Tlingit?]. The person said,

"You ought to keep quiet now! You can never quit barking!"

She knew her brother's dogs. She is inside. And then the dogs go out.

And the man told his wife, "Those are your brothers. They are going to kill me, but when they do kill me, see that you get my skull! Get my whole head. You go get it. When they stretch my skin, make a fire right along where they are stretching it, and put my head in the fire and burn it up."

That day when the brother came to kill him, he did not fight back. He never threw him down the creek. He never rolled down. He just lay there quietly. The three brothers below came to meet the fourth one, because they heard the dogs barking up on the mountain. They went to meet the youngest brother.

When they were skinning the bear, the oldest brother told the youngest one to go into the cave and get the arrow he had shot in there. When he went into the bear-hole the girl was way in the back holding her two babies—one on each side. She tells her brother,

"You skin the bear good. That's your brother-in-law, *i kani* [your brother-in-law]! Treat him good. It's good to use to eat," she said.

When they skinned him, they cut one side of the ribs out to roast it. When they finish, the sister is sitting on the bear-nest.

When the youngest brother saw his sister inside the den, he came out. He tells his oldest brother,

"I see my sister in the bear-hole."

And they don't believe him. "You're no good! You're no good to your sister."

"I know I see her good! She has two babies. On both sides she has a baby. I see it!"

So the oldest brother says, "Let's go look at them! All right, go ahead."

Then they go fast. The first thing, the oldest brother looks in the back of the bear-hole. And then he starts to cry when he sees his sister. He cries and cries, and his sister keeps still. Then she says,

"Keep quiet, brother! I'm not going to be lost much longer!"

Then the man stops crying, and the girl says to him, "When you go back home, *ik*, younger brother, tell my mother to come meet me and bring snowshoes for me."

So just as though it's nothing, they go back home without packing anything. They want to get home quick.

Just as soon as they see the camp, they holler out, "We got our *dlUk* [sister]!"

Nobody believes them. They tell their mother, " *'ax dlUk* [my sister], she calls for you to come with snowshoes." Their mother doesn't believe them either. When they say that, she too doesn't believe them. All the same, she puts on her moccasins and goes, and she packs an extra pair of snowshoes. And she walks and goes to where her daughter is.

When the girl starts to walk out from the hole, she starts to cry and cry to be back at home. She tells them,

"Someone can fix a camp for me, out of the way, way out from where the townspeople stay."

She wants to camp alone.

And they fixed the camp there already. She came home and stayed in there.

That same spring she tells her youngest brother who got her that she wants to have a good time bear hunting. She tells her brother,

"I see smoke, *ik* [younger brother], bear-smoke." [Jake explained as an aside: "The bear has a camp in wintertime. But the bear lives just like a person. He has a fire, and it smokes right in his den."]

"Where?" her brother asks.

"Out there. You see that tree standing up? Right there. You go there and look for it."

He goes and he sees a bear right there every time she says that. Anytime when he is lonesome he asks his sister,

"Can you see any bear-smoke?"

"Wait," she says. "I'll see some!" Then she looks across at the hill, and after a while she sees some. And she tells her brother, "There's a bear there!" She can tell how many bears there are too. Just the woman can see the smoke. Nobody else can see it. She tells them to look by the tree.

After a while it is summer again, and they fish again. And after a while in the fall, they go to get berries again. And they hunt bear again in the fall time. They see three grizzly bears coming out of the side of the mountain. A family. There is a female with two cubs about a year and a half old. She sees them first, and she tells her brother.

"There are more bears up there," she says. "There are three of them. First thing when you clean them up [kill them], don't fool with them," she tells him. "If you fool with them when you kill them, they are going to take me away," she said.

And then they go up there, and they kill the bears—all three of them. And they skin them, and they bring the feet and the skin. And they eat some in the evening. Before the sun goes down they finish their eating somewhere.

Then they tell their mama,

"Mama, can you tell our sister? Let's play with her. We want her to put on the big bearskin, and the cub skins are for our sister's sons!"

And the mother starts crying and crying. And they keep on telling her they want to play with their sister. After a while the mother goes to the daughter and tells her,

"Your brothers tell me they want to play with you. You put on that bearskin and walk just like a bear coming out on the side of the mountain."

And the girl starts to cry. And she gets mad and sore, and she says, "How can they talk that way? I am going to be a bear forever now!" she says.

And the girl is crying and crying. And after a while the menfolk come themselves. They tell her,

"*dlUk*, we want to play with you. We want you to put this bearskin on. And these here are for our nephews."

"What for do you say that? I used to tell you not to fool with those bears! Now I am going to put the skin on. You come quick and see us in the mountain!"

She takes the bearskins with her. And she takes the little one, and she shakes it on the child. She turns the little kid around this way and puts the bearskin on the baby's back. She puts it on four times that way, and then it fits right on. She grabs the other kid and does the

same way again. And a real bear comes out again. Then she picks up
the big skin and puts it on herself that way and walks out. She's a bear.

The oldest brother told his sister, "*dlUk*, we are going to shoot our
bow and arrows, but we are going to use spruce bark for the arrowheads
instead of iron points."

When the brothers were sneaking up to where their sister was eating
berries like a bear, the youngest brother looked at her, and it didn't look
like a person, but just like a bear. When he saw that his sister looked just
like a bear, he took off the spruce and put a bone [sic] point on. A strong
one too. When he saw her, the oldest brother hit her first. She goes right
behind a tree. The other two watch. The youngest brother has a good
arrow. When they shot their bows and arrows, the bear turned around
and just grabbed the three brothers. And those young bears come behind and just tear them up, the three brothers.

The younger brother that is behind, he hits the bear-sister good—
right in the throat. He does it because his sister has turned into a bear.
The arrow goes through and stays in the bear's collarbone—just as big
as a finger. That is where the younger brother shot the bear.

Then the bears went away from their home forever. They never
came back to the camp any more. They had killed the three brothers.
Only the youngest brother was left. He was all right. This is the end
of the story.

How Whiskey-Jack Man Got Married
◇ N A S K A P I   I N D I A N ◇

An old woman had a camp with her daughter on the Notakwanon
River just north of here. All this old woman ever did was scrape caribou
skins. But she wouldn't eat the caribou meat, oh no. She ate people.
Best eating of all was men. Young, good-looking men. She'd send off
her daughter and the daughter'd come back with some trapper from
the bush. Well, he was in *her* trap now. She'd crack his head between
two large stones and suck out all his blood and then eat him.

So Whiskey-Jack Man comes along. The girl she takes off all her
clothes and dances around and lures him back to camp. The old creature

was scraping away at her skins. She was real hungry, like. Whiskey-Jack Man picks up what she's scraped off and eats it, just like a whiskey jack itself, eating hell's worth. The old woman she tried to crack his head on her stones, but Whiskey-Jack Man's too smart for her. They fight. He hops around, she hops around, cracks the two stones together, nothing. Then he grabs her by the neck and swings her round and round and throws her far as the Torngats. Dead.

The girl claps her hands. She's free at last. For she's just like any other girl, but she happened to be under the bad influence of her mother. A mother that ate men. Whiskey-Jack Man he married the girl.

The Woman and the Octopus

◇ E Y A K   I N D I A N ◇

Once there was a woman who went out picking blueberries with her child. While she was standing about berry picking, something interfered with her.

Something grabbed her foot. Something interfered with her foot, and she said, "What's this clinging to my foot?" She looked at it. It was an octopus sitting there. "What are you doing?" she said to it. "Long-Fingers," she called it, and it immediately wrapped itself around her. It wrapped itself around her and started dragging her down toward the shore. She cried out, but who was there to hear her? There was no one to hear her because she was alone with her child. The child wailed for her mother. She said, "It's taking me into the water!" As it dragged her away into the water, she said to the child, "Go home. Tell what has happened to me, that the octopus has wrapped itself around me. Tell my uncles of me. This is already my last breath."

Nothing happened to that woman. The octopus dragged her into the water and it turned into a man with her. He took her into a house, a big house. It was probably a chamber under a rock, but in her eyes it was a house. The octopus married her and she lived with him.

He would always go hunting for all kinds of things, fish, anything, which she would eat. When he caught a seal, he would lie down on top of it to cook it. That's how he cooked them, by lying down on top of them, and she ate them. Cockles, all those kinds of things too, he would cook them that way, by lying over them and right away they would start to cook.

Some time after that the woman's brothers were traveling along in their boat. The woman was sitting on a rock, a skerry. The octopus had gone hunting and she had climbed up onto a skerry and was sitting on it when her brothers saw her. "There she is, our sister, sitting on a skerry there." They landed by her and said, "It's time to come with us. That's enough of living with him. You've been missing a long time already."

She said, "Let me stay here a little while yet. Let me stay here a little while yet. Your brother-in-law will hunt for you," she said to them. So they let her stay there. They went back without her. Only she did say this, "You'll come back here sometime, won't you?" she said to her brothers, and they went back without her.

The octopus came back and she said to him, "Your brothers-in-law came here to get me. I said to them, 'Let me stay here a little while yet. Your brother-in-law will hunt for you,' that's what I said to them. That's why they let me be here." He must have been a big octopus, her husband.

Then he said to his wife, "You had better tell them that they must not kill me, your brothers. Let them not kill me. Killing things is all they have on their minds."

"Yes, I'll tell them that, that you'll help them when you see them," said the woman to the octopus.

That woman had gotten to know him. In fact, she had gotten quite used to the octopus. She had octopus-babies, two of them. Octopus young.

Then he said to her, "We'll go there. We'll go to my brothers-in-law. Take those babies of yours." He had become a person, he wasn't an octopus. They arrived there and she said, "Where's that octopus you were saying had taken me away? He's a person. He has become a man." He lived with them.

Then one day he went out to sea. He made a mistake. He fought with this whale. The whale got the better of him. It killed him. The whale killed the octopus.

After that she went back to his sisters for a last visit, along with her brothers. She didn't stay alive long after that. She soon died.

The young octopuses, however, grew big and went into the water. After their mother died they went into the sea. They said, "We'll get revenge on that whale for our father. We'll kill him." After their mother died they went and fought with the whale, those children. They killed that big whale for their mother's brothers. That big whale, they killed it for their uncles.

After that, they went to sea for good. They never came back. Their uncles never knew where they went.

That's all.

The Marriage of Mink

◇NOOTKA INDIAN◇

Mink was chewing gum as he went to the place on the beach where the daughters of Sawbill Duck were working at mat weaving; both sisters were at work. He had strands of white gum extending out of his mouth as he approached. "Say! Look! My gum is white," said Mink. The pure white gum was hanging out of his mouth in long strands. "Heh, give it here, you rascal! Please pinch off a piece and give it to us," the girls said to Mink. "I won't. Mine is sweet inside, I prize it very much and won't part with it," said Mink. "Still, you rascal, pinch off a piece and give it here," the girls said again. "Well, princess, I believe I will, but only because you persist in asking for a piece. My gum is sweet inside. Don't you go spitting out its foam! Keep swallowing it!" he said. Then he pinched off some of his gum and gave it to the older sister, but did not give any to the younger sister. Then Mink went home.

The young woman started chewing the gum in the way she was told; she kept swallowing the foam. Sawbill's daughter finished chewing. Not long after, she became pregnant. The father was ashamed that, chief as he was, his daughter had become pregnant in an irregular way, and that no one had had the courage to woman-purchase from him. He kept asking his daughter by whom she was pregnant. The young woman did not know, and said she had never done anything with anyone. The father asked, "Who has been coming secretly to lie with you?" The young woman insisted that no one ever came to lie with her, that she did not know what could have caused her to become pregnant.

Sawbill's daughter gave birth to a boy. The Sawbill people were ashamed of what their princess had done; they had been disgraced. The baby became aware of things. It began to say "dada." The chief of the Sawbills gathered his younger brothers together. "We will have that baby look for his father. We will do it over there in the middle of the beach on a canoe platform." "Very well," said the younger brothers, "let us do so." In the morning they made a canoe platform and paddled off, to the middle of the beach at Maakoa. Each one of the Sawbill family had a board in front of him on his canoe and was holding a beating-stick. They took Wren, the senior chief, first. "Now then, Wren, come down to the beach, that it be yours as father! Daddy! daddy!," ran the song. Wren went down to the beach; while he was yet at a distance, the child turned away from him. Wren was ashamed that he was turned away from.

"Now then, come down to the beach, Red Woodpecker, that it be yours as father! Daddy! daddy!" sang the Sawbill band again. While he was yet at a distance, Red Woodpecker too was turned away from. He too was ashamed. There on the ground were all the people, for that was the time when all kinds of birds and animals were still human beings. The Sawbill people picked up the song again: "Now then, come down to the beach, Redheaded Woodpecker, that it be yours as father! Daddy! daddy!" Redheaded Woodpecker also came down to the beach. He too was turned away from while yet at a distance. "Now then, come down to the beach, Fish Hawk, that it be yours as father! Daddy! daddy!" Fish Hawk came down to the beach. He too was turned away from while yet at a distance. "Now then, come down to the beach, Eagle, that it be yours as father! Daddy! daddy!" Eagle came down to the beach and he too was turned away from. They called out the names of all the birds there were, and they were all turned away from while yet at a distance.

Now the Sawbills began calling out the names of the animal tribe: "Now then, come down to the beach, Bear, that it be yours as father! Daddy! daddy!" Bear came down to the beach. He also was turned away from while yet at a distance. The animals were called severally by name. Elk came down the beach. He also was turned away from while yet at a distance. Deer came down to the beach. And he too was turned away from while yet at a distance. Land Otter came down to the beach. He too was turned away from while yet at a distance. Raccoon came down to the beach. He too was turned away from. They had called everyone in the animal tribe. The baby turned away from all of them.

Now only Mink remained. The Sawbill people again took up the song: "Now then, Mink, come down to the beach, that it be yours as father! Daddy! daddy!" Mink wore shredded cedar bark about his head. He came down to the beach. "I guess you would be the princess's lover, you who are a slave," they said to him. He came down to the beach and while the rascal was yet at a distance, the baby began waving his hands: he recognized Mink as his father. At once the baby took hold of Mink and hugged him about the neck. He had come to be from the gum Mink had pinched off and given away. It had turned into a person, become a baby, because Mink, it is said, had been chewing his private parts and had given a pinched-off piece to Sawbill's daughter, which had made her pregnant.

So the rascal became her husband, indeed became the husband of both sisters. Mink was nearly killed by the chiefs because they were jealous that he had married beautiful women, that he had married princesses.

"Now take us to gather sea-eggs," said the older daughter of Sawbill to the one who had become her husband—Mink. They set out on the water, all three with the baby in a canoe. They went to the two islands called Burned-Around, where there were many sea-eggs. When they reached the islands, Mink looked down into the sea and saw many sea-eggs on the rocks. "You two, stop! stop! There are sea-eggs on the rocks," he said to the sisters, his wives, who were with him in the canoe. The sisters stopped paddling. Mink took off his clothes. He dived under the water and came up to the surface, holding several sea-eggs in front of him. "I will first have some for myself," he said. When he had eaten all, he dived down again in order to get some more. Again he came to the surface, carrying many sea-eggs. "I will first have some for myself," he said again and once more he ate them himself. His wives were longing to have some, but he ate them all and again dived under.

The younger sister now looked down under the water. "You old hag, look and see what our husband is like!" she said to her older sister. The older sister looked under the water and there was Mink, moving about, dragging hemorrhoids which extended out some distance. "We will leave him behind on the rocks; he is too nasty," said the older sister. Mink came up to the surface again and once more ate up all the sea-eggs. As soon as he dived under again, the older sister jumped out of the canoe and went to the stern. The Sawbill sisters paddled off hard. They left Mink behind on the rocks. He found that his wives were far off yonder, paddling away. "Say! come here now! I've got some for you," called out Mink. "Get some for yourself now, you with your head cut off," said the daughters of Sawbill. They only paddled along with more force, both sisters together. "Come back! I might say things about you," said Mink. "Go ahead and say things, you beheaded one," said the young women. "Ya! you with your urethras fastened on with gum," said the rascal Mink. He swore at his former wives. The Sawbill sisters continued to paddle away toward home.

They left their former husband behind on the rocks. They disliked him for being bad in that he always put the hemorrhoids out of his anus. Mink was abandoned on the rocks. That is why the Burned-Around Islands are now stocked with many minks, for it is said it was there on the rocks that Mink was stranded. Well, that is what Mink did.

The Wolf's Bride

◇ C A P E   P R I N C E   O F   W A L E S   E S K I M O ◇

There were two people, a man and his wife, living alone with their only child on the seashore. They didn't know that other people existed, until their daughter reached womanhood. One morning she rose as usual while her parents were still asleep, and went outside to look around the horizon. As she gazed, she saw something black a little way inland, which she watched for a while, then went over to examine. She found a freshly killed caribou, so she returned home and told her parents. They immediately rose, and all three went over, cut it up, and carried it home. That day they had a good feast, and in the evening retired to bed just as usual. While they were sleeping, the daughter woke with a violent throbbing of the heart. She started up and looked around, and saw what seemed to be a wolf's tail. However, it disappeared, so she went to sleep again and was not disturbed any more that night.

The following day there was no sign of anything, and when evening came the family all retired to bed as usual. For the second time, the girl was awakened by the violent throbbing of her heart. She opened her eyes rather sleepily and saw again what looked like a wolf's tail; but just as before it immediately disappeared, and she fell asleep again and did not see it any more. When she again went outside and scanned the horizon in the morning, leaving her parents still asleep, she saw something black down on the sea ice. She went over and found a freshly killed seal, so she returned and told her parents. Her father told her to bring it in, and when this was done, he cut it up, and they ate heartily of seal meat that day; then at night they went to bed. Once more the girl was awakened in exactly the same way, but as she looked slowly around she saw, not a wolf's tail, but a wolverine's. This time she rose and took her lamp-stick and went outside; but whatever it was had disappeared, so she went inside again.

Next day she could find no trace of anything, but in the evening they heard the footsteps of a man outside. Then the door opened and there entered a young man whose clothes were fringed with wolf fur. He sat down opposite the girl and said, "I have come at my father's bidding," but before he could proceed any further more footsteps were heard outside. The door opened a second time and another youth entered. This one wore clothes fringed with wolverine fur. He sat down beside the first youth and said to him, "You may have got here before me, but I am going to marry the girl, not you." "No, you are not," the other replied, and the two began to wrangle. Then the girl's father told them that if they wanted to quarrel they had better go outside, so they both got up and went out. Presently the family within the hut heard heavy stamping up and down outside. However, they took no notice, and after a time the noise died away, so they all went to bed.

In the morning the girl saw two tracks outside, one a wolf's, the other a wolverine's. They were covered with bloodstains, and when she followed them along, she saw something black ahead of her. It was a wolverine, dead, with a great gash visible in its side. She went home and told her parents, and her father warned her not to go away. They sat up that night, and about the same time as the two youths had appeared the previous evening, they heard the sound of footsteps again. Then a man entered, and he too had clothes fringed with wolf fur; but he was not so young. As soon as he came in he said, "My son is very ill, so I came to get your daughter. He may be dead already, so it is no use wasting time here talking over the matter." The two old people were unable to travel themselves, but they agreed to let the girl go, though they said that she couldn't walk very far and asked if he had brought a sled. He said he had not, but when he left with the girl, he took her hand and led her inland. Then as soon as they were out of sight of the hut, he put her on his back and, warning her not to look about, started to run; only, as he ran, the motion became more like galloping. At last he set her down just as it was growing light, and taking her hand, dragged her along until they reached his house. There he drew her down into the long passage, and they entered. In the rear of the house sat the son, with his back toward them. "Am I too late after all?" said the father; but at the sound of his words the youth looked around, and seeing both his father and his bride, he smiled. Then his mother said, "Let the bride take charge of his food and feed her future husband." The father told his wife to bring in some clothes, so she went out and after a time brought in some fine clothing. They stripped off the old clothes that the girl was wearing and gave her the new ones to put on, after which she took over the care of her husband.

The young man was woefully thin, but after a time he began to walk again, and soon was able to resume caribou hunting. Then his parents bade them return to his wife's father and mother, for they thought they might be in want of food. So the young man made ready his sled. First he set a load of caribou meat on it, then laid deerskins in the middle and made a kind of tent for his wife to sit in. When all was ready, he placed her inside, warning her not to look around. At first they traveled rather slowly, but soon their speed greatly increased. After a time he bade her to get down, and they walked a little farther until, just as dawn was breaking, they saw her parents' home. As soon as they reached it, they went inside and told the old people that they had brought them some food, and the old man asked his daughter to bring in some from the sled. She went out and brought food in. When they got up in the morning the young man wanted to go hunting, but before he left he warned them not to go outside about noon. They stayed indoors at that time, and after a while he came back with the news that he had killed some deer close by. Her parents went over and found five caribou lying in a row one after the other, so they cut them up and stored them away. The young man was very successful in his caribou hunting, but never managed to catch any seals. How could he be expected to seal when he had always lived on the land? But his father-in-law gave him his own sealing weapons, and taught him to seal as he himself used to in his younger days. After that the young man would go down to the sea, spear a bearded seal, and drag it home with a special harness that he made for the purpose.

In this way they finally filled two stagings with food of various kinds. The girl's parents sent them back to the young man's father and mother, who would be waiting for them. So they got ready again. He piled blubber on his sled, then made a kind of tent on top for his wife and told her to get in. She climbed in and the two started out, traveling first slowly, then very swiftly. After a while he told his wife to get down. By this time it was broad day, for their sled was very heavy, so they rested where they were that day, not far from the houses. Later they continued their journey and reached home. They stayed with his parents, but only for a short time; soon some men came to invite the young man, Irelaq, to a dance at another place. His parents warned him that his wife would die if he took her there, adding further that there was a big bird in that country which would kill them both. However, as the runners who had brought the invitation began to make their preparations for returning, Irelaq and his wife did the same. One morning they all started out, the men pulling their own sleds and Irelaq's as well, while his wife sat on top.

They had not traveled far before they came to a river with steep banks, and the men, who until then had been walking in front of their sleds, went behind them. Irelaq and his wife dropped into the rear. The men walked down the slope, but Irelaq and his wife stopped as soon as they came to the cliff. Meanwhile the men in front crossed the river without stopping and ascended the other bank, which was so steep that they had to lean back as they neared the top. No sooner were they on top, however, than they returned to help Irelaq. They lashed his wife inside the sled-cover and lowered her down the cliff in front of them by means of ropes, themselves descending slowly behind. They managed to reach the river below. There they took her on their shoulders and carried her across, then began the ascent of the opposite bank. After they had dragged the sled up a little way, it began to rise into the air. For a moment it seemed to pause, then it rose straight up. The men climbed on top of it, and it was pulled up the cliff the remainder of the distance till finally it came to rest on the top. They moved on a little farther and at last stopped altogether, everyone uttering a deep sigh of relief.

Irelaq's wife was lashed on top of the sled again, and they traveled along to another river, which they crossed in the same way. This time, hard as they pulled on the sled, it did not move as fast as before. On reaching the top, they lashed the woman on again and continued their journey a little farther until they came in sight of some houses where the inhabitants were already singing. On their arrival, the visitors entered the dance-house and began to exchange presents. When Irelaq produced his and gave them to his host, everyone cheered and said they had nothing of equal value to give in return. At the conclusion of the exchange of presents Irelaq and his wife retired to the house of their host.

Bedtime came, and Irelaq's wife went outside. A little girl came up to her and, taking hold of her, said, "My grandmother over there wants to speak to you about something or other. Come quickly." The woman hesitated, but the girl began to drag her along, so at last she followed. The girl led her along the bank of a river till they reached what appeared to be a cavern in a small knoll. As they were entering the door the woman smelled something like blood, and as soon as they were inside she saw what seemed to be blood boiling in a pot. The old grandmother, with many gestures of affection, requested her to undress so that she might wash her. Her clothes were laid all in one place; then the old woman took down a large pan that had been hanging up, emptied the contents of the pot into it, and washed her visitor. As soon as she had finished she washed the little girl, her grandchild, and told her to pour the bathwater into the river and wash out the pan. But the child, as she passed Irelaq's wife with the pan in her hand, poured it all over her. Immediately the woman shriveled up to the size of the girl and the girl took the form of the woman. The false woman then put on the other's clothes and escaped with them. Irelaq's wife tried to speak, but her voice had changed. The old witch asked her to put on her grandchild's clothes, which she did very unwillingly and returned to her host's house. There she found the witch's grandchild hugging her husband. Irelaq, not recognizing his wife when she entered, ordered her out, and kicked her to make her go. So the poor wife had to stay out-of-doors; she could not go back to the witch's house, for the witch was not her relative.

When they rose in the morning, Irelaq and his new wife danced, the latter making a great flourish and display. At the conclusion everyone went home to sleep. The real wife was trying to get a little sleep out-of-doors, but as she dozed someone took hold of her by the front hair and raised her head. It was a little girl, who said to the woman, "My grandmother over there asks you to visit. Your kinfolk are going away soon." Then the child departed. The woman, not caring any longer what happened to her, followed the child to the river, along which they proceeded until they reached an old hut. They entered, this time through a real door, and inside the woman saw a pot full of hot water. The old grandmother said that to show her affection for

Irelaq's wife she wanted to wash her, so she stripped again while the old woman brought in a pan and filled it with hot water from the pot. Then she washed her for a while, and finally asked her if she had the same shape as before. The woman said she had, and thanked the old woman for restoring her speech, for she had believed herself incapable of speaking. The old woman asked her to throw the water out into the river, then took clean water and washed the old coat that Irelaq's wife was wearing, and because she had no clothes of her own, the old woman gave her a loincloth of squirrel skin and a pair of slippers. She handed her another pot and asked her to empty it into the false wife's ear, after which she was to throw the squirrel skin, the slippers, and the pot into the passage and wish them to return to their donor.

After receiving these instructions from the old woman, Irelaq's wife went straight back to the house, naked except for the loincloth. She slipped in quietly without disturbing anyone and emptied the pot over the false wife. Then she threw the squirrel skin, the slippers, and the pot into the passage, wishing them to return to their donor, and went and crouched down in the corner. The false wife immediately changed to her real shape, and Irelaq, springing up, seized her by the hair and flung her out of the house into the passage. Then he went over to his true wife and tried to take her up onto the sleeping platform, but she broke away from him and asked him why he did not wish to keep his new wife. Irelaq became very angry and threatened to kill everyone in the settlement. This so alarmed his hosts that they begged his wife to return to him, which she did out of affection for them.

Next morning Irelaq and his party left and traveled to the river. There they let the woman down the cliff without any difficulty, but when they tried to carry her up the other side they could not keep their footing. They made another attempt, but failed to reach even as far as they had gone before, and at last could not even lift the sled. So they made a boat of it, and laid skins one above the other on top of it. Then they made a little door in the top, and filled the boat with food and sewing materials and various other things, with a lamp to give light and heat. They told the woman that the river would take her to her parents' home. Whenever she wanted to go ashore, she had only to wish and the boat would obey her. Irelaq also told her that she would pass three villages on the way but that he would protect her. Then, after she reached her parents, he would send a messenger to her about the same time of year as his father had visited her before.

The woman entered the boat and the men pushed it off. She sewed a little, and slept whenever she felt inclined. When she wanted to go ashore she merely wished, and the boat put in to the bank of its own accord. She tried to push it off again, but it would not move; she re-embarked, and it moved off by itself. She floated down the river. Once, just after she had re-embarked, she heard a noise, and looking out, she saw a crowd of people outside their houses; but they did not see her. So it happened that every time she reached a settlement she passed unseen. Then one day she awoke to find her boat aground, and looking out, she saw that its bow was resting on the beach. Getting out, she recognized the place; it was her old hunting ground for berries; climbing a low hill, she could see her parents' hut. First she unloaded her boat and pulled it up onto the beach; then she went home.

As soon as she entered, her mother asked her if her husband had not come also. But she told them that she was alone, that her husband, after the dance was over, had set out on his return journey and she did not know when he would arrive. However, if there were any messenger he could send, he would send him in the winter at the same time as he himself had come before. The three lived very happily on the food that she had brought, and when the time came, watched for the messenger. Irelaq's father appeared. He had come for his son's wife, he said, though he did not know whether her husband would be dead or not before they got back. If he lived, however, he would conduct himself better in the future. The two set out, and the father took her on his back, telling her not to look about. After galloping for some time, he told her to get down, just a little before daybreak, and they entered the house. On the sleeping platform was Irelaq, but only his head was of normal size, so thin and shriveled had he become. His wife took a spoon and fed him on soup that contained a few scraps of meat, and with this diet he began to recover his strength. Then she fed him on a thicker broth until at last he recovered and was able to go hunting again.

They returned to his wife's parents and lived with them until the parents died of old age. Then they went to live with Irelaq's parents until they too died, worn out with years. Finally Irelaq made a distribution of all his food, two sleds laden with meat of various kinds. He told the people that he and his wife were going away to live in a place

where sorrow and pain could never enter, and then the two turned
into wolves and departed.

The Girl Who Married a Whale

◇CHUKCHEE◇

Old maid.
Many young people were together there.
She's living together with her girlfriends.

Says to her girlfriends:
"Let's go get ourselves husbands."

Went out looking.

The others got themselves husbands
who'd been husbands-to-be.
She got herself
an old whale-head,
empty bone.

Head trembles,
moves about,
puts out to sea . . .

Girl wants to break away,
struggles,
can't do it—
clings to the head.

The girlfriends run after
to pull her back,
can't hold her back
and can't tear her away—
she clung.

It got deep,
he dove,
carried her into the water.
Carried her to the open sea,
arrived at that opposite shore.

There they went as far as the cliffs that shut together,
   passed through the cliffs.
       Arrived there at a village,
          lay down to sleep there.

The head became a whale;   X
he was covered with barnacles.
The wife constantly scratched   X
the barnacles with her fingers,
pulled out worms, wore her fingers   X
down to the bone.

The wife's brother's still at home,
he made a boat,
he's all the time testing it,
all the time untying it,
again redoing it.

It's still not fast enough;
again untying it,
again redoing it.

Then he sailed out on the boat.

Birds are flying above;
he's competing with them.
They're leaving him behind.

Small white bird *katajalin*,
so quick in flight—
with her

he's competing,
he's sailing together with her.

Left searching for the tracks of the sister.
 Went out on the sea-road,
  arrived at those cliffs.
   Went as far as the country
   of the wife's husband.

Eight people are traveling there,
only two walked out into that country.
(The wife's brother
left the others in the boat.)

On the road these two men are killing,
each of them a seabird,
each of them an ermine.

The two arrived there;
hid themselves there in the house,
since the sister,
having seen this,
is saying:
"Hide yourselves,
you'll be killed!"

⸰⸱ Husband says to her:
  "How strange—
  Something smells!
  Someone's come!"

"Who could have come?
You carried me
so far away!"

  "It smells,
  it smells!

        Where are they?
        Let them come out!"

The sister told them to come out.
They came out.

        "Kako!
        So you've made it?"

"Yes!"

Says to the wife:
        "Bring the fanciest meat—
        let's eat!"

The fanciest meat,
all different kinds,
she brought it.
They're eating.
Having finished,
says to her:
        "You go out,
        I'll enjoy myself
        with our guests!"

She went out.
They also went out . . .
with their teeth they bit
the dried skins
of the birds they had just killed.

They went back in.
Water came through the door—
the whole sea.

They put on the birdskins,
walked out on the water like birds—

he's not able to destroy them;
the water left.

They lit the lamp.
They're sitting just as before.
The people took off their bird-dress.
The wife's husband says:
>"Kako!
>They came here in spite of everything!
>I couldn't kill them!"

Says to the wife:
>"Carrry out the lamp!"

She carried out the lamp.
With their teeth they bit
the ermine skins.
The wife brought in a spinning-top,
then she went out.
As she went out,
they put on the skins,
hid themselves in cracks like ermines.

He started spinning the spinning-top.
In all directions of the house
he's spinning, whirring,
he can't get at them.
Says:
>"Carry in the lamp!"

She carried it in.
It became light.
They took off the ermine skins,
they're sitting in their former places.

>"Kako!
>In spite of it all they're here!"

Person says:
"Let's go out,
visit the boat!"

He says:
        "Well,
        I couldn't kill you!"

The brother says to the sister:
"Put your husband to sleep,
lullaby your husband at night!"

She made him sleep,
she caressed him well at night.

Before daybreak arrived,
the whale wanted to sleep,
fell into a light sleep.
He's fast asleep.

They arrived.
Said to the sister:
"Bring all your clothes with you!"

Arrived at the boat,
soon sat down,
ran out,
abandoned the sleeping husband.
Hid themselves.

The husband woke up,
searching for the wife;
saw the track,
went after her.

Reached them on the sea:
swimming—
barely touching the water.

They flung the wife's boot in the water.
     He stopped to look at it there.

Again he overtakes them.
They flung the other boot in the water.
     He slowed down a little.
Piece by piece they threw away all of the outer dress.
     For a long time he's there, looking at it.
They began to near land,
she became completely naked,
the brother threw away the underwear.
     He's looking at the underwear
     for a long time sniffing it,
     it smells like her skin.
Again he follows them to the land.

People stood on shore,
ready with spears.
They stabbed the wife's husband,
killed him.

At home the girl gave birth to a little whale.
Says to his mother:
     "Put me in a bowl of water!"

She put him there,
swimming there.

She's collecting all sorts of worms,
bringing them to the child,
raising him.

He grew up—
it's tight for him in the old tub—
they took him away to a lake.
When he wants to suck,
leans his head out from the lake—
his mother feeds him with her breast.

Again there's not enough food in the lake—
worms. Says to his mother:
  "Carry me to the sea!"

"O, you'll run away!"

  "No!"

He grew up.
He's leaving, going out and
bringing the whales back;
the people are killing those whales.

When he was still not completely grown,
people started to say:
"Look, if we don't recognize him, we'll kill him!
We'd better sew a mark on his back."

They sewed dog-hair tassels on him.
Then the whales stopped coming.
He remained there alone.
A stranger stole in,
killed him.

The uncles are saying:
"Ah!
Where did he disappear to?"

Others are walking back and forth along the soul-passage.
They told the uncles about it,
the uncles found out about it.

They started to fight with the murderer.
They arrived there and all of them
killed one another.

The Man Who Married a Fox

◇EAST GREENLAND ESKIMO◇

This is the old story of a wifeless man. His fellow villagers had often told him to take a wife, but this he would not do.

One day he set a trap for foxes. When he went to look at it, there was a fox in it, and this he killed.

The next time he went to look, there was again a fox, this time a vixen.

This he took home with him, and kept as a dog under the window of his house. Whenever he had a meal himself, he gave the bones to the fox, and there it lay, gnawing at them.

Thus he treated that fox. Then one morning he went out hunting in his kayak.

It was not long before the skins of the seals he caught lay ready and finished when he came home; at last he even found them hung up to dry on the frame outside.

Soon after, he noticed that his lamp was kept in order while he was away, so that it never went out. And when he came home, he would find the pot boiling over the lamp, although there was not a single person in the house.

Now, he could not make out how all these things came about, and therefore one day he hid behind a rock to see what was going on. And lo! There was a beautiful woman with broad hips and a great knot of hair. It was the vixen, who was able to change into human form.

When she went in, the wifeless man hurried in after her. As he entered the house, all that he saw was something dark, which vanished beneath the window. The pot had been turned around, but there was not a single human being in the place.

Next day he hid again, and again there came a beautiful woman with a fine knot of hair. She came out of the house, and when she went in again, he ran after her and caught hold of her before she could reach the window. And now he took her to wife.

She was so beautiful that she might have been one of the white men's women!

Now while he was living there with her as his wife, a stranger came to visit them.

"Shall we change wives?" said the stranger one day when they were out in their kayaks.

"It cannot be done, for she is so jealous," said the other.

And the stranger went his way, without having got his will.

But the truth was that the wifeless man was unwilling to lend his wife to anyone, because of the strange smell of fox that hung about her body as soon as she began to sweat.

But one day the stranger came again on a visit, and again he offered to change wives, and as the wifeless man saw no way of refusing, he agreed.

Now the stranger lay down on her bed, and it was not long before she began to sweat, and she, who was more beautiful than other women, lo, she smelled of fox!

For a long time the man refrained from saying anything about it, but the smell grew stronger and stronger, and at last he burst out:

"Where ever can that foxy smell be coming from?"

Then he heard the barking of a fox: "Ká-ká-ká-ká!"

The woman had sprung up from the couch and dashed out. The man ran after her, but all he saw was a fox running swiftly up the hillside.

Then he went home and told the other what had happened.

"Did I not tell you she was easily angered, and that you were not to say anything if she happened to smell?" said the wifeless man, with words of abuse.

And now he went out to seek the fox-woman, and called to her to come back, but this she never did. Men say that he still wanders about among the hills calling for her.

Go Away

◇ S N O W D R I F T   C H I P E W Y A N ◇

A long time ago, there was a man named Crazy River. He fell in love with a woman named One-Who-Squints, who was very beautiful. She did not love Crazy River. Everyone knew about this. When Crazy River visited a village, people there said to him, "Do you still love her?" He'd have to say yes.

Crazy River was in love with her a long time, but she didn't care. She married someone else. When she married, Crazy River called her out in the nighttime, and said, "How could you do this?"

"Go away," she said.

So it went. Crazy River would have to travel far away for a long time. But eventually he'd come back to her village, call her out in the nighttime, and say, "Tell me, how could you marry someone else?"

"Go away."

Well, Crazy River became a great hunter. He was known all over for his hunting skills. And people would say of him, "He will make a fine husband."

One night, he called One-Who-Squints out into the nighttime. "Have you heard people say I'd make a fine husband?" he asked.

"You'll wake up my children," she said. "Go away."

She said go away again.

So she went back inside her house, and Crazy River went out hunting. He had a reputation for it.

More time passed, and Crazy River would come around and call her out into the nighttime, only to hear "Go away."

But one winter, starvation came to her village. People were very hungry. There was no food. One-Who-Squint's husband was a poor hunter. He wasn't much help. There was bad luck all around.

One day Crazy River showed up with some caribou shoulders, some ptarmigan, some fish. "Here," he said. "This is yours."

It was terrible out, very cold, a blizzard stayed around for many days. But now the people there had food. They set up a place for Crazy River to stay. He slept a long time, as he was tired from lugging food through a blizzard. When he woke, he asked for some broth. The people there brought it to him and he sipped it. Then he fell back asleep for another few days. It is well known that certain blizzards can wear a hunter out in this manner.

Now, when he was asleep, his beloved came around to look at him. She snuck up to him and whispered in his ear, "Go away." He was asleep, but he heard it.

That night, when he was sleeping, Crazy River stood right up and began to sleepwalk. He walked out of the village into the blizzard, and he stood there. He stood there, and snow rose around him. But some people noticed he was gone and found him. They carried him back and thawed him out. They made him drink more broth. He went back to sleep.

All this time the people in the village ate well, and they were grateful. Now they kept watch, so that their guest did not sleepwalk into the blizzard again and die.

That is the story. There's not much else.

Crazy River walked through the blizzard to bring food to his beloved's village in hopes.

In hopes she would want to marry him. She knew he was a great hunter. Still she said, "Go away."

Later, it is known that he did not marry. All through the rest of his life he called her out into the nighttime. Even when he was old, hobbling about. "Go away" was what he heard.

Source Notes

INTRODUCTION

Eskimo and Indian peoples: David Damas, in vol.5 of *The Handbook of North American Indians* (Washington: Smithsonian Institution, 1985), pp. 5–7, delineates the complex evolution of the word "Eskimo" (originally from the Montagnais, reaching a more modern usage via the French *Esquimaux*). Today, among native peoples, the word "Eskimo" has fallen into great disfavor. "Inuit" is widely used to designate indigenous peoples of the eastern Canadian arctic. Peoples of the Bering Strait region prefer "Yup'ik." Peoples of the north slope of Alaska are called "Inupiat," and those of the Mackenzie Delta, "Inuvialuit."

Anthony Woodbury, in the same volume (pp. 51–60), breaks Yup'ik down into Siberian Yup'ik and Alaskan Yup'ik. Further, the Inuit-Inupiaq language is a continuum of dialects, stretching from the Seward Peninsula in Alaska across arctic Canada down to the coasts of Quebec and Labrador and up again to the coasts of Greenland.

Subarctic linguistics is equally diverse. According to Richard Rhodes and Evelyn M. Todd in *The Handbook of North American Indians* (vol. 6, pp.52–66): "The indigenous languages of the Subarctic Shield, except for the northwest sector, belong to two of the branches of the Algonquian language family. The northern branch, here called Cree, comprises the local varieties of speech (dialects) known as Cree, Montagnais, and Naskapi, and the southern branch, here called Ojibwa, includes the dialects also known locally (and in some historical and technical writings) as Chippewa, Saulteaux, Ottawa, and Algonquin. Dialects of Cree fall into two groups, Eastern and Western Cree. Dialects of Western Cree are Plains Cree, Woods Cree, Western Swampy Cree, Moose Cree, and Attikamek (Tête de Boule). Dialects of Eastern Cree are East Cree, Naskapi, and Montagnais. Ojibwa falls into eight distinct dialects: Saulteaux, Northwestern Ojibwa, Southwestern Ojibwa, Severn Ojibwa, Central Ojibwa, Ottawa, Eastern Ojibwa, and Algonquin."

In that same volume, Michael Krauss and Victor K. Golla name twenty-three languages that form a recognized geographical subdivision of the Athapaskan language family, usually referred to as Northern Athapaskan. They are: Koyukon, Holikachuk, Ingalik, Tanaina, Ahtna, Kolchan, Lower Tanana, Tanacross, Upper Tanana, Han, Kutchin, Tutchone, Tsetsaut, Tahltan-Kaska-Tagish, Sekani, Beaver, Chipewyan, Slavey-Hare, Dogrib, Babine, Carrier, Chilcotin, and Sarcee.

"Stories are not just about living things": Mark Albert Blackfish, in a taped conversation with Helen Tanizaki. Author's personal collection.

"Storytelling is a common pastime": Hiroko Sue Hara, *The Hare Indians and Their World*, Canada, National Museum of Man, Mercury Series, Ethnology Service Paper no. 63 (Ottawa, 1980), p. 199.

"Oqaluttuarpoq!": Jean Malaurie, *The Last Kings of Thule* (New York: E. P. Dutton, 1982), p. 240.

"I was sitting in a tent": Lawrence Millman, *A Kayak Full of Ghosts* (Santa Barbara, Calif.: Capra Press, 1987), p. 11.

"In 1823, Lewis Cass, governor of Michigan Territory": Victor Barnouw, *Wisconsin Chippewa Myths and Legends* (Madison: University of Wisconsin Press, 1977), p. 3.

"As for myself, I achieved most of my progress": Malaurie, *Last Kings of Thule*, p. 172.

"Descriptions of the Polar Eskimo": Henry B. Collins, in *Handbook of North American Indians*, vol. 5, p. 8.

"Anna Nelson Harry was one of the last": Michael E. Krauss, ed., *In Honor of Eyak: The Art of Anna Nelson Harry* (Fairbanks: Alaska Native Language Center, 1982), p. 11.

PART ONE. THE EMBARRASSMENT OF THE CRANBERRY PARTNERS: TALES OF VILLAGE LIFE

"Some elderly man of a household": James Alexander Teit, *The Thompson Indians of British Columbia*, Memoirs of the American Museum of Natural History, no. 2 (New York, 1900), p. 367.

"The children repeated the story": Catherine Holt, *Shasta Ethnography*, University of California Anthropological Records, vol. 3, no. 4 (Berkeley, 1946), p. 338.

The Embarrassment of the Cranberry Partners: Told by Tealie Denis.

Eviksheen the Grass-User: Told by Niyuk. From J. L. Giddings, *Kobuk River People*, University of Alaska Studies of Northern Peoples, no. 1 (Fairbanks, 1961), p. 106.

The Girl Who Watched in the Nighttime: Told by Nipe'wgi, in the village of Uni'sak at Indian Point, May 1901. Translated by Waldemar Bogoras. From Bogoras, *The Eskimo of Siberia* (1913; reprint ed., New York: AMS Press, 1975), pp. 422–24.

Uteritsoq, the Obstinate One: Told by Napa. Translated by Knud Rasmussen. From Hother B. S. Ostermann, ed., *Knud Rasmussen's Posthumous Notes on East Greenland Legends and Myths*, Meddelelser om Grønland, vol. 109, no. 3 (Copenhagen, 1939), pp. 58–60.

The Chuginadak Woman: Translated by V. I. Jochelson. From Jochelson, *History, Ethnology, and Anthropology of the Aleut*, Carnegie Institute of Washington Publication no. 432 (Washington, 1933).

The Boy Who Became an Arctic Tern: Told by Paul Monroe, Noatak, Alaska. From Edwin S. Hall, Jr., *The Eskimo Storyteller: Folktales from Noatak, Alaska* (Knoxville: University of Tennessee Press, 1975), pp. 224–27.

The Little Old Lady Who Lived Alone: Transcribed by James Kari. From John W. Chapman, *Athabaskan Stories from Anvik*, ed. James Kari and Jane McGary (Fairbanks: Alaska Native Language Center, 1981).

Qasiagssaq, the Great Liar: Told by Sabine Igdlukasik. Translated by Knud Rasmussen. From Ostermann, *Knud Rasmussen's Posthumous Notes on East Greenland Legends and Myths*.

Witiko Father and Son Bested by a Conjuror: Told by Harvey Smallboy at Moose Factory, Ontario, in 1933. Transcribed by Regina Flannery. From Flannery, Mary Elizabeth Chambers, and Patricia A. Jehle, "Cree Witiko Accounts," *Arctic Anthropology* 18, no. 1 (1981): 62–64.

Alder-Block: Told by Katherine Rumiantzeu in the village of Pokhotsk, Kolyma country, Siberia, in summer of 1895. Translated by Waldemar Bogoras. From Bogoras, "Tales of the Yukaghir, Lamut, and Russianized Natives of Eastern Siberia," *Anthropological Papers of the American Museum of Natural History* 20, no. 1 (1918).

The Crow Story: From Bill Vaudrin, *Tanaina Tales from Alaska* (Norman: University of Oklahoma Press, 1969), pp. 28–44.

Stingy Reindeer Owners: Told by Ivashkan, on the upper course of the Molonda River, Kolyma country, Siberia, in summer of 1895. Translated by Waldemar Bogoras. From Bogoras, "Tales of the Yukaghir, Lamut, and Russianized Natives of Siberia," pp. 30–32.

Fourteen with One Stroke: Told by Tom Batiste at Court Oreilles, Wisconsin, in 1942. Interpreter: Prosper Guibord. From Barnouw, *Wisconsin Chippewa Myths and Legends*, pp. 214–18.

PART TWO. WHY OWLS DIE WITH WINGS OUTSPREAD: HOW THINGS GOT TO BE THE WAY THEY ARE

How the Earth Was Made and How Wood-Chips Became Walrus: Told by Attin'qeym at Marinsky Post, Siberia, in October 1900. Translated by Miriam Olisensky in Leningrad. From Waldemar Bogoras, *The Chukchee* (1904; reprint ed., New York: AMS Press, 1975).

The First Snowshoes: Told by Mrs. Kitty Smith, Whitehorse, Alaska. From Julie Cruikshank, *Athapaskan Women: Lives and Legends*, Canada, National Museum of Man, Mercury Series, Ethnology Service Paper no. 57 (Ottawa, 1979), p. 177.

Gambling Story: Told by Peter Kalifornsky. English version by Katherine McNamara, from Peter Kalifornsky's oral tellings and literal translation.

Story While Pointing at a Constellation: Told by Ritchie Feathers and Ruth Leaves Abernon. Recorded in 1979.

Why Owls Die with Wings Outspread: Told by Joby Maskunow near Family Lake, Manitoba, in August 1972. Translated by Alaric Holt.

When Musk Oxen Spoke Like Humans: Told by Amos Crouches Harbison. Translated in 1949 by Edward Bukkard, a missionary.

Why the Path Between Fish-Camps Is Always Worn Down, and No One Walks It Any More: Told by Peter LeCou. Recorded and translated in 1966 by Jukichi Shindo.

What Is the Earth? From several Greenlandic sources. Translated by Lawrence Millman. From Millman, *A Kayak Full of Ghosts*, p. 201.

How the Narwhal Got Its Tusk: Told by Pioopiula to Michael and Severance Rosegood in 1975. Translated by Severance Rosegood.

Ayas ̇ e and the Origin of Bats: Translated by Frank G. Speck. From Speck, *Myths and Folklore of the Timiskaming Algonquin and Timagami Ojibwa*, Canada Department of Mines, Geological Survey Memoir no. 71 (Ottawa, 1915).

The Loon and the Raven: Told by Thomas Nassiquiurt, a King William Island Eskimo. Translated by Michael Weller.

The Giant Skunk and His Offspring: Told by Frances Tshasha-Giberson in summer of 1952. Translated by Howard Norman and Israel Crane.

A Yukaghir Tale of the Origin of the Chukchee: Told by Yegor Shamanoff on the Kolyma tundra in April 1902. Translated by Waldemar Bogoras. From Bogoras, "Tales of the Yukaghir, Lamut, and Russianized Natives of Siberia."

Which Animals Are on the Moon: Told by Aluniq (Jenny Mitchell). Translated by Puyuk (Della Keats). From Hall, *The Eskimo Storyteller*.

Why Rattlesnakes Don't Cross the River: Translated by James Alexander Teit. From Teit, *The Thompson Indians of British Columbia*, pp. 339–40.

The First White Men: Told by Frances Pike.

PART THREE. ENDLESS TROUBLE, ENDLESS WANDERING:
TRICKSTERS AND CULTURE HEROES

Smart Beaver Cycle: Told by Mrs. Angela Sidney. From Cruikshank, *Athapaskan Women,* pp. 83–92.

Kuloscap Tales: Told by Mrs. Constance Traynor, Nova Scotia. From correspondence with Howard Norman.

The Wenebojo Myths: Told by Tom Badger, Lac du Flambeau, Wisconsin, in 1944. Interpreter: Julia Badger. From Barnouw, *Wisconsin Chippewa Myths and Legends,* pp. 13–44.

PART FOUR. THE STUBBORNNESS OF BLUEJAYS:
STORIES ABOUT ANIMALS

The Bear Goes on His Long, Solitary Journey: Related by Jean Malaurie. From Malaurie, *Last Kings of Thule,* p. 345.

Bluejay's Revenge: Told by Sixwi'lexken. Translated by James Alexander Teit. From Teit, *The Thompson Indians of British Columbia.*

The Wolverine Loses His Shoes: Told by John Fredson. Transcribed by Katherine Peter. Translated by Edward Sapir. From Fredson and Sapir, eds., *Stories Told by John Fredson to Edward Sapir* (Fairbanks: Alaska Native Language Center, 1982), p. 86.

Skunk's Tears: Translated by James Alexander Teit. From Teit, *The Thompson Indians of British Columbia,* pp. 233–36.

The Duck Whose Grandmother Was Out of Her Wits: Told by Mary Alin in the village of Markova, Siberia, in winter of 1900. Recorded by Mrs. Sophie Bogoras. From Waldemar Bogoras, *The Eskimo of Siberia.*

The Helldiver and the Spirit of Winter: Told by Pete Martin, Court Oreilles, Wisconsin, in 1942. From Barnouw, *Wisconsin Chippewa Myths and Legends,* pp. 154–55.

The Stubbornness of Bluejays: Told by Enuch Oschewensaw near Pigeon Lake, Ontario.

Coyote and Fox: Told by Sixwi'lexken. Translated by James Alexander Teit. From Teit, *The Thompson Indians of British Columbia.*

The Owl Woman: Told by Tommy Bruneau in Calgary, Alberta.

Crow and Camp Robber: Told by Peter Kalifornsky. English version by Katherine McNamara, from Peter Kalifornsky's oral tellings and literal translation.

Why Brown Bears Are Hostile Towards Men: Told by Makaka. From F. C. Johnson, *Chugach Legends* (Anchorage: Chugach Alaska Corporation, 1984), p. 48.

The Wolverine Grudge: Told by Moses Sandy near the Winisk River, Ontario, in August 1981.

The Whale, the Sea Scorpion, the Stone, and the Eagle: Told by Ivaluardjuk. Translated by Knud Rasmussen. From Rasmussen, *Intellectual Culture of the Iglulik Eskimos* (1929; reprint ed., New York: AMS Press, 1976), pp. 281–84.

PART FIVE. CARRIED OFF BY THE MOON: SHAMAN STORIES

"Blow away the sickness": Jean Blodgett, *The Coming and Going of the Shaman* (Winnipeg: Winnipeg Art Gallery, 1979).

Iglulik tradition about birth of first shaman: Knud Rasmussen, *Intellectual Culture of the Iglulik Eskimos,* pp. 110–11.

"Qaqortineq had just come home": Knud Rasmussen, *The Netsilik Eskimos* (1931; reprint ed., New York: AMS Press, 1976), p. 298.

"Niviatsian, when out hunting": Rasmussen, *Intellectual Culture of the Iglulik Eskimos*, p. 121.

Carried Off by the Moon: Told by Kuvdluitsoq. Translated by Knud Rasmussen. From Rasmussen, *The Netsilik Eskimos*, p. 236.

Story of a Female Shaman: Told by Gale at the Anui Fair, Siberia, in spring 1896. From Waldemar Bogoras, *The Eskimo of Siberia*.

How the False Shaman Was Flung by Walrus: Told by Moses Nucaq.

Things Seen by the Shaman Karawe: Told by the shaman Karawe on the Poginden River, Siberia, in 1896. Recorded by Waldemar Bogoras. From Bogoras, *Materials for the Study of the Chukchee Language and Folklore* (St. Petersburg: Imperial Academy of Sciences, 1900), pp. xxx–xxxi. Translated by Barbara Einzig.

The Curing-Fox Windigo: Told by John Rains near Lake Winnipegosis, Manitoba.

Kinigseq: Told by Autaruta at Igdluluarssuit, Greenland. Translated by Knud Rasmussen. From Ostermann, *Knud Rasmussen's Posthumous Notes on East Greenland Legends and Myths*.

How a Bagpipe Drew Hunters from the Outskirts: Told by Moses Nucaq.

Song of Spider Goddess: Translated by Donald L. Philippi: From Philippi, *Songs of Gods, Songs of Humans* (San Francisco: North Point Press, 1982), pp. 78–82.

Desire for Light: Told by Jennie Thompson. Translated by Diamond Jenness. From Jenness, *Myths and Traditions from Northern Alaska, the Mackenzie Delta, and Coronation Gulf*, vol. 13A of *Report of the Canadian Arctic Expedition 1913–1918* (Ottawa: F. A. Acland, 1924).

Aksikukuk and Kukrukuk: Told by Paul Monroe, Noatak, Alaska. From Hall, *The Eskimo Storyteller*, pp. 109–14.

Encounter with the Shaman from Padlei: Told by Moses Nucaq at Eskimo Point, Northwest Territory, in summer 1979.

PART SIX. THRASHING SPIRITS AND TEN-LEGGED POLAR BEARS: STORIES OF STRANGE AND MENACING NEIGHBORS

"We fear the weather spirits of earth": Knud Rasmussen, *Intellectual Culture of the Iglulik Eskimos*, p. 56.

The Birth of Tchakapesh: Told by Jean-Baptiste Rich in Davis Inlet, Labrador. Translated by Lawrence Millman.

The Thrashing Spirit with a Bearded Seal for a Whip: Told by Ivaluardjuk. Translated by Knud Rasmussen. From Rasmussen, *Intellectual Culture of the Iglulik Eskimos*, p. 217.

The Mother of Sea Beasts: Told by Nalungiaq. Translated by Knud Rasmussen. From Rasmussen, *The Netsilik Eskimos*, p. 225.

Brushmen: From Douglas Leechman, "Folk-lore of the Vanta-Kutchin," in National Museum of Canada Bulletin no. 126 (Ottawa, 1952), pp. 76–93.

Ayaje's Wives with Forearms Like Awls: Told by Mary Muini. Translated by the Reverend Samuel Kinder.

Three Sisters and the Demon: Translated by Emiko Ohnuk-Tierney. From Ward Goodenough, ed., *Sakhalin Ainu Folklore*, American Anthropological Association, Anthropological Studies, no. 2 (Washington, 1969).

The Giant Rat: Told by Anna Nelson Harry. Translated by Michael E. Krauss. From Krauss, *In Honor of Eyak,* pp. 56–58.

The Ghost: Told by Jennie Thompson. Translated by Diamond Jenness. From Jenness, *Myths and Traditions from Northern Alaska.*

The Giants: Told by Angotitsiaq of Point Hope.

The Woman Who Ate Men: Translated by Knud Rasmussen. From Ostermann, *Knud Rasmussen's Posthumous Notes on East Greenland Legends and Myths.*

The Wrong-Chill Windigo: Told by Andrew Nikumoon near Cormorant Lake, Manitoba.

Ipiup Inua, the Spirit of the Precipice: Told by Inugpasugjuk. Translated by Knud Rasmussen. From Rasmussen, *Intellectual Culture of the Iglulik Eskimos,* p. 219.

Inugpasugssuk the Giant: Told by Manelaq. Translated by Knud Rasmussen. From Rasmussen, *The Netsilik Eskimos,* p. 252.

The Four Cannibals: Told by Sixwi'lexken. Translated by James Alexander Teit, From Teit, *The Thompson Indians of British Columbia.*

Kivioq, Whose Kayak Was Full of Ghosts: From versions heard in both West and East Greenland. Recorded by Lawrence Millman. From Millman, *A Kayak Full of Ghosts,* p. 199.

The Ten-Legged Polar Bear: Translated by Robert F. Spencer. From Spencer, *The North Alaskan Eskimo: A Study in Ecology and Society,* Bureau of American Ethnology Bulletin no. 171 (Washington, 1959; reprinted 1969), pp. 425–26.

The Monster Fish in the Lake: Told by John Fredson. Transcribed by Edward Sapir. Translated by Jane McGary. From Fredson and Sapir, *Stories Told by John Fredson to Edward Sapir,* p. 94.

The Attainable Border of the Birds: Told by Yatirgin on the Wolverine River, Siberia, c. 1900. From Waldemar Bogoras, *Material for the Study of the Chukchee Language and Culture,* pp. xxx–xxxi. Translated by Barbara Einzig.

PART SEVEN. THE DAY AUKS NETTED HID-WELL: HUNTING STORIES

Polar Eskimo song: Howard Norman, personal archives.

"Human existence depends on a morally based relationship": Richard K. Nelson, *Make Prayers to the Raven* (Chicago: University of Chicago Press, 1983),p. 240.

"Those of us in the boat were watching intently": Malaurie, *Last Kings of Thule,* p. 65.

The Dream That Came Back: Told by Charlie Kanatiwat. From Richard I. Preston III, *Cree Narrative Expressing the Personal Meaning of Events,* Canada, National Museum of Man, Ethnology Service Paper no. 30 (Ottawa, 1975).

The Hunter and the Goats: Translated by James Alexander Teit. From Teit, *The Thompson Indians of British Columbia,* pp. 261–64.

Agdlumaloqaq, Who Hunted the Blowholes in a Far, Foreign Land: Told by Inugpasugjuk. Translated by Knud Rasmussen. From Rasmussen, *Intellectual Culture of the Iglulik Eskimos,* p. 286.

The Moose Among the Chandalar River People: Told by John Fredson. Transcribed by Edward Sapir. Translated by Jane McGary. From Fredson and Sapir, *Stories Told by John Fredson to Edward Sapir,* p. 50.

The Woman Who Put a Bucket over a Caribou's Head: Translated by Robert F. Spencer. From Spencer, *The North Alaskan Eskimo,* pp. 413–14.

The Day Auks Netted Hid-Well: Told by William Etajuak. Translated by Peter Stolper and Howard Norman.

Lake-Dwarves: Told by Anna Nelson Harry. Translated by Michael E. Krauss. From Krauss, *In Honor of Eyak,* p. 39.

The Mammoth Hunters: Told by Michael Peglirook. From Giddings, *Kobuk River People,* p. 71.

Why Woolly Mammoths Decided to Flee Underground: Told by Mark Nucaq.

Sometimes a Seal Hunt Goes Like This: Told by Charles Fort Franklin Bird.

PART EIGHT. WOLF'S BRIDE, STAR HUSBANDS: STORIES ABOUT ALL SORTS OF MARRIAGES

Raven Didn't Stick Around: Told by Billy Sees.

Kivioq, Who Left His Home Because His Wife Was Unfaithful: Told by Tingmiaq. Translated by Knud Rasmussen. From Ostermann, *Knud Rasmussen's Posthumous Notes on East Greenland Legends and Myths.*

The Windigo Almost Prevents a Marriage: Told by John Rains near Lake Winnipegosis, Manitoba.

The Star Husbands: Told by Mrs. Kitty Smith, Whitehorse, Alaska. From Cruikshank, *Athapaskan Women,* p. 128.

The Girl Who Married the Bear: Told by Jake Jackson. Recorded by Catherine McClelland. From McClelland, *The Girl Who Married the Bear: A Masterpiece of Indian Oral Tradition,* Canada, National Museum of Man, Publications in Ethnology, no. 2 (Ottawa, 1970), pp. 15–23.

How Whiskey-Jack Man Got Married: Told by Silas Noke in David Inlet, Labrador, to Lawrence Millman.

The Woman and the Octopus: Told by Anna Nelson Harry. Version by Michael E. Krauss. From Krauss, *In Honor of Eyak,* p. 99.

The Marriage of Mink: Told by Tom Tsishaath. Recorded by Alex Thomas. From Edward Sapir, *Nootka Texts* (Philadelphia: Linguistic Society of America, University of Pennsylvania, 1939).

The Wolf's Bride: Told by Ugiarnaq to a household at Cape Halkett, Alaska, January 1, 1914, and dictated afterwards by two of his audience, Itaqluq and Alfred Hobson, both of Barrow. From Bogoras, *The Eskimo of Siberia.*

The Girl Who Married a Whale: Recorded by Waldemar Bogoras on the Molonda River, Siberia, c. 1895. From Bogoras, *Materials for the Study of the Chukchee Language and Folklore,* pp. 297–99.

The Man Who Married a Fox: Translated by Knud Rasmussen. From Ostermann, *Knud Rasmussen's Posthumous Notes on East Greenland Legends and Myths.*

Go Away: Written by Mary Pigeon.

Bibliography

Ager, Lynn Price. "Storytelling: An Alaskan Eskimo Girls' Game." *Journal of the Folklore Institute* 11, no. 3 (1974):189–98.

Alaska Native Language Center. *Ugiuvangmiut, Quliapyiut: King Island Tales.* Fairbanks: University of Alaska Press, 1988.

Allen, Henry T. *Report of an Expedition to the Copper, Tanana, and Koyukon Rivers, in the Territory of Alaska, in the Year 1885.* Washington: Government Printing Office, 1887.

Anderson, Wanni W. "Song Duel of the Kobuk River Eskimo." *Folk* (Copenhagen) 16–17 (1974–1975):73–81.

Arima, Eugene Y. *Report on an Eskimo Umiak Built at Ivujivik. P. Q. in the Summer of 1960.* Anthropological Series, no. 59. National Museum of Canada Bulletin no. 189. Ottawa, 1963.

Armstrong, Sir Alexander. *A Personal Narrative of the Discovery of the Northwest Passage: With Numerous Incidents of Travel and Adventure During Nearly Five Years' Continuous Service in the Arctic Regions While in Search of the Expedition Under Sir John Franklin.* London: Hurst & Blackett, 1857.

Baer, John L. "Language of the Indian Tribe on the Island of Chak-lock." Pp. 19–26; "List of Tchuktchi Words Collected in Glasenap Harbor, Straits of Seniavine West Side of Behrings Straits." Manuscript no. 338-C in National Anthropological Archives, Smithsonian Institution, Washington, 1855.

Balikei, Asen. "The Eskimos of the Quebec-Labrador Peninsula: Ethnographic Contributions." Pp. 375–94 in *Le Nouveau-Quebec: Contribution à l' étude de l'occupation humaine.* Ed. J. Malaurie and J. Rousseau. Paris: Mouton, 1964.

Banfield, Alexander W. F. *The Mammals of Canada.* Toronto: University of Toronto Press, 1974.

Barnouw, Victor. *Wisconsin Chippewa Myths and Legends.* Madison: University of Wisconsin Press, 1977.

Beechey, Frederick W. *Narrative of a Voyage to the Pacific and Beering's Strait, to Co-operate with the Polar Expeditions: Performed in His Majesty's Ship "Blossom," Under the Command of Captain F. W. Beechey, in the Years 1825, 26, 27, 28.* 2 vols. London: Colburn & Bentley, 1832.

Birket-Smith, Kaj. *The Caribou Eskimos: Material and Social Life and Their Cultural Position.* Trans. W. E. Calvert. Vol. 5, pts. 1–2, of *Report of the Fifth Thule Expedition, 1921–24.* Copenhagen: Gyldendal, 1929.

———. *The Chugach Eskimo.* Nationalmuseets Skrifter, Etnografisk Raekke, no. 6. Copenhagen, 1953.

———. *Contributions to Chipewyan Ethnology.* Trans. W. E. Calvert. Vol. 6, pt. 3, of *Report of the Fifth Thule Expedition, 1921–24.* Copenhagen: Gyldendal, 1930.

———. *Ethnographical Collections from the Northwest Passage.* Vol. 6, pt. 2, of *Report of the Fifth Thule Expedition, 1921–24.* Copenhagen: Gyldendal, 1945.

————. *Ethnography of the Egedesminde District, with Aspects of the General Culture of West Greenland*. Meddelelser om Grønland, vol. 66. Copenhagen, 1924.

————, and Frederica De Laguna. *The Eyak Indians of the Copper River Delta, Alaska*. Copenhagen: Levin & Munksgaard, 1938.

Black, Mary. "Legends and Accounts of Weagamow Lake." *Rotunda: Bulletin of the Royal Ontario Museum* 3, no. 3. (1970):4–13.

Blodgett, Jean. *The Coming and Going of the Shaman: Eskimo Shamanism and Art*. Winnipeg: Winnipeg Art Gallery, 1979.

Boas, Franz. *The Central Eskimo*. Pp. 399–699 in *6th Annual Report of the Bureau of American Ethnology for the Years 1884–1885*. Washington, 1888. Reprint. Lincoln: University of Nebraska Press, 1964.

————. *The Eskimo of Baffin Land and Hudson Bay*. Bulletin of the American Museum of Natural History no. 15. New York, 1901–1907.

————. "Traditions of the Ts'ets' aut. I." *Journal of American Folklore* 9, no. 35 (1896): 257–68.

————. "Traditions of the Ts'ets' aut. II." *Journal of American Folklore* 10, no. 36 (1897):35–48.

————. *Tsimshian Mythology: Based on Texts Recorded by Henry W. Tate*. Pp. 29–881 in *31st Annual Report of the Bureau of American Ethnology for the Years 1909–1910*. Washington, 1916. Reprint. New York: Johnson Reprint Corp., 1970.

————, and Pliny E. Goddard. "Ts'ets' aut, an Athapascan Language from Portland Canal, British Columbia." *International Journal of American Linguistics* 3, no. 1 (1924): 1–35.

Bogoras, Waldemar. "Chukchee." Pp. 631–903 in pt. 2 of *Handbook of American Indian Languages*. Ed. Franz Boas. Bureau of American Ethnology Bulletin no. 40. Washington, 1922.

————. *The Chukchee*. Vol. 7 of *Publications of the Jesup North Pacific Expedition*. Ed. Franz Boas. 12 vols. New York: G. E. Stechert, 1904–1909. Also issued as Memoirs of the American Museum of Natural History, no. 11. Reprint. New York: AMS Press, 1975.

————. "Early Migrations of the Eskimo Between Asia and America." Pp. 216–35 in vol. 1 of *Proceedings of the 21st International Congress of Americanists*. Göteborg, 1924.

————. "Elements of the Culture of the Circumpolar Zone." *American Anthropologist* 31, no. 4 (1929):579–601.

————. *The Eskimo of Siberia*. Vol. 8, pt. 3, of *Publications of the Jesup North Pacific Expedition*. Ed. Franz Boas. 12 vols. New York: G. E. Stechert, 1913. Also issued as Memoirs of the American Museum of Natural History, no. 12. Reprint. New York: AMS Press, 1975.

————. *Materials for the Study of the Chukchee Language and Folklore*. St. Petersburg: Imperial Academy of Sciences, 1900.

————. "Tales of the Yukaghir, Lamut, and Russianized Natives of Siberia." *Anthropological Papers of the American Museum of Natural History* 20, pt. 1 (1918).

Boyle, David. "The Killing of Wa-Sak-Apee-Quay by Pe-Se Quan and Others." Pp. 91–120 in *Annual Archaeological Reports for 1907: Being Part of Appendix to the Report of the Minister of Education, Ontario*. Toronto, 1908.

Brooke, John M. "Vocabularies of Tchucktches on Tchuklook." P. 1 in "Vocabularies of Central Siberian Yupik and Chukchi, from Arakamchechen and Yttygran Islands,

Strait of Seniavin." Copy by George Gibbs; manuscript no. 341 in National Anthropological Archives, Smithsonian Institution, Washington, 1855.

Chapman, John W. *Athabaskan Stories from Anvik*. Ed. and trans. James Kari and Jane McGary. Fairbanks: Alaska Native Language Center, 1981.

———. "Athapascan Traditions from the Lower Yukon." *Journal of American Folklore* 16, no. 62 (1903): 180–85.

———. *Ten'a Texts and Tales from Anvik, Alaska, with Vocabulary by Pliny Earle Goddard*. Publication of the American Ethnological Society no. 6. Leyden: E. J. Brill, 1914.

Chernenko, M. C. "Puteshestviia po Chukotskoi zemle i plavanie na Aliasku kazach 'ego sotnika Ivana Kobeleva v 1779 i 1789–1791 gg." [The travels in Chukchi country and voyages to Alaska of the Cossack captain Ivan Kobelev in 1779 and 1789–1791]. *Letopis'Severa* (Moscow) 2 (1957):121–41.

Clavering, D. C. "Journal of a Voyage to Spitzbergen and the East Coast of Greenland in His Majesty's Ship Griper." *Edinburgh New Philosophical Journal* 9 (1830):1–30.

Cooper, John M. "The Cree Witiko Psychosis." *Primitive Man* 6, no. 1 (1933):20–24.

———. *The Northern Algonquian Supreme Being*. Catholic University of American Anthropological Series, no. 2. Washington, 1934.

———. "Notes on Ethnographic Fieldwork Among the Attikamek–Tete de Boule, Mostly at Obedjiwan." Manuscript in Department of Anthropology, Catholic University of America, Washington, 1926–1937.

Cruickshank, Julie. *Athapaskan Women: Lives and Legends*. Canada, National Museum of Man, Mercury Series, Ethnology Service Paper no. 57. Ottawa, 1979.

Davidson, Daniel S. "Folk Tales from Grand Lake, Victoria, Quebec." *Journal of American Folklore* 41, no. 160 (1928):275–82.

———. "Some Tête de Boule Tales." *Journal of American Folklore*. 41, no. 160 (1928):262–74.

De Laguna, Frederica, and Marie-Françoise Guedon. "Ahtna Fieldnotes." Manuscripts in authors' possession. Microfilm copy at American Philosophical Society, Philadelphia, 1968.

De Laguna, Frederica, and Catharine McClellan. "Ahtna Fieldnotes." Manuscripts in authors' possession. Microfilm copy at American Philosophical Society, Philadelphia, 1954–1960.

Dorais, Louis-Jacques. *The Inuit Language in Southern Labrador from 1694–1785*. Canada, National Museum of Man, Mercury Series, Ethnology Service Paper no. 66. Ottawa, 1980.

Elias, Douglas, "Gossip." Unpublished manuscript in University of Winnipeg, Department of Anthropology, 1967.

Farrand, Livingstone. "The Chilcotin." Pp. 645–47 in *Report of the 68th Meeting of the British Association for the Advancement of Science, 1898*. London, 1899.

———. "Traditions of the Chilcotin Indians." Pp. 11–54 in Memoirs of the American Museum of Natural History, vol. 4, no. 1. New York, 1900.

Fidler, Peter. "Journal of a Journey with the Chipewayans or Northern Indians to the Slave Lake and to the East and West of the Slave River, in 1791 and 1792." Pp. 493–556 in *Journals of Samuel Hearne and Phillip Turnor Between the Years 1774 and 1792*. Ed. J. B. Tyrrell. Toronto: Champlain Society, 1934.

Flannery, Regina. "Some Magico-religious Concepts of the Algonquians on the East Coast of James Bay, Canada." Pp. 31–39 in *Themes in Culture: Essays in Honor of Morris*

Opler. Ed. Mario D. Zamora, J. Michael Mahar, and Henry Orenstein. Quezon City, P. I.: Kayumanggi Publishers, 1971.

―――――, Mary Elizabeth Chambers, and Patricia A. Jehle. "Cree Witiko Accounts." *Arctic Anthropology* 18, no. 1 (1981):57–64.

Formorzov, A. N. *The Snow Cover as an Integral Factor of the Environment and Its Importance to the Ecology of Mammals and Birds.* Trans. William Prychodko and William Pruitt. University of Alberta, Boreal Institute Occasional Publication no. 1. Edmonton, 1964.

Giddings, J. L. *Kobuk River People.* University of Alaska Studies of Northern Peoples, no. 1. Fairbanks, 1961.

Goddard, Pliny E. "Analysis of Cold Lake Dialect, Chipewyan." *Anthropological Papers of the American Museum of Natural History* 10, no. 2 (1917):67–170.

―――――. "Beaver Dialect." *Anthropological Papers of the American Museum of Natural History* 10, no. 6 (1917):399–546.

―――――. "The Beaver Indians." *Anthropological Papers of the American Museum of Natural History* 10, no. 4 (1917):201–93.

―――――. "Beaver Texts." *Anthropological Papers of the American Museum of Natural History* 10, no. 5 (1917):295–397.

―――――. "Chipewyan Texts." *Anthropological Papers of the American Museum of Natural History* 10, no. 1 (1917):1–65.

Godfrey, W. Earl. *The Birds of Canada.* Biological Series, no. 73. National Museum of Canada Bulletin no. 203. Ottawa, 1966.

Golder, Frank A. "Eskimo and Aleut Stories from Alaska." *Journal of American Folklore* 22, no. 83 (1909):10–24.

―――――. "A Kodiak Island Story: The White-faced Bear." *Journal of American Folklore* 20, no. 79 (1907):269–99.

―――――. "Tales from Kodiak Island." *Journal of American Folklore* 16, no. 60 (1903): 16–31.

Goodenough, Ward. *Sakhalin Ainu Folklore.* American Anthropological Association, Anthropological Studies, no. 2. Washington, 1969.

Gruhn, Ruth. "Summary of Field Work at Calling Lake, Northern Alberta." *Archaeological Society of Alberta Newsletter* 16 (1966): 2–4.

―――――. "Summary of Field Work at Calling Lake, Northern Alberta, Summer 1968." *Archaeological Society of Alberta Newsletter* 19 (1969): 8–14.

―――――. "Summary Report of 1967 Fieldwork at Calling Lake, Northern Alberta." Unpublished manuscript no. 87 in National Museum of Man, Archaeological Survey of Canada, Ottawa, 1967.

Guedon, Marie-Françoise. *People of Tetlin, Why Are You Singing?* Canada, National Museum of Man, Mercury Series, Ethnology Service Paper no. 9. Ottawa, 1974.

Gulløv, Hans C., and Hans Kapel. *Haabetz Colonie 1721–1728: A Historical-Archaeological Investigation of the Danish-Norwegian Colonization of Greenland.* National Museum of Denmark Ethnographical Series, no. 16. Copenhagen, 1979.

―――――. "Legend, History, and Archaeology: A Study of the Art of Eskimo Narratives." *Folk* (Copenhagen) 21–22 (1979–1980):347–80.

Hall, Edwin S., Jr. *The Eskimo Storyteller: Folktales from Noatak, Alaska.* Knoxville: University of Tennessee Press, 1975.

Hallowell, A. Irving. "Ojibwa Ontology, Behavior, and World View." Pp. 19–52 in

Culture in History: Essays in Honor of Paul Radin. Ed. Stanley Diamond. New York: Columbia University Press, 1960.

Hanzeli, Victor E. *Missionary Linguistics in New France: A Study of Seventeenth- and Eighteenth-Century Descriptions of American Indian Languages.* Janua Linguarum Series Major, no. 29. The Hague: Mouton, 1969.

Hara, Hiroko Sue. *The Hare Indians and Their World.* Canada National Museum of Man, Mercury Series, Ethnology Service Paper no. 63. Ottawa, 1980.

Hardisty, William L. "The Loucheux Indians." Pp. 311–20 in *Notes on the Tinneh or Chepewyan Indians of British and Russian America. Annual Report of the Smithsonian Institution for the Year 1866.* Washington, 1872.

Harper, Francis. *Caribou Eskimos of the Upper Kazan River, Keewatin.* University of Kansas Museum of Natural History Miscellaneous Publications, no. 36. Lawrence, 1964.

Hauser, Michael. "Structure of Form in Polar Eskimo Drumsongs." *Proceedings of the 23d International Folk Music Council.* Kingston, Ont., 1975.

————. *Traditional Music and Music Traditions in Greenland: An Annotated Bibliography.* Meddelelser om Grønland. Copenhagen, 1983.

Helm, June, and Vital Thomas. "Tales from the Dogribs." *The Beaver* 297 (Autumn 1966):16–20; (Winter 1966):52–54.

Holt, Catherine. *Shasta Ethnography.* University of California Anthropological Records, vol. 3, no. 4. Berkeley, 1946.

Holtved, Erik. *The Eskimo Legend of Navaranaq: An Analytical Study.* Acta Arctica, no. 1. Copenhagen: E. Munksgaard, 1943.

————. *The Polar Eskimos, Language and Folklore: Pt. 1: Texts; Pt. II: Myths and Tales.* Meddelelser om Grønland, vol. 152, nos. 1–2. Copenhagen, 1951.

Hooper, William H. *Ten Months Among the Tents of the Tuski with Incidents of an Arctic Boat Expedition in Search of Sir John Franklin as Far as the MacKenzie River, and Cape Bathurst.* London: John Murray, 1853.

Hughes, Charles C. *Eskimo Boyhood: An Autobiography in Psychosocial Perspective.* Lexington: University Press of Kentucky, 1975.

Irving, Laurence. "Naming of Birds as Part of the Intellectual Culture of Indians at Old Crow, Yukon Territory." *Arctic* 11, no. 2 (1958):117–22.

Jenness, Diamond. *Myths and Traditions from Northern Alaska, the Mackenzie Delta, and Coronation Gulf.* Vol. 13A of *Report of the Canadian Arctic Expedition 1913–18.* Ottawa: F. A. Acland, 1924.

Jette, Jules. "On the Language of the Ten'a." *Man* 7 (1907):51–56; 8 (1908):72–74; 9 (1909):21–25.

————. "On the Medicine-men of the Ten'a." *Journal of the Royal Anthropological Institute of Great Britain and Ireland,* n.s., 37 (1907):157–88.

————. "On Ten'a Folk-Lore." *Journal of the Royal Anthropological Institute of Great Britain and Ireland,* n.s., 38 (1908):298–367; 39 (1909):460–505.

————. "L'Organisation sociale des Ten'as." Pp. 395–409 in vol. 1 of *Proceedings of the 15th International Congress of Americanists.* 2 vols. Quebec, 1906–1907.

Jochelson, V. I. *History, Ethnology, and Anthropology of the Aleut.* Carnegie Institute of Washington Publication no. 432. Washington, 1933.

Johnson, F. C. *Chugach Legends.* Anchorage: Chugach Alaska Corporation, 1984.

Keim, Charles J., ed. "Kutchin Legends from Old Crow. Yukon Territory." *Anthropological Papers of the University of Alaska* 11, no. 2 (1964):9.

Kleivan, Inge. *The Swan Maiden Myth Among the Eskimo.* Acta Arctica, vol. 13. Copenhagen: E. Munksgaard, 1962.

Knight, James. *The Founding of Churchill, Being the Journal of Captain James Knight, Governor-in-Chief in Hudson Bay, from the 14th of July to the 13th of September, 1717.* Ed. J. F. Kenney. Toronto: J. M. Dent & Sons, 1932.

Krauss, Michael E., ed. *In Honor of Eyak: The Art of Anna Nelson Harry.* Fairbanks: Alaska Native Language Center, 1982.

———, ed. and trans. *The Alaska Native Language Center Report for 1973.* Fairbanks, 1973.

———, ed. and trans. *Alaska Native Languages: Past, Present and Future.* Alaska Native Language Center Research Paper no. 4. Fairbanks, 1980.

———, ed. and trans. "Eskimo-Aleut." Pp. 796–902 in *Linguistics in North America.* Vol. 10 of *Current Trends in Linguistics.* Ed. Thomas A. Sebeok. The Hague and Paris: Mouton, 1973. Reprint. New York: Plenum Press, 1976.

———, ed. and trans. "Eyak Texts." Mimeo. University of Alaska and Massachusetts Institute of Technology, 1963–1970.

———, ed. and trans. "Na-Dene and Eskimo Aleut." Pp. 803–901 in *The Languages of Native America: Historical and Comparative Assessment.* Ed. Lyle Campbell and Marianne Mithun. Austin: University of Texas Press, 1979.

———, ed. and trans. *Native Peoples and Languages of Alaska.* Map. Fairbanks: Alaska Native Language Center, 1975.

———, ed. and trans. "St. Lawrence Island Eskimo Phonology and Orthography." *Linguistics* 152 (May 1975):39–72.

———, ed. and trans. "Siberian Yupik Prosodic Systems and the Yupik Continuum (with Inupiaq Connections)." Paper read at the Third Inuit Studies Conference, London, Ont., 1982.

Krenov, Julia. "Legends from Alaska." *Journal de la Société des Américanistes,* n.s., 40 (1951):173–95.

Lantis, Margaret. "The Mythology of Kodiak Island, Alaska." *Journal of American Folklore* 51, no. 200 (1938):123–72.

Leechman, Douglas. "Folk-Lore of the Vanta-Kutchin." Pp. 76–93 in National Museum of Canada Bulletin no. 126. Ottawa, 1952.

———. "Loucheux Tales." *Journal of American Folklore* 63, no. 248 (1950):158–62.

Lucier, Charles B. "Buckland Eskimo Myths." *Anthropological Papers of the University of Alaska* 2, no. 2 (1954):215–33.

———. "Noatagmiut Eskimo Myths." *Anthropological Papers of the University of Alaska* 6, no. 2 (1958):89–117.

MacLachlan, Bruce B. "Notes on Some Tahltan Oral Literature." *Anthropologica* 4 (1957):1–9.

MacNeish, June Helm. "Contemporary Folk Beliefs of a Slave Indian Band." *Journal of American Folklore* 67, no. 264 (1954):185–98.

———. "Folktales of the Slave Indians." *Anthropologica* 1 (1955):37–44.

Malaurie, Jean. *The Last Kings of Thule.* New York: E. P. Dutton, 1987.

Mandelbaum, David G., ed. *Selected Writings of Edward Sapir.* Berkeley: University of California Press, 1951.

Martijn, Charles A. "The 'Esquimaux' in the 17th and 18th Century Cartography of the Gulf of St. Lawrence: A Preliminary Discussion." *Etudes/Inuit/Studies* 4, nos. 1–2 (1980):77–104.

McClellan, Catharine. *The Girl Who Married the Bear: A Masterpiece of Indian Oral Tradition.* Canada, National Museum of Man, Publications in Ethnology, no. 2. Ottawa, 1970.
––––––. "Indian Stories About the First Whites in Northwestern America." Pp. 103–33 in *Ethnohistory in Southwestern Alaska and the Southern Yukon: Method and Content.* Ed. Margaret Lantis. Studies in Anthropology, no. 7. Lexington: University Press of Kentucky, 1970.
––––––. "My Old People's Stories: Oral Literature of the Indians of Southern Yukon Territory." Manuscript in McClellan's possession; copy in National Museum of Man, Ottawa, 1975.
Millman, Lawrence. *A Kayak Full of Ghosts: Eskimo Tales.* Santa Barbara, Calif.: Capra Press, 1987.
Nelson, Edward W. *The Eskimo About Bering Strait.* Pp. 3–518 in *18th Annual Report of the Bureau of American Ethnology for the Years 1896–1897.* Washington, 1899. Improved reprint, intro. W. W. Fitzhugh, Washington: Smithsonian Institution Press, 1984.
Nungak, Zebedee, and Eugene Arima. *Unikkaatuat sanaugarngnik atyingualiit Puvirngniturngmit: Eskimo Stories from Povungnituk, Quebec.* Anthropological Series, no. 90, National Museum of Canada Bulletin no. 235. Ottawa, 1969.
Osgood, Cornelius. *The Ethnography of the Tanaina.* Yale University Publications in Anthropology, no. 16. New Haven, Conn., 1937.
––––––. *Ingalik Mental Culture.* Yale University Publications in Anthropology, no. 56. New Haven, Conn., 1959.
Ostermann, Hother B. S., ed. *Knud Rasmussen's Posthumous Notes on East Greenland Legends and Myths.* Meddelelser om Grønland, vol. 109, no. 3. Copenhagen, 1939.
––––––. *Knud Rasmussen's Posthumous Notes on the Life and Doings of the East Greenlanders in Olden Times.* Meddelelser om Grønland, vol. 109, no. 1. Copenhagen, 1938.
Oswalt, Wendell H. "Traditional Storyknife Tales of Yuk Girls." *Proceedings of the American Philosophical Society* 108, no. 4 (1964):310–36.
Paul, Gaither, and Ronald Scollon. *Stories for my Grandchildren.* Told by Gaither Paul; ed. Ron Scollon. Fairbanks: Alaska Native Language Center, 1980.
Peter, Katherine, ed. *Dinjie Zhuu Gwandak: Gwich'in Stories.* Anchorage: Alaska State Operated Schools, 1974. Reprint. Austin, Texas: Dissemination and Assessment Center for Bilingual Education, 1976.
––––––. *Elders Speak.* Anchorage: University of Alaska, National Bilingual Materials Development Center, 1979.
––––––. *Sapir John Haa Googwandak* [Sapir-Fredson stories]. 3 vols. Fairbanks: Alaska Native Language Center, 1974.
Philippi, Donald L. *Songs of Gods, Songs of Humans: The Epic Tradition of the Ainu.* San Francisco: North Point Press, 1982.
Preston, Richard I., III. *Cree Narrative Expressing the Personal Meanings of Events.* Canada, National Museum of Man, Mercury Series, Ethnology Service Paper no. 30. Ottawa, 1975.
––––––. "Eastern Cree Attitudes Towards Hardship: Emotional Responses to the Contingencies of Bush Life." Unpublished paper read at the Second Conference on Algonquian Studies, St. John's, Newf., 1969.
Rasmussen, Knud. *The Eagle's Gift: Alaska Eskimo Tales.* Trans. Isobel Hutchinson. Garden City, N.Y.: Doubleday, Doran, 1932.

————. *Eskimo Folk-Tales*. Ed. and trans. W. Worster. London and Copenhagen: Gyldendal, 1921.

————. *Intellectual Culture of the Copper Eskimos*. Vol. 9 of *Report of the Fifth Thule Expedition, 1921–24*. Copenhagen: Gyldendal, 1932.

————. *Intellectual Culture of the Hudson Bay Eskimos*. Vol. 7, pts. 1–3, of *Report of the Fifth Thule Expedition, 1921–24*. Copenhagen: Gyldendal, 1930.

————. *Intellectual Culture of the Iglulik Eskimos*. Vol. 7, pt. 1, of *Report of the Fifth Thule Expedition, 1921–24*. Copenhagen: Gyldendal, 1929. Reprint. New York: AMS Press, 1976.

————. *The Netsilik Eskimos: Social Life and Spiritual Culture*. Vol. 8, pts. 1–2, of *Report of the Fifth Thule Expedition, 1921–24*. Copenhagen: Gyldendal, 1931.

Renner, Louis L. "Julius Jette: Distinguished Scholar in Alaska: A Jesuit Priest and Accomplished Linguist on the Yukon." *Alaska Journal* 5, no. 4 (1975):239–47.

Ridington, Tonia, and Robin Ridington. "Beaver Tales, as Told or Translated by Johnny Chipesia and Others at Mile 232, Alaska Highway, British Columbia." Mimeo, 1967.

Rink, Hinrich J. *Tales and Traditions of the Eskimo: With a Sketch of Their Habits, Religion, Language and Other Peculiarities*. Ed. Robert Brown. Edinburgh and London: W. Blackwood & Sons; Copenhagen: C. A. Reitzel, 1875.

Schmitter, Ferdinand. *Upper Yukon Native Customs and Folk-Lore*. Smithsonian Miscellaneous Collections, vol. 56, no. 4. Washington, 1910.

Silook, Roger S. *Seevookuk: Stories the Old People Told on St. Lawrence Island*. Anchorage: Alaska Publishing Company, 1976.

Skinner, Alanson B. "Plains Cree Tales." *Journal of American Folklore* 29, no. 113 (1916):341–67.

Spencer, Robert F. *The Northern Alaskan Eskimo: A Study in Ecology and Society*. Bureau of American Ethnology Bulletin no. 171. Washington, 1959. Reprinted in 1969.

Teit, James Alexander. "Kaska Tales." *Journal of American Folklore* 30, no. 118 (1917): 427–73.

————. "Tahltan Tales." *Journal of American Folklore* 32, no. 124 (1919):198–250; 34, no. 133 (1920):223–53; 34, no. 134 (1921):335–56.

————. *The Thompson Indians of British Columbia*. Memoirs of the American Museum of Natural History, no. 2. New York, 1900.

————. "Two Plains Cree Tales." *Journal of American Folklore* 34, no. 133 (1921): 320–21.

————. "Two Tahltan Traditions." *Journal of American Folklore* 22, no. 85 (1909): 314–18.

Thalbitzer, William. *The Ammassalik Eskimo: Contributions to the Ethnology of the East Greenland Natives*. Meddelelser om Grønland, vols. 39–40, 53. Copenhagen, 1914–1941.

————. "Ethnographical Collections from East Greenland (Angmagsalik and Nualik) Made by G. Holm, G. Amdrup and J. Petersen and Described by W. Thalbitzer." Pp. 319–755 in vol. 1, pt. 7, of *The Ammassalik Eskimo*. Meddelelser om Grønland, vol. 39. Copenhagen, 1914.

————. *A Phonetical Study of the Eskimo Language Based on Observations Made on a Journey in North Greenland 1900–1901*. Meddelelser om Grønland, vol. 31. Copenhagen, 1904.

Turner, David H. "Windigo Mythology and the Analysis of Cree Social Structure." *Anthropologica*, n.s., 19, no. 1 (1977):63–73.

Turner, Lucien M. "Ethnology of the Ungava District, Hudson Bay Territory." Ed.

John Murdoch. Pp. 159–350 in *11th Annual Report of the Bureau of American Ethnology for the Years 1889–1890.* Washington, 1894.

———. "Language of the 'Koksoagmyut' Eskimo at Fort Chimo, Ungava, Labrador Peninsula." 3 vols. Manuscript no. 2505a in National Anthropological Archives, Smithsonian Institution, Washington, 1882–1884.

VanStone, James W. *The Snowdrift Chipewyan* (NCRC 63–64). Ottawa: Department of Northern Affairs and National Resources, Northern Co-ordination and Research Centre, 1963.

Vaudrin, Bill. *Tanaina Tales from Alaska.* Norman: University of Oklahoma Press, 1969.

Williams, Frank, and Emma Williams. *Tongass Texts.* Ed. Jeff Leer. Fairbanks: Alaska Native Language Center, 1978.

Permissions Acknowledgments

Grateful acknowledgment is made to the following for permission to reprint previously published material:

Canadian Museum of Civilization: "Smart Beaver Cycle" narrated by Angela Sidney and "The First Snowshoes" narrated by Kitty Smith from *Athapaskan Women: Lives and Legends,* compiled by Julie Cruikshank, paper no. 57 of the Canadian Ethnology Service, Canadian Museum of Civilization Mercury Series; "Bushmen" by Douglas Leechman in *Folklore of the Vanta-Kutchin,* National Museums of Canada Bulletin 129; "The Dream That Came Back" narrated by Charles Kinatiwat in *Cree Narrative: Expressing the Personal Meaning of Events* by Richard Preston, paper no. 30 of the Canadian Ethnology Service, Canadian Museum of Civilization Mercury Series; and "Ayas'e and the Origin of Bats" by Frank Speck in *Myth and Folklore of the Timiskaming Algonquin and Timagami Ojibwa,* Canada Dept. of Mines, Geological Survey Memoir 71, no. 9, Anthropological Series (1915). Reprinted by permission of the Canadian Museum of Civilization.

Michael E. Krauss: "Giant Rat," "Lake-Dwarves," and "Woman and Octopus" from *In Honor of Eyak: The Art of Anna Nelson Harry,* compiled and edited with introduction and commentary by Michael E. Krauss. Copyright © 1982 by the Alaska Native Language Center, University of Alaska. Reprinted by permission of Michael E. Krauss.

North Point Press: "Song of Spider Goddess" from *Songs of Gods, Songs of Humans,* copyright © 1982 by Donald Philippi. Published by North Point Press and reprinted by permission.

University of Oklahoma Press: "The Crow Story" from *Tanaina Tales from Alaska* by Bill Vaudrin. New edition copyright © 1969 by the University of Oklahoma Press. Reprinted by permission.

The University of Tennessee Press: Material from *The Eskimo Storyteller: Folktales from Noatak, Alaska* by Edwin S. Hall. Copyright © 1975 by The University of Tennessee Press. Reprinted by permission of The University of Tennessee Press.

HOWARD NORMAN has worked and traveled extensively in the arctic and subarctic regions of Canada, writing documentary and ethnographic film scripts, radio plays, and articles on northern language, culture, and wildlife. He has received fellowships from the John Simon Guggenheim Foundation, the National Endowment for the Humanities, and the National Endowment for the Arts, and was a Hodder Fellow at Princeton University. His first novel, *The Northern Lights*, won a Mrs. Giles Whiting Writers Award and was a final selection for the National Book Award in 1987. He is also the author of a collection of short stories, *Kiss in the Hotel Joseph Conrad*, and several children's books. He has taught and lectured at a number of universities. Currently, he teaches folklore and fiction writing at the University of Maryland, and divides his time between Washington, D.C., and Vermont. He is at work on a new novel and a number of film scripts.